LANGUAGE, DISCOURSE, SOCIETY
General Editors: *Stephen Heath, Colin MacCabe* and *Denise Riley*

published titles

VISION AND PAINTING: The Logic of the Gaze   *Norman Bryson*

ALICE DOESN'T: Feminism, Semiotics and Cinema
FEMINIST STUDIES/CRITICAL STUDIES (*editor*)
Teresa de Lauretis

THE DESIRE TO DESIRE: The Woman's Film of the 1940s
Mary Ann Doane

CONDITIONS OF MUSIC   *Alan Durant*

FEMINISM AND PSYCHOANALYSIS: The Daughter's Seduction
Jane Gallop

UNDERSTANDING BECKETT: A Study of Monologue and Gesture in the Works of Samuel Beckett   *Peter Gidal*

LEGAL DISCOURSE: Studies in Linguistics, Rhetoric and Legal Analysis   *Peter Goodrich*

ON LAW AND IDEOLOGY   *Paul Hirst*

AFTER THE GREAT DIVIDE: Modernism, Mass Culture and Postmodernism   *Andreas Huyssen*

THE POLITICS OF IMAGINATION IN COLERIDGE'S CRITICAL THOUGHT   *Nigel Leask*

EPOS: WORD, NARRATIVE AND THE *ILIAD*
Michael Lynn-George

JAMES JOYCE AND THE REVOLUTION OF THE WORD
THE TALKING CURE: Essays in Psychoanalysis and Language (*editor*)
Colin MacCabe

PORTRAIT OF THE KING   *Louis Marin*

PSYCHOANALYSIS AND CINEMA: The Imaginary Signifier
Christian Metz

GENEALOGIES OF MORALS: Nietzsche, Foucault, Donzelot and the Eccentricity of Ethics   *Jeffrey Minson*

LANGUAGE, SEMANTICS AND IDEOLOGY   *Michel Pecheux*

LANGUAGE, SEXUALITY AND IDEOLOGY IN EZRA POUND'S *CANTOS*   *Jean-Michel Rabaté*

'AM I THAT NAME?'   *Denise Riley*

THE CASE OF PETER PAN OR THE IMPOSSIBILITY OF CHILDREN'S FICTION   *Jacquelin Rose*

SIGNIFYING NOTHING: The Semiotics of Zero   *Brian Rotman*

NOT SAUSSURE: A Critique of Post-Saussurean Literary Theory
Raymond Tallis

CIRCULATION: Defoe, Dickens and the Economies of the Novel
THE MAKING OF THE READER: Language and Subjectivity in Modern American, English and Irish Poetry   *David Trotter*

forthcoming titles
SCIENCE AS POWER   *Stanley Aronowitz*
ITALIAN WOMEN BETWEEN CHURCH AND STATE
Lesley Caldwell
TO REPRESENT WOMAN: The Representation of Sexual Difference in the Visual Media   *Elizabeth Cowie*
THE QUESTION OF EDUCATION: Essays on Schooling and English Culture, 1790–1987   *James Donald*
SOUNDTRACK AND TALKBACK   *Alan Durant*
MODERNISM AND THE MODERN   *Piers Gray*
THREE ESSAYS ON SUBJECTIVITY   *Stephen Heath*
CULTURE AND GOVERNMENT: The Emergence of Literary Education
Ian Hunter
ON PORNOGRAPHY   *Ian Hunter, David Saunders and Dugald Williamson*
CONTEMPORARY BRITISH POETICS   *Rod Mengham*
FOR THE LOVE OF LANGUAGE   *Jean-Claude Milner*
GENESIS AND AUTHORSHIP
PERSONAL POLITICS AND ETHICAL STYLE   *Jeffrey Minson*
VISUAL AND OTHER PLEASURES: Collected Writings
Laura Mulvey
POETS ON POETICS   *Denise Riley*
POLITICS AND CULTURE   *Michael Ryan*
SEEING BLACK: A Semiotics of Black Culture in America
James A. Snead and Cornel West

Series Standing Order

If you would like to receive future titles in this series as they are published, you can make use of our standing order facility. To place a standing order please contact your bookseller or, in case of difficulty, write to us at the address below with your name and address and the name of the series. Please state with which title you wish to begin your standing order. (If you live outside the United Kingdom we may not have the rights for your area, in which case we will forward your order to the publisher concerned.)

Customer Services Department, Macmillan Distribution Ltd
Houndmills, Basingstoke, Hampshire, RG21 2XS, England.

Improvement and Romance

Constructing the Myth of the Highlands

Peter Womack
Lecturer in English Literature
University of East Anglia

© Peter Womack 1989

All rights reserved. No reproduction, copy or transmission of this publication may be made without written permission.

No paragraph of this publication may be reproduced, copied or transmitted save with written permission or in accordance with the provisions of the Copyright Act 1956 (as amended), or under the terms of any licence permitting limited copying issued by the Copyright Licensing Agency, 33-4 Alfred Place, London WC1E 7DP.

Any person who does any unauthorised act in relation to this publication may be liable to criminal prosecution and civil claims for damages.

First published 1989

Published by
THE MACMILLAN PRESS LTD
Houndmills, Basingstoke, Hampshire RG21 2XS
and London
Companies and representatives
throughout the world

Typesetting by Footnote Graphics
Warminster, Wiltshire

Printed in China

British Library Cataloguing in Publication Data
Womack, Peter, *1952–*
Improvement and romance : constructing the myth of the Highlands. —(Language, discourse, society).
1. Scotland. Highlands. Portrayal by printed media in Great Britain, 1700–1815
I. Title II. Series
941.1'5
ISBN 0-333-40708-3

For my parents

Contents

	List of Plates	ix
	Preface	xi
1	Introduction	1
2	Converting the Uncouth Savage	4
	1 Integration	4
	2 The Fool	7
	3 The Rogue	11
	4 The Beggar	14
	5 The History of Civilisation	20
3	Warriors	27
	1 Barbarians	27
	2 Recruiting	29
	3 Battles Long Ago	34
	4 Virtue	39
	5 Regimentals	44
	6 Reaction	48
	7 The Peninsula	55
4	The Land	61
	1 The Picturesque	61
	2 Trees	65
	3 Ruling the Waves	68
	4 The Sublime	72
	5 Bounty	82

5	Ghosts		87
	1	The Superstitions of the Highlands of Scotland, Considered as the Subject of Poetry	87
	2	The Well-Taught Hind	94
	3	The Tale of Other Times	101
	4	Memorials	109
6	Social Tribes		115
	1	A Stay of Execution	115
	2	Poetry and Emigration	118
	3	Sacred Retreats	125
	4	The Language of Nature	131
	5	Caledonia	140
7	Holidays		149
	1	Make-believe	149
	2	The Tourist in the Text	154
	3	The Huntsman	158
	4	Leisure and Industry	163
8	The Structure of the Myth		166
	1	Peripheralisation	166
	2	Nature	169
	3	Community	176
	Notes		181
	Index		207

List of Plates

1a 'The Scrubbing Post', from *The Scots Scourge*, a collection of anti-ministerial prints of 1762–3. Reproduced by permission of the Trustees of the National Library of Scotland.

1b 'God Bless the Duke of Argyle for his Claw Post', postcard c. 1914. Reproduced by permission from the collection of Murray and Barbara Grigor.

The 'beggarly Scot' survives 150 years of romanticisation. In images of the Scotch itch Highlanders are not only dirty and infected, but also subhuman, deriving satisfaction from the animal pleasure of scratching. The early cartoon is explicitly political; the postcard explicitly a bit of fun. The difference that makes to the images themselves, however, is limited.

2a 'Colonel Alastair Macdonell of Glengarry', a portrait by Sir Henry Raeburn. Reproduced by permission of the Scottish National Portrait Gallery.

2b 'W. Macdonald in the Dress of an Officer of the Highland Society of Scotland' (c.1800), from *A Series of Original Portraits and Caricature Etchings* by John Kay. Reproduced by permission of the Trustees of the National Library of Scotland.

Highland dress as costume. The sitters are dressed and posed similarly, but Raeburn, as a commissioned portrait-painter, supports Glengarry's 'True Highland' self-image in the composition as a whole. Kay, a mildly satirical recorder of the Edinburgh social scene, isolates the fancy dress from its proper context in national fantasy.

3a 'View in Strathtay', by Paul Sandby (1747). Reproduced by permission of the National Library of Wales.

3b 'View in Strathtay', engraving after Sandby (1780). Reproduced by permission of the National Gallery of Scotland.

'We must ... enlarge the scale a little beyond nature to make nature look like herself'. Gilpin's paradox is put into practice by the engraver of Sandby's drawing; Strathtay acquires the wild and rugged aspect which is known (by 1780) to be what a Highland scene *ought* to look like.

4a 'Loch Hourn', from *A Tour in Scotland and voyage to the Hebrides* (1772), by Thomas Pennant. Reproduced by permission of the Trustees of the National Library of Scotland.

4b 'Loch Lomond', from *Remarkable Ruins, and Romantic Prospects, of North Britain* (1795), by Charles Cordiner. Reproduced by permission of the Mitchell Library, Glasgow.

Mountains humanised. For Pennant on Loch Hourn, 'the wildest scene in nature', the presence of fishing boats confirms the ultimate usefulness of the remotest parts of Britain. Comparably, Loch Lomond figures as the perfect union of beauty and sublimity, in which stern mountains close off the prospect and enhance by contrast the placid fertility of the foreground.

5a 'Cascade near Carril', from *Antiquities and Scenery of the North of Scotland* (1780), by Charles Cordiner. Reproduced by permission of the Trustees of the National Library of Scotland.

5b 'Fingal and Conban Cargla' (c.1772–4), by Alexander Runciman, from *Painting in Scotland*, by Duncan Macmillan. Photograph by courtesy of Joe Rock.

Ossian: sensibility and sublimity. The engraving features, not the epic, but the blind bard in a sympathetically twilit natural setting. Runciman's sketch seizes on the other natural correlative for Macpherson's imagery: Highland weather. The wind-blown protagonists appear as animated clouds.

6 Inveraray Castle and village in 1824, from the slopes of Duniquaich. Engraved after a drawing by John Clark. Courtesy of the British Museum.

Improvement and romance in estate architecture. At the seat of the Dukes of Argyll, the landscaped park embraces both an Enlightenment model village and a (mid eighteenth-century) Gothic castle.

Preface

I did the research for this book while reading for a Ph.D. at Edinburgh University. The book is shorter and, I hope, more lucid than the thesis: additional detail on many points can be found in the latter, which is called 'Improvement and Romance: the Scottish Highlands in British Writing After the Forty-Five' and dated 1984.

Both versions have benefited from the generosity of friends in Edinburgh and elsewhere. It's a pleasure to record my thanks to my supervisor Geoffrey Carnall and to my external examiner David Craig. I have also greatly appreciated the less official help of Robert Bartlett, Ian Carter, Sue Hemmings, Glen Murray and Randall Stevenson. Given the political and national issues I have touched on, it's particularly to the point to add that any uncorrected errors and prejudices are mine.

The longest-serving encourage and critic of the project is my wife Ruth, who has been around, not only at the discoveries, but also at the dead ends. Many thanks.

The bourgeois viewpoint has never advanced beyond the antithesis between itself and the romantic viewpoint, and the latter will accompany it as its legitimate antithesis up to its blessed end.

Karl Marx, *Grundrisse*

All of Scotland's a stage.

ScotRail advertisement, 1986

1
Introduction

We know that the Highlands of Scotland are romantic. Bens and glens, the lone shieling in the misty island, purple heather, kilted clansmen, battles long ago, an ancient and beautiful language, claymores and bagpipes and Bonny Prince Charlie – we know all that, and we also know that it's not real. Not that it's a pure fabrication: on the contrary, all the things on that rough-and-ready list actually exist, or existed. But the romance is not simply the aggregate of the things; it is a message which the things carry.

Around 1730, an English gentleman called Edward Burt described the mountains near Inverness: they were, he observed, 'of a dismal gloomy Brown, drawing upon a dirty Purple; and most of all disagreeable, when the Heath is in Bloom'.[1] Here, preserved by chance, is one of the things without the message. Burt doesn't know what heather 'means'; for him, the plant is innocent of romance. This is because when he was looking at it, the romance had not yet been invented.

It is not a question of personal taste. Burt thought the heather-covered mountains ugly, but he might have liked them; most people nowadays find them beautiful, but it's perfectly possible for a modern individual to dislike them. What it is *not* possible to do today, whatever our personal tastes, is to see the heather he saw. Trying to see that neutral, unappropriated flower would be like trying to see, say, a swastika as nothing but an abstract design. For us, the moment when we set eyes on a heather-covered Highland hillside, and *see what it is*, is also the moment when we register the presence of the Highland romance. Thus, while Burt's observation is an exemplary demonstration that the things and the romance are separable in principle, it is equally a reminder that they are inextricable in practice. The Highlands are no longer just a place where people and animals and plants live; they have been colonised by the empire of signs; they are what Roland Barthes called a myth: that is, an object which is signified within an ordinary linguistic sign, but at the same time serves as the signifier within a secondary sign, having been, so to speak, pressed into the service of a concept. The concept, the mythic signified, is vague: as Barthes also notes, 'the knowledge contained in a mythical concept is confused, made of yielding, shapeless associations ... not at all an abstract, purified essence [but] a formless, unstable, nebulous condensation'.[2] It would be about right to say that Highland heather signifies Scottishness, wild freedom, naturalness, antique valour. But that is talking loosely; it is not the point of myth that it should specify denotations in that way; this is not a question of symbolism. Rather, the heather (together with the other Highland *differentiae*) is made the instrument of an intention, saturated with ideological imperatives which, by merging themselves with its incontestably organic fibres, win for themselves the opaque and self-evident charm of a natural contingency. The concept, no longer recognisable as such, is *just there*, for all to see. Botanically, no doubt, *calluna vulgaris* is exactly as it was in the 1730s. Semiotically, it has been irrevocably hybridised.

For historians of Highland society, economy, literature or ecology, this is a serious inconvenience, because it means that their sources appear to be contaminated by quantities of colourful nonsense, which they must separate out and discard in order to get at the truth. But the contamination is not just an arbitrary historiographical interference. It is also, itself, the outcome of a historical process: the Highlands are romantic because they have been romanticised. This *happened*, at an identifiable point in time, in response to specific ideological requirements and contradictions which are both exhibited and disguised by its eventual form.

In the chapters which follow, I have tried to tell the story of that process – to present the formation of the Highland romance as a historical event, albeit an event of a particularly bizarre and protracted kind. It began, fairly decisively, with the military defeat of the Jacobite clans in 1746, and can be regarded as complete by 1810–11, when a flurry of publications, including most notably Scott's *The Lady of the Lake*, both depended on and confirmed a settled cultural construction of the Highlands as a 'romantic country' inhabited by a people whose ancient manners and customs were 'peculiarly adapted to poetry'.[3] Although I have strayed across both these chronological boundaries in pursuit of particular motifs and developments, the 65 years between them are the essential epoch in which the story is set.

During this period, the dominant theme in British discourse concerning the Highlands was Improvement. I have tried to give a sort of cumulative definition of this charged term in the course of the book as a whole, so I shan't offer to sum it up here. A rich and detailed sense of its economic implications is provided by A.J. Youngson's study, *After the Forty-Five*.[4] What is worth pointing out at once, though, is that the primary meaning of the word, etymologically and historically, is the narrowly economic one — the cultivation of an asset in order to profit from it. The ramifications of eighteenth-century usage, in social, aesthetic, moral, juridical and religious applications, are transferences of that basic idea. The growth, in this semantic field, of the vaguer sense which is current now — the process of making something better — is thus quite specifically an instance of capitalist ideology: it makes managing a stock so that it increases in value the universal type of beneficent change. The 'Improvement' of the Highlands, then, signified (a) that the region was to yield a better return on capital; (b) that it was to become, very generally, a better place; and (c) that (a) and (b) were substantially identical.

This was evidently a project fraught with contradictions both internal and external; and it was out of its contradictions that the Highland myth was generated. At every stage of its elaboration, the code of Improvement gave rise to discordant tones, dysfunctional ideological traces which it was obliged to elide or exclude: these, precisely because of the hegemonic unity of Improvement itself, formed a coherent counter-image to it, matching its powerful but limited rationale with a utopian but impotent irrationalism, mirroring its economism in a quixotic denial of self-interest, haunting its progressivism with a voluptuous love of the past. These oppositions can occasionally make the romance look like a counter-ideological formation, but as their symmetry suggests, the conflict is illusory. Rather, it is the ideological function of the romance that it removes the contradictory elements from the scope of material life altogether; that it marks out a kind of reservation in which the values which Improvement provokes and suppresses can be *contained* — that is, preserved, but also imprisoned. I began by pointing out that the romantic Highlands are not real; this is not an incidental drawback; not to be real is what they are for. Officially, Romance and Improvement were opposites: native and imported, past and present, tradition and innovation. But in reality they were twins.[5] The story of Highland romanticisation is essentially the story of that covert complementarity.

2
Converting the Uncouth Savage

1 INTEGRATION

That spirit of industry which begins to take place among them, together with a more free and liberal education, will soon, it is to be hoped, polish their manners, take off the rust of barbarity, sloth and ignorance, and convert the uncouth savage into an industrious and useful member of society.[1]

As soon as the Forty-five was over, the Scottish Highlands became the target of a legislative programme designed to efface their historical distinctiveness. The military challenge had been destroyed at Culloden; now the aim was to pre-empt any possible revival by making the area as much as possible like the rest of Britain. In 1746 the Disarming Act outlawed not only the carrying of weapons but also, no less severely, the wearing of Highland dress. In 1747 heritable jurisdictions were abolished, thus 'rendering the Union more complete' by imposing on Scotland the state monopoly in the administration of justice which already obtained in England. The estates of the rebels were forfeited to the Crown, and in 1752 the Annexing Act arranged for the management of these lands on enlightened capitalist principles which would, it was hoped, diffuse an ethos of rational self-interest in place of what the House of Lords agreed in calling an 'enthusiastical clannish spirit'.[2] Education was to be centralised too: the Disarming Act tried to license Highland schools in such a way as to place children everywhere under the influence of the established Kirk, whose presbyterianism made it solidly anti-Jacobite, and whose language of instruction was English.[3] The whole thrust of the legislation was neatly summarised in the brief of the Commissioners appointed under the 1752 Act: revenues from the annexed estates were to be devoted

Converting the Uncouth Savage

to the purposes of civilising the inhabitants upon the said estates, and other parts of the highlands and islands of *Scotland*, [and] the promoting amongst them the protestant religion, good government, industry and manufactures, and the principles of duty and loyalty to his Majesty.[4]

The formula is typical in shifting effortlessly from principles to manufactures and back to principles again: the seamless unity of religious, political, economic and cultural themes speaks the confident ideology of Improvement.

Of course, this battery of measures did not emerge spontaneously from the general ideological formation. In order to decide what to do about the Highlands, it was first necessary to have some definite picture of what they were actually like. Accordingly, the legislative programme was accompanied by a flurry of reports, articles and speeches analysing the state of the region. Ironically, the government's determination that Highland difference should end led to its representation, with unprecedented concreteness and detail, within official discourse. The Highlands, as a distinct historical society, were grasped in the act of consigning them to oblivion.

The picture which was elaborated may be summarised as follows.[5] The people of the Highlands are liable to be led into Jacobite adventures for three reasons: that they are, both by sentiment and in practice, the slaves of a numerous class of hereditary clan chiefs; that the primitive state of agriculture makes them poor and underemployed (that is, it gives them both the motive and the leisure to prey upon their wealthier neighbours); and that the differences between them and other British people, seen in their manners, their religion, their language and their dress, combine to make them feel like foreigners who owe no allegiance to the British state. These three factors tend to reinforce one another: the multiplicity of petty princes leads to a general lawlessness inimical to the accumulation of productive capital; the clansmen's poverty seals their dependence on their chiefs; the poor communications attendant on the poverty and lawlessness keep the greater part of the region remote and preserve its peculiarities. Minuter connections can also be traced: for example, the Highlanders' houses are often mere hovels, which they are not afraid of losing in the course of an insurrection; again, the Highland dress, to which the people are enthusiastically attached, is much better adapted to sport and fighting than to working, so that their prejudice on this point prolongs the material conditions which are its ultimate cause. The picture, in short, shows a system of greater and lesser vicious circles, in which disorder, idleness, ignorance and remoteness all feed on one another, and popery and the Stuarts on all.

Even bating its hostility, this account is not the innocent fruit of observation. Its guiding lines mirror those of eighteenth-century constitutionalism, in which liberty and property are the joint and mutual guarantors of law, since law secures property, which in turn confers the independence necessary to defend liberty, thus creating a constituency with both the interest and the power to uphold the rule of law.[6] The vicious circle is this benign circle reversed: the state of the Highlands appears as an *idealised and inverted* image of the Constitution.

Thus, through the historical circumstances of its insertion into British ideology, Highland difference has the formal character of a negation. A minor anomaly in the diagnosis suggests the kind of regularity this imposes. 'The Camerons', we learn, 'are a Lazy Silent Sly and Enterprising People.'[7] How can they be both lazy and enterprising? The words have a covertly restricted meaning. Forbes of Culloden implicitly glosses 'lazy' when he suggests a secondary reason for disarming the Highlanders — that the 'diversion which is the greatest incentive to their idleness, i.e. hunting, is cut off'.[8] And another commentator sheds some light on 'enterprising' when he explains how inter-clan 'jealousies, feuds, depredations and thefts ... affect the common sort, and in so far open their understandings, and sharpen their judgments'.[9] When they're read together, it's clear that these writers expect the poor to engage in lower-class pursuits (manual labour), and when they find them engaged in upper-class ones (hunting or diplomacy), they don't recognise the activity, but see it as a form of doing nothing.

In other words, Highland life, within this discourse, has no *autonomy* — no internal order which would make it intelligible in its own terms. Rather, it is given as the opposite of order in general. Conformably with this, we find that anglophone culture identifies the Highlander, in the first instance, with the traditional stereotypes of the social reject. In particular, the Highlander is textualised as the fool, as the rogue, and as the beggar.

2 THE FOOL

As far as I know, the Highlander made his theatrical debut at Drury Lane in 1731, in a ballad-opera called *The Highland Fair; or the Union of the Clans*, by Joseph Mitchell. The lightweight plot concerns the efforts of a Captain in one of the newly formed Independent Companies (effectively the first Highland regiment) to bring about the ceremonial reconciliation of two clans who are hereditary enemies. One or two of the obstacles retarding the eventual union are tinged with local colour − one of the clans, for example, can't be prevented from stealing the other's cattle − but on the whole the play eschews social realism and concentrates on the amorous complications which threaten the marriages involved in the settlement. The picture of the Highlands is therefore a faint one for most of the show. One of the lovers is foppish, another a man of sense; the intrigues are resolved with the aid of a sardonic but good-hearted widow − the setting is an exotic touch within a secure world of Restoration comic types.

In this familiar dramatic context, the distinctive Highland characteristics appear as a kind of folly, to be laughed out of countenance from the standpoint of 'sense'. The Chief's insistence on the antiquity of his family and the absolute submission of his vassals is a monomania like the ones in Molière. The Captain, in an expository scene, wonders at the rival leaders' pretensions, and adds: 'But to expect Homage, and insist on Punctilio's of Honour and Ceremony, among Equals too, is a peculiar Instance of their Romantic Pride and Grandeur!'[10] 'Romantic' has no shadow of its later positive sense, I think: it merely promises the audience an exhibition of behaviour laughably at odds with reality. The assured formulas of the genre render Highland manners eccentric. Even the chiefs' supposed claims to independent sovereignty (the most formidable objection to them from the point of view of the British Crown) are sweetly assimilated into the comic world via the *Beggar's Opera* joke of using diplomatic language to talk about domestic business: 'There's as much difficulty in bringing about the happy Union of our *Clans*, as in settling the Peace of *Europe*.'[11] The conflicts are depoliticised by the smoothing and reconciling rhythms of the marital ending; it can be assumed of Highlanders, as of any other misguided comic protagonists, that 'If their Eyes were once Open'd and their Prejudices removed they would See and Act as others do.'[12] Just like the state papers, the comedy establishes a discursive order within which the Highlands take their place as nonsense.

This is typical of a persistent subculture of jokes and snap judgements. In 1706 Defoe found the same 'Romantic Pride':

> They are all gentlemen, will take affront from no man, and insolent to the last degree. But certainly the absurdity is ridiculous to see a man in his mountain habit, armed with a broadsword, target, pistol, at his girdle a dagger, and staff, walking down the High Street ... as if he were a lord, and withal driving a cow! bless us — are these the gentlemen! said I.[13]

And the delusions of sovereignty are mocked in this story retailed by Burt in the 1730s:

> They say a *Spanish* Ship being stranded upon the Coast of Barra ... one of the Members proposed, 'If she was laden with Wine and Brandy, she should be confiscated as an illicit trader upon the Coast; but if she was freighted with other Merchandize, they should plunder her as a Wreck.' Upon this, one of the Council, more cautious than the rest, objected that the King of *Spain* might resent such Treatment of his Subjects; but the other replied, We have nothing to do with that, McNeal *and the King of Spain will adjust that Matter between themselves.*[14]

Nor was this tradition of humour cut short by the later romanticisation of the Highlands: in 1828 Sir Walter Scott was telling the story about the chief who ordered one of his people to be hanged; the man 'was shy of mounting the Ladder: his wife called "Hoot Mon, make haste or ye'll anger the Laird."'[15] In all these examples, as in Mitchell's play, Highland social attitudes are presented in isolation from the social relations within which they make sense; they thus appear as a kind of insanity.

The image of the fool was also produced in a fool's language, analogous to the comic dialects spoken by Irishmen and Frenchmen on the eighteenth-century stage. Mitchell had no Highland equivalent for these farcical jargons; his characters all speak standard English, and the chiefs who eventually appear for the reconciliation remain silent. At this early stage, before the Forty-five, the Highlands were too remote for such a joke to gain

Converting the Uncouth Savage

currency. Stage Highlandese appears later, in Smollett's patriotic comedy *The Reprisal*, in 1757. A briefly introduced piper declares to his master, 'her nain sell wad na pudge the length of her tae, without your honour's order'.[16] Here the comical English is of a piece with the un-English servility of the sentiment; like all theatre clowns, 'Tonalt' garbles both language and reason.

This curious dialect, for which 'her nain sell' is the crude call-sign as 'bigard' is for stage Frenchmen, seems to descend from derisive Lowland Scots balladry of the early Jacobite period;[17] it's not an accident that it was introduced on the London stage by a Scottish writer. The earliest example I've seen is in William Cleland's satire on the Highland Host, the royalist clansmen who were punitively quartered on the Covenanters of the south-west in the 1670s; but the style of use there expects a quick recognition, as if the formula were already well known. As a notation of Highland speech it is whimsically inaccurate ('I doubt', an irritated Celticist remarked in 1889, 'if one Highlander in a hundred would know what "her nain sell" meant'[18]); and this probably reflects hostility rather than ignorance. But after the Forty-five, at least, its uses are farcical rather than vituperative: the Highlander who speaks like that is not so much a barbarian as an innocent. The master of this fantasy language is Dougal Graham, the Glasgow bellman and literary pedlar, who wrote a handful of stylish ballads in which 'her nain sell' gives his views on the changing condition of the Highlands.[19] The best known of them is 'The Turnimspike': dating from the 1760s, it protests topically and impotently about incomers who 'mak a lang road on the crund' and then make you pay to go on it. Its opening self-portrait duplicates Defoe's 'gentleman', but doesn't have Defoe's hard class appraisal:

> First when her to the Lowlands came,
> Nain sell was driving cows, man:
> There was nae laws about hims narse,
> About the breeks or trouse, man.
>
> Nain sell did wear the philapeg,
> The plaid prik't on her shouder;
> The gude claymore hung pe her pelt,
> The pistol sharg'd wi' pouder.

The softening is partly a sociological matter: all these imposing accoutrements are now illegal, and the tone deftly catches the new vulnerability. The speaker tamely pays his toll, and vows never to come near the Turnimspike again 'Unless it pe to purn her' — a threat which is evidently no more than cheeky.

The character, drawing on old Lowland prejudice but also on new historical experience, isn't a simple one. The 'shentleman', with his vanity, his wholly unfounded self-confidence, his ingenuous bloodthirstiness and timidity, and his spectacular grammatical incompetence, has something of the elusiveness of a folk-tale fool. Sometimes, as in the popular 'John Highlandman's Remarks on the City of Glasgow', the language is so fantastically at odds with ordinary modern life that the poem reads like a series of riddles. All these qualities are seen in the pay-off of 'Tugal McTagger', the story of a Lochaber lad's career in the Glasgow retail trade:

She'll got a big shop, an' she'll turn'd a big dealer;
She was caution hersel', for they'll no sought no bailer,
But Tugal McTagger hersel' mak's a failure —
    They'll call her a bankrumpt, a trade she'll not know.

They'll called a great meeting, she'll look very quate now,
She'll fain win awa', but they'll tell her to wait now;
They'll spoket a lang time, 'pout a great estate now;
    She'll thocht that they'll thocht her the laird o' Glendoo.

They'll wrote a long while about a trust deeder,
She'll no write a word, for hersel' couldna read her,
They'll sought compongzition, hoogh, hoogh, never heed her —
    There's no sic a word 'mang the hills o' Glendoo.

But had she her durk, hersel' would devour them,
They'll put her in jail when she'll stood there before them;
But faith she'll got out on a hashimanorum,
    And now she's as free as the win's on Glendoo.

A 'hashimanorum' (*cessio bonorum*) is a deed whereby a debtor escapes prison by ceding all his effects to his creditors: Tugal has lost everything through processes which we deduce with difficulty from his uncomprehending narrative. Written about 1772, during the first major exodus from the Highlands, the piece is not without sympathy for the predicament of the Gaelic immigrants in the literate commercial city. But at the same time, Tugal's blind irresponsibility, his mental fog, his immediate impulse to sneak off when things look bad, lightly and maliciously sketch the Highlander as a person incapable of property rights. (This is perhaps the historical content of the relentless joke about personal pronouns: in the terms of possessive individualism the clansman can't even claim an identity firmly enough to say 'I'.) Graham was anything but an official spokesman; nevertheless, what emerges from his laughter is an ideological position inseparable from that of the state — the constitutional interlocking of liberty, property and law, and the definition of the Highlander as opposed to all three.

On the other hand, it's impossible to miss a lyric note amid the knowing urban patronage. 'The win's on Glendoo' vindicate Tugal as a free spirit, above all the legal palaver. The ideology of Improvement, by making a fool of the Highlander, opens him up to the traditional ambivalences of motley. Ridicule is shadowed by a dream.

3 THE ROGUE

Somebody observing that the Scotch Highlanders, in the year 1745, had made surprising efforts, considering their numerous wants and disadvantages: 'Yes, Sir, (said he,) their wants were numerous; but you have not mentioned the greatest of them all, — the want of law.'[20]

This comment of Samuel Johnson's expresses a far-reaching judgement on the Highlands. Immediately, it alludes to the military proposition that the clans were formidable only in agility and impetuosity, and could gain only temporary advantages over disciplined troops; this was a well-established commonplace. But by implicitly linking indiscipline to that other dimension of the Jacobite army's lawlessness — the fact of its being in rebellion — Johnson suggests how the category defines the whole relationship of the Highlands to the British state. Personally, politically and juridically, the clansman is a person without law. For many of the post Forty-five commentators this is the essence of the 'Highland problem':

> Here the laws have never been executed, nor the authority of the magistrate ever established. Here the officer of the law neither

dare nor can execute his duty, and several places are above thirty miles from lawfull persons. – In short, here is no order, no authority, no government![21]

Well before 1745 this formidable 'want' had concentrated itself in the figure of the blackmailer, that is, the cattle thief or patron of cattle thieves who instituted a protection racket along the boundary of Highland and Lowland. This 'heavy and shamefull tax' was noticed in the 1720s by General Wade, the Commander-in-Chief for North Britain; and at about the same time one of the culprits, Rob Roy Macgregor, then still alive, was launched upon national notoriety by a pamphlet published in London, entitled *The Highland Rogue*.[22]

What was particularly offensive about blackmail was that it was not simply a crime but also a system: as one post Forty-five analyst sarcastically put it, a 'famous Company had the Honour to Methodize Theft into a Regular Trade'.[23] The regularity meant that they stole only cattle; that ordinary people looked on them as heroes; and that they scrupulously kept the undertakings which they gave in return for their money – indeed, the system flourished because the outlaws' protection was so much more worth having than that of the state that even respectable and law-abiding proprietors came to terms. In short, it was 'black' in the sense that it implied, not just illegality, but an alternative legality – a territorial jurisdiction and a right to tax. In this it resembled, at least from a metropolitan point of view, the old sovereignty of the clan: the blackmailing brigand is a criminalised image of the Chief.

It's an image which in its popular form works rather ambivalently. *The Highland Rogue*, though it portrays Rob Roy as an almost animal figure, an enormous man covered in red hair, nevertheless implies that he was forced into outlawry by the injustice of the Duke of Argyll, and features anecdotes in which he pays (and steals back) a poor man's rent arrears, or bewilders a captured clergyman with the mock-Calvinist argument that he was predestined to be a cattle-rustler. This atmosphere of Renaissance picaresque clearly creates the conditions for Rob Roy's conversion into Robin Hood, and thirty years or so after his death the parallel was being explicitly drawn.[24] The political problem of lawlessness inverts easily into a folk-tale image of freedom – the more so because of the success of government repression after the Forty-five; within a dozen years of Culloden the Highlands were (if we exclude excise and game laws, both special cases) more law-abiding than Hampstead Heath.[25] The same reversal is noticeable in Lowland popular song, where long-standing prejudices against the Highlander as a thieving vagabond soften imperceptibly into romance. For example, what is the tone of 'The Highland Balou', collected, and probably reshaped, by Burns?

> Hee-balou, my sweet, wee Donald,
> Picture o' the great Clanronald;
> Brawlie kens our wanton Chief
> Wha got my wee Highland thief . . . [26]

The implications are consciously libellous: the Highland character is certainly being denigrated. But the lyric's outlaw tenderness makes a converse, sentimental appeal. Similarly in the 'Highland Laddie' vein of ballads,[27] the girl who goes off with Donald is choosing freedom instead of respectability with her 'Lawland Kin and Dady'. The aims of Improvement are directly refused:

> I'll sell my rock, my reel, my tow,
> My gude gray mare and hacket cow,
> To buy my love a tartan plaid,
> Because he is a roving blade.

The social defiance is vitally, in the songs, a sexual dynamism: Liza Baillie, in a much-hymned seduction, elopes with Duncan Grahame:

> But she's cast aff her bonny shoon,
>   Made of the Spanish leather,
> And she's put on her Highland brogues
>   To skip amang the heather[28]

and the invariable features of costume (dirk, pistol, enveloping plaid) shade readily into innuendo. The plaid in particular becomes something of an erotic symbol because so many ballad heroines are 'row'd' in it. It is then doubly illicit: it confers a gipsy freedom by allowing the 'ranting, roving laddie' to bed down anywhere, and it was, itself, a prohibited garment between 1746 and 1782.

The two analogous themes, banditry and sexual licence, combine literally in the string of songs about girls who, like Bonny Babbie Livingstone, were abducted to the Highlands more or less by force; the most popular of these in the later part of the century seems to have been the one about Robin Oig, Rob Roy's son.[29] This libertine tradition arguably reaches its peak in the song of the 'raucle Carlin' in Burns's *Love and Liberty* cantata,[30] where 'John Highlandman', now in the 1780s a half-militarised figure, is the carrier of a rowdy vagabond energy verging menacingly on a newer political radicalism.

In these notations, admiring or deploring, of outrageous Highland freedom, there is an obvious conflict with the idea, equally powerful and equally the product of the state's efforts to erase Highland particularity, that Highlanders were all slaves. It was not a formal inconsistency: the official view was that the people were not free because the Chiefs' power over them was not sanctioned, and therefore not controlled, by law, and so that 'the Common People are Slaves, in Proportion to the Distance of their Country from the Centre of Justice'.[31] Tyranny and lawlessness are on this account two sides of the same coin; Bonny Babbie Livingstone would perhaps have agreed. But the contradiction was none the less felt. It meant for example that the extension of 'liberty' to the Highlanders took the form of heavy policing – of 'keeping garrisons', as one writer of 1746 put it, 'in proper places all over the Highlands, till the people are acquainted with their own interests'.[32] It's an uneasy position: the people are too benighted to want freedom, so it will have to be forced upon them. After 40 years of the attempt, a visitor found the 'spirit of clanship' persisting, and concluded that 'if certain appearances prove that human nature pants after freedom, there are others which seem to indicate a propensity to voluntary slavery'.[33] The freedom which is caught in this paradox is of an ideologically particular kind; and the case of the poor Highlander, for whom it meant new labour discipline, new state power, and new rights of private property, was calculated to strain its limits. The image of an outlaw freedom registers the strain: the slavish mountaineer becomes the exponent, against the abstract juridical liberty of the constitution, of a utopian liberty of desire.

4 THE BEGGAR

The fool and the rogue are texts which incorporate the superior stability of an observer. Tonalt wanders alone through a Lowland society whose values are perhaps less appealing than his, but certainly stronger. In crises at which Highlanders in a body were temporarily formidable, the tone is harsher. William Cleland, a Cameronian lieutenant-colonel, saw the Highland Host of 1678, who were being used to intimidate his own people, as exploiters: violent, cowardly, uncouth. Yet even here the underlying disadvantage of the Highlanders is preserved in the terms of the invective:

> There swarms of vermine, and sheep kaids,
> Delights to lodge beneath the Plaids,
> For they like not in frostie Weather
> To sit upon her open leather.
> Her nane sell lapp and clapt her narse,
> More like a Monkie, nor like *Mars*.[34]

The invaders are not powerful and hard, but cold, hungry and lice-ridden. Not that the denunciation is tempered by any sympathy: on the contrary, it's exactly the destitution of the Highlanders, their bestial neediness, which makes them hateful. A closely similar idea appears, with the same rough command of grotesque, in verses quoted in *The Highlander Delineated*, a somewhat panic-stricken pamphlet published in London in late 1745. For example:

> Whene'er his craving Thirst or Hunger calls
> For due Subsistence, on his Knees he falls,
> And in the Impression of a *Hobby's Hoof*,
> Where Rain lies mix'd with other nasty stuff,
> He drops his *Oatmeal*, stirs it well about,
> And, leaning on his Hands, sucks up the *Grout*.[35]

This extravagantly sordid person is not only repellent but dangerous: if he survives on little more than mud, it's hard to see how he can be conclusively defeated, and impossible to guess what he might do on reaching London. The same pamphlet, which is an anthology of quotations, also refers the reader to Joel, ii, 3:

> A fire devoureth before them; and behind them a flame burneth: the land is as the garden of Eden before them, and behind them a desolate wilderness; yea, and nothing shall escape them.

Here again the Highlanders pose the special threat of people who have nothing. They are not so much an invading army as a plague – vermin, as well as verminous – locusts, banditti, beggars coming to town. The topical version of 'Lillibulero' – 'O Brother Sandie, hear ye the News?/An army's just coming without any shoes' – is a terse memento of the mixture of sneering and fearing which met the invasion. A similar tone later justified the atrocities that followed Culloden; Brigadier Mordaunt, according to one account, went 'to Lord Lovat's House, that Nest and Cage of unclean Birds, where much Treason and Rebellion had been hatched; he only found the Nest, for the Birds were flown, however, he thought proper to purge it from all Pollutions by Fire'.[36]

At this point, however, the image of the Highlander gets interestingly mixed up with that of the Scot in general. As Defoe puts it, when James VI came to the English throne,

> *Scots* from the *Northern* Frozen Banks of *Tay*
> With Packs and Plods came *Whigging* all away:
> Thick as the Locusts which in *Egypt* swarm'd,
> With Pride and hungry Hopes compleatly arm'd:
> With Native Truth, Diseases and No Money,
> Plunder'd our *Canaan* of the Milk and Honey.[37]

That union of courts, and therefore of preferment pyramids, between a rich nation and a poor one; the complex subsequent Scots involvement in the Civil War; the new suspicions consequent on the negotiation of parliamentary union in 1707; the spectacular electoral corruption of the Scottish burghs down to 1832 – a whole history of Anglo-Scottish enmity lay behind the sour Scotch stereotypes of eighteenth-century English prejudice. Many of the types were Lowland,[38] as of course were most of the alleged plunderers. But Defoe's Scot (from *The True-Born Englishman* of 1701), like John Cleveland's much-quoted 'Rebell Scot' from half a century earlier,[39] is poor, proud, plaided and infected, and clearly overlaps with the locust-like Highlander. Some Highland insignia, such as the bagpipes, early acquired a role as identifiers of any Scot; and even well-informed writers don't scruple to mingle the types. Smollett's Maclaymore,[40] for example, though he's supposed to be from Lochaber and has a parodically clannish name, is given a Lowland accent and a legalistic pedantry drawn from a different Scotch formula. Highland and national caricatures tended to fall together.

They were also pushed. Lord Hardwicke, speaking to the Heritable Jurisdictions Bill in 1747, felt obliged to dissociate the government from 'the notion of a general disaffection in Scotland', and to threaten to prosecute the distributors of 'infamous incendiary pamphlets' designed to 'make a breach between the two nations'.[41] Typical of these would be the letter in the journal *Old England*, December 1746, urging Englishmen 'to keep in remembrance their [that is, the *Scots'*] late odious attempt to subvert our Laws'; an attempt which originated 'as well in the brutal Ignorance of the barbarous *Highlander*, as in the politer Treachery of the false *Lowlander*'. As this last distinction shows, the writer is not confounding the two parts of Scotland out of ignorance, but deliberately tarring the whole country with the brush from Culloden. His real concern, it soon transpires, is not the Rising, but the old competition for government places: the way to protect the constitution from sedition by Scots turns out to be to 'exclude them from sharing in the Benefit of our Plenty'. Once it was safely defeated, the Forty-five could be used as a propaganda advantage within factional London politics.

It was most obviously an advantage for English over Scots, but it also served, by a supplementary smear, as an advantage for Whigs over Tories: since Tory die-hards had presumably welcomed the prospect of a Jacobite restoration, they could be linked to the beggarly Highland army too. This association spread easily to all Tories, and then to all and any opponents of the ruling Whig oligarchy. A pro-ministerial election rhyme of 1754 makes light work of the tortuous connections:

> Don't, like asses, cloud your glory;
>   Will you change your reds and blues
> For the livery of a Tory,
>   For a Highland plaid and trews?[42]

It was this associative web — Tory–Jacobite–Scot–Highlandman — which was activated in early 1761 by the rise of the Earl of Bute.

As is well known, Bute became the object of a furious press onslaught led by John Wilkes.[43] Within it, the victim's Scottish origins were turned to account in three separable ways. One was, of course, the struggle for places. Bute's success was part of, and must have furthered, a general increase in the proportion of Scots in political and military posts; Wilkes encouraged the widespread belief that the London Scots did each other systematic good turns, and dwelt on the scandalous commissioning of Sir Gilbert Elliot's ten-year-old son. Secondly, there was Bute's invidious status as a royal favourite asserting the rights of monarchy against oligarchy: this his opponents interpreted as a neo-Jacobite plot to subvert the constitution and reinstate autocracy. And thirdly, much of the attack was directed at the administration's winding-up of the Seven Years War, detecting in every concession the spirit of the auld alliance. All three accusations were calculated to revive the themes of 1745. As organised place-hunters, the Scots were beggarly and clannish; as monarchists, they were slavish and unconstitutional; and as French pawns they were Jacobitical and treacherous.

The manner of the *North Briton* blends all these aspersions together so that their mutual contradictions disappear. For example, Wilkes, writing in the character of a Scot, argues that the rising of 1715, which cost millions to suppress, only happened because the subsidies to the clans were stopped:

> I therefore most sincerely hope, that as we have now a *Scottish* nobleman at the head of the treasury, his lordship will consider it as the truest *oeconomy* to give some proper pensions to his countrymen the Highland chiefs, which may save England the severe and expensive operation of quelling another insurrection ... If this is done, I make no doubt but they will as implicitly follow the Earl of BUTE as they did the Earl of MAR.[44]

The knack is to bring Whitehall and Highland politics together to their mutual discredit: place-hunting Scots are denounced as rebels while at the same time rebel chiefs are belittled as place-hunters. The overall implication is that Bute is at the head of a system of national blackmail. Stereotypical details casually cement the link. For example, the London Scot recommends a bridge over the Tweed 'as my family are very impatient to pay me a visit, and I have not seen any of them since I took a walk up hither' – implying that Scots are clannish and backward. Or again, in a discussion about Canada, a Scots aristocrat dismisses the importance of furs since 'such delicacy is rarely found in our hardy, naked-thighed country' (Scots are uncivilised kilted Highlanders).[45] Pro-Hanoverian Scotland is relentlessly elided: Smollett's youthful Culloden poem, 'The Tears of Scotland', is joyfully quoted against him with all its national rhetoric,[46] and the fact that Bute's family name is Stuart is repeated *ad nauseam*. All Scots are Highlanders, all Highlanders are rebels, and all rebels are out for loot.

Further down the market the identifications were yet cruder. In the prints collected in the much supplemented *British Antidote to Caledonian Poison* (1763–6), Scots almost invariably appear in skimpy plaids and Scotch bonnets, often with harsh faces and lank unkempt hair; and whole sectors of abuse are devoted to the bagpipe, and to the Scotch itch (in unconscious homage to the Scot Cleland, kilted figures scratch themselves and make faces). These nasty characters get everywhere: they fly to London on Moggy Mackenzie's broomstick under an insignia compounded of thistle, money-bags, and claymore and target; they gather round the standard of the Boot (a universal punning symbol of the minister) as the wild chiefs of the Hebronites from the satire *Gisbal, an Hyperborean Tale* (1762); they are seen conniving, between ignorance and malice, at the gross 'evacuation' of the conquests of 1759–60.[47] For a brief but rather horrifying period, the Highlander takes on the role of political devil. As a commentator in 1763 remarked of another fictional diatribe, *Le Montagnard Parvenu, or the new Highland Adventurer* (the old Highland adventurer was of course the Pretender), 'Poor Scotland! how unfortunate art thou in having produced a B–! Poor B–! how unhappy art thou in being a Scotsman!'[48]

It was, though, a temporary misfortune for Scotland, and for the Highlands in particular. The war years were those not only of Bute but also, as we shall see, of the Highland regiments and of Macpherson's Ossian, both of which had a more lasting, as well as more positive, impact on perceptions of the region than topical lampoons. In the early 1770s came the first and most influential of many books by southern visitors to the Highlands: Thomas Pennant, a Flintshire landowner and zoologist, went there in 1769 and 1772, and produced what became the standard guides for the rest of the century; and in 1773 Johnson and Boswell made their still more famous journey. Changes in the Highlands' relationship with metropolitan culture were making the reflexes of 1745 obsolete. In 1772 the shift of attitudes was staged in Richard Cumberland's successful comedy *The Fashionable Lover*.

The lover of the title is a foppish heir who is going to the bad through flattery and gaming; his one honest dependant is Colin Macleod from Skye, an immediately recognisable comic Scot. Thus when, on Colin's first exit, the fop exclaims, 'What a Highland savage it is',[49] the 'fashionable' sentiment is being unmistakably reproved as a piece of metropolitan affectation. Colin's part in the subsequent plot is wholly benign, though occasionally misguided; and some vestigial North Britonish character traits, such as an unreasoning devotion to genealogy, pipe music and Scotland, are set against a naive good-heartedness which is authorially identified as far more significant. Only the unsympathetic characters exhibit the prejudices of the Bute years, a point which is made polemically, for instance, when Colin satirically introduces himself to the well-heeled villain as 'Cawdie Macleod, a ragged Highlander, so please you, a wretched gaelly', or when at the end the play's *raisonneur* deplores 'those whose charity, like the limitation of a brief, stops sort at Berwick'.[50] In these touches, the figure of the Highland beggar is revalued in the new terms of the literature of sensibility, with far-reaching implications which will be explored in Chapter 6.

In the mean time, it's worth noting what survived, and survives, of the campaign of vilification: the conflation of Highland and Lowland Scotland. That all Scots wear tartan, are devoted to bagpipe music, are moved by the spirit of clanship, and supported Bonny Prince Charlie to a man – all these libels of 1762 live on as items in the Scottish tourist package of the twentieth century. Absorbed into the cultural nationalism of the age of Scott, and thence transmitted via royal Scotomania throughout the Victorian Empire, they acquired a nostalgic glow without ever, as Murray Grigor's 'Scotch Myths' exhibition demonstrated,[51] quite losing their power to express derision and loathing.

5 THE HISTORY OF CIVILISATION

The stereotypes which I have been discussing project the Highlanders as aliens. Speakers of an outlandish jargon, vagabonds outside the law, foreign despoilers of the country, they are apparently people originally and irreducibly different from ourselves. Such a cultural construction of the stranger is consistent with the ethnography, dominant in the earlier part of the century, which explains differences of manners by mapping them on to a taxonomy of 'peoples', each having its own distinct character. This is the academic model derived by early chroniclers of the Forty-five from antiquarian classics such as Camden, Buchanan and Tacitus. Camden, for example, says that the Caledonii are 'of a fiercer temper from the extream coldness of their climate, and more bold and forward from their abundance of blood'.[52] The historians of the Rising not only reproduce judgements of this kind, but also apply the principle to their own observations. Thus Andrew Henderson in 1748 characterises individual clans: the Camerons are lazy, the Munros 'like the Grants for selfishness, but not so enticing', and so on.[53] And James Ray in 1749 remarks that 'The Highlanders have been reckoned an indolent people; although, by what I have said, it may appear that they are ingenious and industrious';[54] he evidently assumes that in the end one or the other of these descriptions must be the true one. Weightier historians share the same frame of reference: Pelloutier's *Histoire des Celtes* (1750) and Maitland's *History and Antiquities of Scotland* (1757) both deploy etymological and archaeological evidence to fit the modern Scottish Highlander into a transhistorical ethnic unity — that of the Scythian-Celt and the Gaul-Gael respectively.

However, this structuring of difference was clearly incompatible with the ideology of Improvement. In positing a permanent distinction of peoples, it shut off the perspective of British unification: its political conclusions were logically drawn by John Pinkerton, who unfashionably argued in the 1790s that the Highlanders were savages and would 'infallibly remain so till the race be lost by mixture'.[55] And as socioeconomic changes did in fact become visible to observers of the region in the 1760s and 70s, fixed ethnic categories offered no explanation of what was happening. Improvement required, and developed, a more subtly articulated theory of cultural difference.

The appearance of this alternative can be identified quite exactly. In 1755 William Robertson, the future historian, church leader and Principal of Edinburgh University, preached a sermon before the Society in Scotland for Promoting Christian Knowledge, in which his main theme was that Christ had come to earth at exactly the right historical moment: had he come sooner, the progress of civilisation would not have been far enough advanced for the reception and diffusion of the gospel; yet he came soon enough to mitigate the corruption which accompanied the excessive prosperity of Rome. The moral for Scotland, as it moved to shake off its 'barbaric' past and emulate the ambivalent polish of its wealthier sister kingdom, was pregnant; and at the end Robertson turned to the main field of the Society's missionary activities – the Highlands and Islands:

> There, society still appears in its rudest and most imperfect form: Strangers to industry, averse from labour, inured to rapine; the fierce inhabitants scorn all the arts of peace, and stand ready for every bold and desperate action. Attached to their own customs, from ignorance and habit, they have hitherto continued a separate people.[56]

The epithets are the same as Pelloutier's, or as those of the State in 1746. From all three points of view, Highlanders are idle, thievish, warlike and separatist. But Robertson deliberately sets the received traits in a schematic historical context: the state of the Highlands is that of an *early stage of society*. What lies behind this formulation is a theory of society which had taken shape, after a lengthy pre-history, in Adam Smith's Glasgow lectures of 1751–2: the concept of the four universally determinate stages of social development.[57] Thus, at the outset of his literary career, Robertson explicitly connects philosophical history – the essential discourse of the Scottish Enlightenment – with the partnership of Church and State to civilise the Highlands.

The operative distinction of the theory is the general comparability it permits between different societies. The most diverse observations about laws, manners, arts and beliefs can all be ranged along a single line leading from the hunting stage of development through the pastoral and agricultural to the commercial. This unifying principle permeates the articulation of Highland questions. As early as 1746, a paper in the *Craftsman* based policy proposals on the view that the Highlands were now what England had been in the time of Henry VIII.[58] In 1767 Sir James Steuart paused over the example of Highland agriculture 'because I imagine it to be, more or less, the picture of Europe 400 years ago'.[59] Adam Smith himself, in 1762, traced the growth of predatory pastoral tribes in the rugged valleys of pre-classical Greece and commented, 'The several clans ... would plunder on one another as the clans did in this country and in every country where they are established'.[60] Hugh Blair in 1763 made the universality of the 'four great stages' the explicit basis of his influential comparison of Ossian and Homer: 'For though Homer lived more than a thousand years before Ossian, it is not from the age of the world, but from the state of society, that we are to judge of resembling times.'[61] In each of these widely different contexts, the Highlanders appear, no longer as different from ourselves, but as *what we once were*.

To see what difference this makes, we can take as an exemplary issue, once again, the local sovereignty of the chiefs. Edward Burt in the 1730s describes this in some detail: he explains how loyalty to one's chief overrides 'the Government, the Laws of the Kingdom, or even ... the law of God'; how Scots law acknowledged the fact by making chiefs answerable for depredations committed by their followers; how this power is 'not supported by Interest, as they are Landlords, but as lineally descended from old Patriarchs'; and so on.[62] In all this, as very often, Burt circumstantially anticipates the discoveries of later travellers. But he does so without their interest in explanation: for him, country gentlemen in Inverness-shire and Surrey are just different.

Forty-five years later Johnson, though by no means sympathetic to Scottish philosophical history, is using very different terms:

> The Laird is the original owner of the land, whose natural power must be very great, where no man lives but by agriculture ... This inherent power was yet strengthened by the kindness of consanguinity, and the reverence of patriarchal authority. The Laird was the father of the Clan, and his tenants commonly bore his name. And to these principles of original command was added, for many ages, an exclusive right of legal jurisdiction.[63]

In a sense, Johnson knows less about the matter than Burt; he hasn't grasped that the functions of clan chief and landowner are separable. But in assigning the phenomenon a set of causes — economic, moral, juridical — which can in turn be derived from the general state of society in the area, he gives his inferior information a superior shaping power. If such are the bases of the chief's ascendancy, then it follows that the introduction of manufactures, or of modern communications, will cause it to decline. The Highland chief acquires a past and a future, and the attitudes which sustain his sovereignty are referred to the situation, rather than to the oddity, of those who hold them.

However, the rationale is not yet universal history. Johnson's hierarchy of causes stops short at the fact of ownership, and he is prepared to accord topographical and legal factors independent weight. The movement of generalisation is completed, appropriately, by Adam Smith, whose *Wealth of Nations* appeared the year after Johnson's *Journey*. Discussing the prevalence of local jurisdictions, not in the Highlands, but throughout medieval Europe, Smith argues that they were not created by feudal law, but were one of its conditions:

> That authority and those jurisdictions all necessarily flowed from the state of property and manners just now described ... We may find in much later times proofs that such effects must always flow from such causes. It is not thirty years ago since Mr. Cameron of Lochiel, a gentleman of Lochabar in Scotland, without any legal warrant whatever, not being what was then called a lord of regality, nor even a tenant in chief, but a vassal of the duke of Argyle, and without being so much as a justice of peace, used, notwithstanding, to exercise the highest criminal jurisdiction over his own people.[64]

The 'state of property and manners just now described' turned on two factors — the impossibility of exchanging an agrarian surplus for luxuries and the consequent distribution of produce to buy dependents at home, and the power vacuum resulting from regional inadequacies of royal authority. These conditions, according to Smith, survived in Lochaber and formed the basis of Lochiel's rule. 'Such effects must always flow from such causes': the chieftainship of the recent Highlands is universalised as an instance of a certain 'state of property'.

In thus systematising the description of Highland society, Smith is also subordinating its peculiarities to a powerful logic of progress. Just as in the post Forty-five state papers, the region is distinguished by its 'wants' — the *absence* of markets, the *failure* of legality. The positive idiosyncrasies registered by Burt's anecdotal style are eroded by the flow of comprehension: the drive to explain is also a drive to assimilate. It's true that in Smith's immediate context the Highlands are only mentioned as an illustration for a more general argument. But many subsequent discussions of the Highlands in particular took place within his immensely influential categories. Take for example one of the most widely discussed

Highland pamphlets of all, the Earl of Selkirk's *Observations on the Present State of the Highlands* (1805). The starting-point of Selkirk's case is the analogy between the mid-eighteenth-century Highlands and medieval Europe. He argues that in this state of society the consequence of a gentleman depended on the number and attachment of his followers; he was therefore obliged to bind them to himself by a 'sacrifice of pecuniary interest', and by assiduous hospitality and condescension. When these are taken into account, the devotion of the people, which so astonished contemporary observers, is 'an effect easily deducible from the general principles of human nature'.[65] Here again the sovereignty of the chiefs is historically generalised, but now with a clear political edge. What Selkirk means by a sacrifice of pecuniary interest is that under the old order the rent paid on a given piece of land was lower than it would have been in conditions of unrestricted economic exploitation. To call this difference a 'sacrifice' is to erect the *laisser-faire* market as a transhistorical norm of valuation and carry the imperatives of landed capitalism deep into the representation of the past.

In this we can see the ideological potency of the 'four stages' theory. It situates the most remote and antithetic social formations in an intellectual landscape where capitalism is *already* present. In part, this is a question of its implicit teleology: the 'commercial' stage of history — that is, the theorist's own — appears as the destination towards which all the others are travelling. It's because of this inevitability that the 'clannish spirit' of the Highlands is characterised in the discourse of Improvement without any of the venom of 50 years before: instead of an executive intention to stamp out the pretensions of the chiefs and the idleness of their followers, there is now a historical narrative in which they are stamped out impersonally by the progress of civilisation. But beyond that, 'philosophical history' deploys the ideology of universalism itself. Converting local particularities of all kinds into a single transhistorical master-code, it mirrors the contemporary elaboration of a world market which functions smoothly in so far as it reduces the diversity of social production to a uniform medium of exchange. Liberated from his unconformable stereotypes by this global abstraction, the uncouth savage is converted into an industrious and useful member of society by the sheer force of reality.

If this logic had been as universal as its claims there would have been no Highland myth. Instead, the story would have been the uncontradictory one which the legislators of 1746 intended: the Gaeltacht would have been swallowed up by the unfaltering expansion of metropolitan capital as totally as the metropolis itself swallowed up the villages of Paddington or Hoxton, and left as little trace of its distinctive identity. In practice, however, the expansion was by no means as lucid as its theory. Under the pressure of its dynamism, the figures of fool, rogue and beggar continued to reverberate, and to mutate. And by defining them as archaic, Improvement inadvertently accorded the Highlands the special, numinous value of relics.

3

Warriors

1 BARBARIANS

The Forty-five was the fourth occasion on which a Jacobite leader had raised a Highland army and thus put himself in a position to threaten the progress of the English Revolution. From a Whig point of view, 1745 was a replay of 1645, 1689 and 1715. This recurring pattern meant that Highlanders impressed themselves on British consciousness first of all as warriors. Economically and politically, Gaelic Scotland was no doubt negligible; but militarily it had made itself impossible to ignore.

How was it that a fairly small number of poverty-stricken tribesmen were periodically able to exert this anomalous influence on the destiny of a great nation? Most of the writers who considered this question had recourse to the same classical parallel. The Highlanders were like the barbarians who brought down the Roman Empire; formidable in battle, not despite their uncivilised way of life, but because of its privations, which rendered them, 'like the ancient Goths, intrepid, bold, daring, and inur'd to Hardships and Fatigues from their infancy'.[1] Thus the historian Alexander Cunningham, writing some time between 1714 and 1737, prepares the ground for his account of Killiecrankie by depicting the Highlanders as a clannish race, addicted to arms, inured to cold, and given to liquor;[2] all these epithets, besides anticipating a Highland stereotype still recognisable today, directly reproduce characteristics of the German nation described by Tacitus. Sir John Dalrymple's similar account, given at the same juncture in his *Memoirs of Great Britain and Ireland*, adds that Highlanders are hospitable, given to feuds, believers in auguries and fond of music, which they use especially to rouse their spirits in war — a different selection from the same chapter of the *Germania*.[3] Less specifically, Pennant's formally characterised Highlanders, with their uncivilised alternation of indolence and violent sport or action, bear a family likeness to Gibbon's Huns.[4]

No doubt these resemblances partly reflect the direct influence of classical historiography on the mental sets of the eighteenth-century writers. But a more cogent factor is the analogy of viewpoint. Tacitus and Gibbon were interested in 'barbarism' only in so far as it impinged on the history of Rome, which it did primarily as a military problem on the frontiers. The models they provided for the delineation of the Highlands therefore exactly matched the immediate concerns of the British state. This common priority had two significant effects on the picture that was constructed. The first was to exaggerate the militarism of Highland society: since the object of the description was to explain the people's effectiveness in war by reference to their social system, it tended to produce the image of a social system wholly geared to war. And the second effect was to suggest the idea of a barbarian whose accoutrements, methods and motivation all emerged spontaneously from his way of life — in short, a *natural* soldier.

This figure implied the question: is a commercial society not then at a crucial disadvantage when it must fight a more primitive one? It was a question posed with obvious insistence by the Government débâcle in Scotland in the autumn of 1745.

A writer in the *Gentleman's Magazine* for March 1746 — just before Culloden — recalls the military disasters of the late Greek Empire, and imagines the reactions of the courtiers in Constantinople. They would blame the generals, or bad luck, or the weather:

> In short, nothing was omitted that could screen the true cause, which was the courage of their enemies, that led them to practise a discipline and method of attack 'till then unknown, and therefore despis'd.[5]

The moral is that imperial troops shouldn't be too proud to learn from 'undisciplin'd Highlanders':

> Can we imagine that a *Camillus*, a *Scipio*, a *Marius*, or a *Caesar*, would have stood upon the decency and conveniency of a fellow's being very neat, and having his hair tuck'd under his cap, while their raggamuffin enemies, by a new method of attacking, discovered the emptiness and folly of their own military discipline.

This recalls the hirsute freedom of the Highland Rogue: the ragged barbarian is, so to speak, expressing himself in battle, while the operations of regular troops are vitiated by artificiality. Of course, that particular anxiety subsided after Culloden, which was seen as precisely a victory of discipline over wild valour. Still, the central thrust of the argument, which is the military importance of 'enthusiasm', continues to reverberate. The writer ends by saying that the national crisis requires 'the assistance of those who are capable of thinking, that they have somewhat to fight for, that ought to be more dear to them than *sixpence a day*'.

Here then, cutting across the region's serried negatives, was a Highland difference which the state positively coveted. Officially, Improvement was a gospel of peace: 'Commerce and Concord',[6] in a typical phrase, were to enter the Highlands hand in hand along the new roads. But the establishment of the global market whose unity was thus celebrated was in fact an extremely violent process. At the beginning of the 1740s, after a generation of peace, Britain had embarked on a war which would last for about 40 of the following 75 years, and which was essentially a contest with France for world domination. Professional fighting men were needed for Canada, India, Ireland, the Low Countries, the sea. The barbarism of the clans, deplorable when perceived as a cause of domestic bloodshed, became an asset if it could be deployed in the far bloodier wars of imperialist expansion.

2 RECRUITING

The deployment was already beginning. Only a month before Charles Edward's landing in the Hebrides in 1745, the 42nd Regiment, in which there was 'not a soldier born south of the Grampians',[7] had distinguished itself at Fontenoy, its first battle. This was regarded as erasing the stain of its mutiny in 1743; the same logic, written large across the Highlands, connects the rebellion of 1745 and the war of 1756–63. There's an early hint of it in Smollett's comic melodrama *The Reprisal*, in which a villainous French privateer with designs upon a genteel English couple is thwarted because his ex-Jacobite lieutenants, Oclabber and Maclaymore, turn against him.[8] In a vulgarised but pointed echo of *Henry V*, the deviant bits of Britain unite behind the English hero. Smollett was, as usual, abreast of the times: in the year of the play (1757) Pitt took his famous decision to raise regiments from the Jacobite clans.

It was an extraordinary response to extraordinary demands. This war was in many ways the showdown between the two potential world empires, British and French, which had been postponed by the peace of 1748. In Britain, the ideological dimension of the global effort was a strenuous national self-consciousness, a recognisably modern 'king and country' jingoism, which crystallised in the war's distinctive myths: Clive, the death of Wolfe, the unstable genius at the helm of state, the 'wonderful year' (1759) of Garrick's 'Heart of Oak'. Among these emblems of imperial ethicity was the romance of the Highland regiments.

A decade after the war ended, Johnson could say, 'England has for several years been filled with the atchievements of seventy thousand Highlanders employed in America';[9] the figure is, as he observes, a vast exaggeration, and suggests how the images of Louisburg, Ticonderoga and the Heights of Abraham were becoming legendary. 'They cut them, and slashed them, and whupt them aboot, and played the vary deevil with them, sir. There is nai siccan a thing as standing a Highlander's Andrew Ferrara', exults Macklin's Sir Archy Macsarcasm in *Love à la Mode*:[10] on the play's first night in December 1759, he would hardly have been recognisable as a Scot if he had not. In 1762 the *Scots Magazine* presented a description by an inhabitant of Minden, who had gathered that these outlandish soldiers

> are caught in the mountains when young; and still run with a surprising degree of swiftness. As they are strangers to fear, they make very good soldiers when disciplined ... They discover an extraordinary submission to and affection for their officers, who are all young and handsome.[11]

In a similar vein, John Knox, a London Scot with Highland interests, records in the 1780s that 'The French tremble at the sight of them, calling out, *the English Lions!*'[12] The Empire, it seems, has been lucky enough to enlist a force of nature.

A different magniloquence was put into circulation by James Macpherson, the promoter of Ossian, whose own wonderful year was 1761, and whose Highland Homerics chimed neatly with the general patriotic enthusiasm for Scottish warriors. A major in Campbell's, killed in 1762, was commemorated in the *Scots Magazine* with Fingalian pomp:

Where is car born Maclean? why lags my son behind?
Foremost was his sword in battle, though last to receive his
praise.
   Say'st thou the mighty is fallen in battle! yet not without his
fame ... [13]

This was to conflate the modern war with a misty tradition of barbaric prowess; John Langhorne's 'Genius and Valour', a poem published in 1763 'in honour of a sister kingdom'[14] as an explicit rebuke to the anti-Bute campaign, was typical in celebrating Canada and Minden as scenes where antique valour was renewed.
   The policy of recruiting from the Jacobite clans in fact proved a triumph on most of its several grounds. It produced half a dozen regiments of quality; it probably did 'drain the Highlands of some disaffected clansmen';[15] it offered career prospects for frustrated and latently rebellious Highland gentry. It may also really have offered its recruits some cultural consolation for the punitive legislation of the post Forty-five era: the soldiers were wearing the otherwise illegal tartan and, in many cases, serving under officers of their own name, so that the regiment became, designedly, a privileged replica of the clan.[16] And it was an ideological success as well. In 1766 Pitt looked back proudly in a much-quoted speech:

I sought for merit wherever it was to be found. It is my boast that I was the first minister who looked for it; and I found it in the mountains of the north. I called it forth and drew it into your service, a hardy and intrepid race of men; men who, when left by your jealousy, became a prey to the artifices of your enemies, and had gone nigh to have overturned the State in the war before the last. These men, in the last war, were brought to combat on your side: they served with fidelity as they fought with valour, and conquered for you in every part of the world: detested be the national reflections against them![17]

The immediate context of the speech is relevant to the nationalist rhetoric. Pitt is attacking the administration's American policy, and here dissociates himself from the anti-Scottish element in the opposition. The digression about the Highland regiments is thus both a declaration of Great British unity and a warning (prophetic, as it turned out) about the dangers of alienating far-flung minorities in the Empire. This gesture, including the Highlands in the oratorical sweep of an imperial ideal, alerts us to a nice ambiguity in Knox's story, mentioned above. That the French should call troops from Scotland 'the English lions' is in one way satisfying because it shows how little the panic-stricken foreigners understand what they're up against. But in another sense the name is accurate. The barbarians who once threatened the English domination of the state are now trained to maul its enemies; the Lyon in Mourning[18] retains its native ferocity, but its victims — and its significations — are selected in London.

Pitt's speech has an extra-parliamentary companion piece: the song 'The Garb of Old Gaul', which was written during the war and adopted as the regimental tune of the 42nd Regiment in 1767.[19] Allegedly translated from a Gaelic original, the lyric begins:

In the garb of old Gaul, wi' the fire of old Rome,
From the heath-cover'd mountains of Scotia we come,
Where the Romans endeavour'd our country to gain,
But our ancestors fought, and they fought not in vain.[20]

The continuation runs through the familiar repertoire of inherited military assets — the 'loud-sounding pipe', the freedom from 'effeminate customs', and so on; until the chorus, with a jolt which is ideological as well as metrical, declares:

Then we'll defend our liberty, our country and our laws,
And teach our late posterity to fight in freedom's cause.

The tone of all this is insecure because the song is trying to be a general description of the 'Highland character' and at the same time an authentic particular manifestation of it. The first person plural, the springy anapaests, the macho meiosis in the fourth line — these features indicate the voice of the fiery Scotians in person. But the allusive and linguistic Latinity, and the Hanoverian constitutionalism, advertise on the contrary the metalinguistic presence of the English political establishment. That the resulting lameness didn't stop the piece becoming very popular says much for the potency of the contradictory ideology it hymns.

The contradiction becomes concrete if we look again at Pitt. He had conducted the war with the support of the City — the merchants, financiers, and to some extent industrialists. As J. H. Plumb says, 'His world and their world were one: he voiced, as no one else could, their aspiration, and he had given a moral purpose to their appetite for wealth, power, and dominion.'[21] The objectives of the war were markets, raw materials, control of trade routes. For the landed classes, who were taxed to pay for it, the adventure had less to offer, and they eventually came to oppose it: it was the commercial nation that was at war. It's thus wholly consistent with the 'Great Commoner's' ideological role that he speaks of his Highland recruiting as an application of the principle of free competition: 'I sought for merit wherever it was to be found.' In fact, however, it was understood to be a clan levy, working through the residual authority of dynastic chiefs; hence the insistence, in many of the literary memorials, that it was the renewal of an *antique* valour. The hardiness and intrepidity represented, not the unleashed energies of the new order, but the habits of an old one intentionally doomed to extinction by the successes of, precisely, the commercial nation. Only three years later, Thomas Pennant observed that the sword and target, 'since the disarming act, are scarcely to be met with; partly owing to that, partly to the spirit of industry now rising among them, the Highlanders in a few years will scarce know the use of any weapon'.[22]

In other words, the recruiting drive ran in tandem with that other model of Highland development, described in Chapter 2, which deliberately sought to douse the fire of old Rome and to substitute labour discipline – hands who would give value for 'sixpence a day'. The state was trying to eat and have the cake of Highland belligerence: as Knox put it: 'At present that barbarous ferocity, which was the offspring of feudal institutions, is completely extinguished; while their native valour, and military character, remain unimpaired'.[23] That pleasing antithesis, at once optimistic and evasive, is an ideological reflection of Pitt's coup.

The same transvaluation of Highland violence was celebrated more indirectly a few years later in a farce called *The Highland Drover; or Domhnul Dubh M'Na-Beinn at Carlisle*. Written by, and starring, a half-pay officer from a Highland regiment, it was staged in Greenock, where there was a large community of Highland immigrants; and its plot ingeniously exploits the bilingualism of its audience.

Domhnul Dubh, who speaks only Gaelic, falls in with young Ramble, who is busy arranging a friend's elopement, and who speaks only English. The two have almost come to blows when the situation is saved by the heroine's bilingual maid Betty, who not only resolves the misunderstandings, but also enlists Domhnul Dubh's help with the intrigue. In the end the couple get away and the drover has a second and more useful quarrel, this time with the girl's unsympathetic old guardian.

Domhnul Dubh, whose haphazard but vigorous involvement in someone else's plot identifies him as a harlequin figure, is akin to Dougal Graham's 'Tonalt'; innocently narrow-minded and, as the scenario suggests, indiscriminately pugnacious. The stereotype is most deftly displayed in Betty's attempts to win him over: she obtains his confidence by claiming to be a Campbell (from which he concludes that they are related), and tells him that the guardian is a man with no chief (Domhnul Dubh, appalled, instantly embraces the lovers' cause against such a pariah). This is the Highlander as clown again, though the caricature — naturally enough in this performing context — is exceptionally friendly: the eventual moral is a regional compliment to the effect that 'though a Highlander through ignorance may be brought to espouse a bad cause, whenever he becomes sensible of his mistake, he thinks himself bound to double his diligence in friendship, to atone for his error.'[24]

Fortuitously or not, the play is a kind of slapstick allegory of Highland recruiting. The Highlander begins by fighting against us through misunderstanding, but once his quaint prejudices are soothed and suitable propositions put to him, he fights no less enthusiastically on our side. What is interesting then, however, is that the inconvertibility of the two languages is not really resolved: Domhnul Dubh's idea of what is happening is hardly more accurate by the end than it was at the start. The dénouement is content, with genial cynicism, to rest on illusions which serve the interests of the English juvenile leads. Farce turns out to be a surprisingly suitable form for the colourful chapter of regimental history which it encodes. With cheerful vulgarity, it reveals how the kilted battalions of Victorian legend, the heroes of Lucknow and Sebastopol, owe their existence to a ruse.

3 BATTLES LONG AGO

'That barbarous ferocity, which was the offspring of feudal institutions' was widely taken to be the normal state of society and morals in the mountains until the institutions were broken by state power. Johnson's theorisation of the matter is both representative and influential:

> A tract intersected by many ridges of mountains, naturally divides its inhabitants into petty nations, which are made by a thousand causes enemies to each other . . . Mountaineers are warlike, because by their feuds and competitions they consider themselves as surrounded with enemies, and are always prepared to repel incursions, or to make them . . . Among a warlike people, the quality of highest esteem is personal courage, and with the ostentatious display of courage are closely connected promptitude of offence and quickness of resentment.[25]

It's a quasi-ethnographic argument of some sophistication, in which geography determines social forms, which in turn determine social values and so, eventually, personal behaviour. As striking as the rationality of the profile, however, is the slightness of its empirical base. The documented facts sustaining it are two stories about clan feuds, whose luridly picturesque particulars jar curiously with the dispassionate generality of their interpretation. (In one, for example, the Campbells take refuge in a cave, and the Macdonalds light a fire at its entrance and suffocate them.) The information is being structured by an unacknowledged hyperbole: Highlanders, we are assured, 'were so addicted to quarrels, that the boys used to follow any publick procession or ceremony, however festive, or however solemn, in expectation of the battle, which was sure to happen before the company dispersed.' (Ibid.) It's easy to imagine Johnson himself, in a different vein, pointing out that the tendency of boys to follow processions does not require such a formidable explanation; or that a society quite this addicted to quarrels would not have survived to be suppressed by legislation. His credulity in this case has to do with the latent fascination of a Highland past imagined as a zone of pure violence. The brief anecdotes claim to be illustrating a generalisation, but really, in their asyntactic and shocking singularity, they are enforcing an image.

A collection of such tales appeared in 1764 in a publication entitled *The History of the Feuds and Conflicts among the Clans*.[26] It consists of thirty-odd accounts, taken from a seventeenth-century manuscript, of violent disputes in the Highlands between 1031 and

1619. Most of them are from the sixteenth-century islands, a bias which probably reflects the instability associated with the long-drawn-out decline of the power of the Lords of the Isles; but the book has no strategies for tracing any such pattern of events. It is simply a catalogue of atrocities. In chronicle fashion, the writing has recourse to formulas – one side enters the other's territory 'with all hostility' and 'spoils' it; fighting normally ensues 'with great slaughter on both sides'; and quite often it is the point of the story that the killing is aggravated by cruelty or by a violation of sanctuary or trust. These details, as they accumulate, generate an atmosphere of unrestrained butchery, though the extent of the destruction actually described is usually very limited. The style is flatly informative, guaranteeing by its very dullness the authenticity of the exotic horrors it relates.

In this form, tales of the Highland savage could be picked up by visitors like geological specimens. William Gilpin, connoisseur of the picturesque, extracted 15 pages of the *History of the Feuds* in his Highland book.[27] One of the earliest tourist guides, Charles Burlington's, repeated the *History's* tale of the slaughter at the North Inch, as well as an independent account of stones being rolled on to the heads of invaders in Glen Lyon.[28] In a tradition of Killiecrankie recorded by Dalrymple, Sir Ewan Cameron, disarmed in hand-to-hand combat, tears out his opponent's throat with his teeth; it's not clear whether it's this resourcefulness or the heroic fidelity of Cameron's servant, related in the sequel, that Dalrymple judges 'characteristic of a Highland engagement'.[29] Of course, many Highland families will have had a few such stories in their traditionary records: what is interesting is their dissemination through the 1760s and 70s – the aftermath of Pitt's war and the golden years of the original Highland Regiment.[30]

At an immediately political level, the image of the Highland past as an endless pageant of bloodshed was ideologically grateful because it made it possible to celebrate the recruiting of Highland warriors for imperial wars not only as a national advantage, but also as a blessing to the people themselves. 'Illustrious CHATHAM'[31] is the hero of several descriptive Highland poems on this basis: if in the dark ages before the coming of 'the blest light of polity sublime',[32]

> Murder was manly deem'd – and deeds most dire,
> Day after day succeeded sword and fire!

Hence rose the FEUDAL STATE. High-minded chiefs
Then dealt their wide demesnes in servile fiefs;
As VASSALS to the field the GAËL were led,
In causes not their own they oft-times bled[33]

then the recruiting officer comes as a saviour, converting fratricidal strife into honourable service.

However, the tone in which the stories are passed on is ambivalent. Burlington's guide, for instance, mentions the Fiery Cross, which picturesque call to arms he interprets as a wordless threat to burn down the draft-evader's house; and comments: 'This was certainly one of the most antient customs in Europe, and seems to have been invented by a ferocious and barbarous people.'[34] Especially in the touristic context, the ferocity seems somehow dignified by the antiquity: the detail, though it isn't different in itself from those in the policing descriptions of 30 years before, is now being offered overtly for the reader's enjoyment. Gilpin's interest in bloody deeds is still more explicitly an aesthetic matter. He offers the savage tale of Maclean's nuptials as a specimen of 'characters drawn from the life' particularly associated with the scenery his book analyses, just as his description of the pass of Killiecrankie is adorned with a dramatic reconstruction of the battle. In the same spirit, he praises a waterfall as 'a continued scene of violence, opposition, and every species of agitation', and deplores the decrenellation of Blair Atholl as a loss of Highland character.[35] Tumult and wild grandeur are the distinctive pleasures of Highland landscape, and the traces of a violent past form an apt text for the pictures.

Most travellers, even programmatic Improvers, register this converse appeal at some point, despite the pleasure they also take in signs of peace and progress. The most self-conscious note of the tension is Boswell's:

> The very Highland names, or the sound of a bagpipe, will stir my blood, and fill me with a mixture of melancholy and respect for courage; with pity for an unfortunate and superstitious regard for antiquity, and thoughtless inclination for war; in short, with a crowd of sensations with which sober rationality has nothing to do.[36]

It hardly flies in the face of 'sober rationality' to feel a mingled respect and pity for the brave prejudices of 1745: indeed, it was a Hanoverian cliché to say that the chiefs had made an honourable stand upon mistaken principles. What Boswell needs to apologise for is rather his sharing, in reverie, the prejudices themselves. The terms of constitutional orthodoxy are disconcerted by a half-articulated romance of war.

The 18-year-old Anne Grant, possessed (in 1773) of a greater share of fashionable sensibility, takes the romance further. On seeing the 'solemn and melancholy grandeur' of the mountains above Loch Lomond,

> I peopled their narrow and gloomy glens with those vindictive clans, that used to make such fatal incursions of old. I thought I saw Bruce and his faithful few ascending them, in his forced flight from Bute. A train of departed heroes seemed to pass on their clouds in long review, and do but guess who closed the procession; no other than the notorious Rob Roy, riding up the Loch side with the lady he forced away, and the 'twenty men in order', who make such a figure in the ballad. My mother knew the family, and tells the whole history of the transaction.[37]

The epithets – 'vindictive', 'notorious', 'narrow and gloomy' – are continuous with the hostile barbarian stereotype of the mid-century; and then their touristic revaluation is detectable in the little flourishes of style ('of old', 'faithful few'), as well as the explicitly active imagination 'peopling' the glens. But what is historically striking is the dreamy conflation of different kinds of story; the heroes on their clouds are unmistakably Ossianic, while Rob Roy was at large within living memory, as she says, and not so much a warrior as a bandit.[38] Legendary kings and modern criminals merge, together with the indigenous clans, in a composed landscape of violence.

Within this composition, violent acts cease to serve real historical intentions and conflicts, and become a part of Highland identity, as natural and as timeless as the hills. Fighting is situated in the cultural construction of the Highlands, not simply as something that happened there, and certainly not as the index of any kind of historical change, but as the expression of an essence: in a romantic realisation of the neo-classical placing of the barbarian, the Highland zone produces warfare from its own dark interior. There is a striking correspondence between that irrationalism and the rational exploitation of the region as a source of military manpower: for the picturesque tourist, as for the Army, Highland belligerence takes on the form of a raw material, conferring value on ground which otherwise contains none. Thus the ideological corollary of the formation of the Highland regiments as heirs and replicas of the clans was that the clans were retrospectively remade in the image of the regiments, as a social system wholly centred on fighting. In one text, we even discover that runrig, the commonest way of arranging the cultivated space in pre-Forty-five Highland communities, was practised in order to render the fields defensible against surprise attack.[39] And the botanical badge of the mountains, conspicuous in 'The Garb of Old Gaul', takes on an extra and distasteful connotation: in a recruiting poem of 1779 – a year of particularly frantic ideological effort following the entry of France into the American War – the Caledonians appear in arms on the 'purpl'd heath' where their ancestors shed the invader's blood.[40] Even the vegetation is militarised.

4 VIRTUE

The heather looked bloodstained to constitutionalist observers who assumed that the only possible guarantee of social order is the law. Johnson bases his picture of interminable feuding on the proposition that so long as the region had lacked any central authority, it had necessarily been anarchic:

> Those who had thus the dispensation of law, were by consequence themselves lawless. Their vassals had no shelter from outrages and oppressions; but were condemned to endure, without resistance, the caprices of wantonness, and the rage of cruelty.[41]

'Outrages', 'caprices', 'cruelty' – the vocabulary unhesitatingly selects the worst that could come of such parcellised jurisdictions. The political ideology underlying the judgment is individualistic and legalistic: that's to say, Lockean. The old Highlands are the place where the social contract doesn't apply. As such, they testify negatively to its value; but at the same time, they harbour latencies which the contract excludes. Might there not be social capacities which are not reducible to individual rights?

The frequent practice of war tends to strengthen the bands of society, and the practice of depredation itself engages men in trials of mutual attachment and courage. What threatened to ruin and overset every good disposition in the human breast, what seemed to banish justice from the societies of men, tends to unite the species in clans and fraternities; formidable indeed, and hostile to one another, but, in the domestic society of each, faithful, disinterested and generous. Frequent dangers, and the experience of fidelity and valour, awaken the love of these virtues, render them a subject of admiration, and endear their possessors.[42]

This is from Adam Ferguson's *Essay on the History of Civil Society*, which appeared in 1767, and may be regarded as yet another literary response to the achievements of the Highland regiments in 1756–63: Ferguson, the only eminent figure in the Scottish Enlightenment actually to come from the Highlands, had for several years from 1745 been chaplain to the 42nd, and in 1761–2 had taken part in the campaign for a Scottish militia. Although the *Essay* never mentions the Highlands, its tracing of an ethically ambiguous progression from barbarism to civility was, as Duncan Forbes has argued,[43] a theoretical representation of their recent history. One element of this is a sort of philosophic militarism, turning on an almost pagan polarity of virtue and languor, vigorous and enervated states of the 'national spirit'. The question of the social order, in this moralised sociology, is not only about peace and prosperity, or even justice; it is first of all about the human 'powers' which an establishment calls forth or allows to decline. In this light, the feud-torn life attributed to the Highlands is unexpectedly revealed as a nursery of virtues.

Ferguson didn't produce this revaluation out of nothing. Philosophically, it perhaps owes something to Sir William Temple, the idealised Scythians of whose paradoxical essay 'Of Heroic Virtue' (1690)[44] conform to the classical barbarian stereotypes I reviewed earlier in this chapter. And within the Highlands, the ethic can be seen in a curious pastoral version of the Forty-five called *Alexis; or the Young Adventurer* (1746), where the rescue of national manners is actually presented as the object of the whole enterprise, to the exclusion of the dynastic issue. Alexis, the Prince, deploring the dejected state of the shepherds of 'Robustia', resolves to lead them 'back to that happy Simplicity and Innocence, for which their *hardy Ancestors* are so famed in Story'.[45] Unfortunately, the shepherds of neighbouring 'Felicia' turn out to be so sunk in 'Luxury and thoughtless Indolence' that it's impossible to rouse them from 'their lethargick and grovelling State', so the band of ascetic and vigorous Robustians are defeated. Nor was Highland virtue a Jacobite monopoly: soon after the Rising a pro-Hanoverian Highlander, John Campbell, writing in indignant correction of the prejudices of his own side, makes the same contrasts: Highland babies

> are pretty roughly handled, wrapt up in a Highland Blanket, and nursed in a very homely and masculine Manner, not bound and painted up in their Trinkets like so many Dolls, but are often carried in and about the House as naked as when they were born, and nourished with good and substantial Cheer, not with Dates and Sugar Plumbs.[46]

The products of this austere regime employ their leisure in hunting, fishing and running up hills, disdaining cards, dice, and the covetousness that goes with them.

In these steadily moralistic oppositions a virtue at once mental and physical defines itself: 'hardy' (a word which clings to the Highlanders for the rest of the century) refers to an admirable elasticity of character as well as muscle. One antiquarian in the 1770s asserts that the ancient Highlanders, if narrow in their views, were strictly honourable: 'Men used to determine their disputes by the sword will detest fraud and duplicity as the true ensigns of cowardice.'[47] In view of the lurid and, as we have seen, well-known annals of Highland treachery, this confidence illustrates how the imagined purity of the region's violence could operate as a paradoxical centre for positive associations.

A typical prospect poet of the 1790s, viewing the Highlands from his vantage-point in Fife, shows by the very naivety and carelessness of his writing how automatic such associations would become:

> Amid those rude incult and dreary wilds,
> The tartan-cinctur'd Caledonians dwell;

> A rough, a brawny, incorrupted race,
> By hardships tutor'd, blood, and dreadful things.[48]

The conflict of valuations, between 'incorrupted' and 'dreadful', doesn't register because the potential contradiction is contained by a habitual rhetoric. The same cliché underlies Lockhart's mock-heroic praise of the phenomenal stair-climbing powers of the largely Gaelic Edinburgh cadies;[49] and from this comic and reductive celebration of Highland vigour it's not far to the broadside image of the sexually potent 'Donald' of the *Merry Muses*[50] – yet another dimension of the prowess arising from austere living and bare legs. At all discursive levels, from philosophical history to pornographic rhyme, Highland virtue is equivocally and unreflectively idealised.

This is clearly the form of a tension within the much more powerful ideal of a peaceful and commercial society: the suspicion that the very success of Improvement undermines qualities such as courage, endurance, or loyalty, whose value can't be reduced to their military utility. Ironically, no one advances this reservation more vehemently than the recognised spokesman of commercial rationality, Adam Smith:

> Even though the martial spirit of the people were of no use towards the defence of the society, yet to prevent that sort of mental mutilation, deformity and wretchedness, which cowardice necessarily involves in it, from spreading themselves through the great body of the people, would still deserve the most serious attention of government; in the same manner as it would deserve its most serious attention to prevent a leprosy.[51]

As Smith's context makes clear, the historical core of the moral problematic is the division of labour. The republican Roman, Ferguson writes, could hardly have foreseen a time so refined that

> citizens and soldiers might come to be distinguished as much as women and men; that the citizen would become possessed of a property which he would not be able, or required, to defend; that the soldier would be appointed to keep for another what he would be taught to desire, and what he would be enabled to seize for himself ...[52]

Ferguson is not a primitivist: he emphasises the rewards, in wealth and politeness, which flow from 'the Separation of Arts and Professions'. But he also identifies the same separation as tending to relax the spirit, and threaten the cohesion, of the society it enriches. This anxiety makes of the Highlands, where military and social institutions were supposed to have been inseparable and 'every person wished to be thought a soldier',[53] an asset of which recruiting is a specifically inadequate use: the image of a lost ideological unity.

Johnson, usually fairly immune to pastoral, warms to this martial one:

> It affords a generous and manly pleasure to conceive a little nation gathering its fruits and tending its herds with fearless confidence, though it lies open on every side to invasion, where, in contempt of walls and trenches, every man sleeps with his sword beside him; where all on the first approach of hostility come together at the call of battle, as at a summons to a festal show.[54]

Johnson doesn't finally, any more than Ferguson, assent to this image, which is embedded in an argument to the effect that the miseries of perpetual feuding outweigh the felicity of communal self-reliance. Still, the fearlessness, the contempt of artifical defences, the 'festal show', celebrate in a more than merely concessive tone the solidarity which is sacrificed in the advance to more specialised forms of production and defence. It's not only that dear associations are dearest in the hour of danger. It's more crucially that the sword beside the bed represents an indissoluble union of public and private commitments, whereas in the mediated, economistic society which is emerging in Britain and imposing itself on the Highlands, individuals 'may, like the inhabitants of a conquered province, be made to lose the sense of every connection, but that of kindred and neighbourhood.'[55]

Against such fragmentation, the warrior idyll remains a dream, not because the verifiable circumstances of traditional Highland life necessarily fail to confirm its details, but because it is generated within an assumption that the 'separation of arts and professions' is rational and inevitable. Ferguson, though not insistently deterministic, speaks only of 'how long the decay of states may be suspended'[56] — he doesn't suggest that the national 'relaxation' can be reversed. However, it can be mitigated, by *cultivating* the character which barbaric circumstances produced naturally. Ferguson insists that the 'weakness and effeminacy' of civilised nations is not physical, but exists only in the mind;[57] to remake in the mind, then, the national virtue which the division of labour mutilates, is the cultural task which the *Essay* adumbrates.[58] The necessary object of patriotic virtue, the affective nation, is not in the gift of the modern commercial state; but it is possible to recreate it from − or more precisely project it on to − the relics of the local past, inventing tradition to retie by conscious effort the bands of society which an insensible historical logic unpicks. It was in the service of this project that the myth of the fiery clans would take the national and imperial stage.

5 REGIMENTALS

The dignity of the region's developing ideological function is signalled by a new sense of the word 'Highlander'. In 1773 Anne Grant, travelling to the Highlands in the company of a dour and materialistic native, complains of his failure to conform to her 'hardy' and 'enthusiastic' stereotype: 'He and I are a complete contrast; he has nothing of a highlander but by his birth; now that is the precise and only circumstance wanting to make me a complete one.'[59] A few years later Donald McNicol implies the same enhanced connotation in wondering who can have told Johnson that 'Earse' is 'the rude speech of a barbarous people': only a Highlander could judge, but no Highlander would have passed such a verdict on his own language.[60] The word is coming to indicate, not only someone from a certain area, but also someone with certain attitudes and loyalties.

What becomes clear about this spiritual Highlander over the following decades of upheaval and clearance is that, unlike the merely geographical one, he is incompatible with historical change. Anne Grant again, in 1811:

> Nature never meant Donald for a manufacturer: born to cultivate or defend his native soil, he droops and degenerates in any mechanical calling. He feels it as losing his cast; and when he begins to be a weaver, he ceases to be a highlander.[61]

Here the assertion of extra-economic values, implied by Ferguson, coarsens into an ethnic type: 'Donald'. An ethos, extracted from its material history to be set as a pseudo-nature *against* history, therefore becomes at one gaudy and immutable. The problem of cultural identity is formulated, not as a choice among ways of living, but as a question of preservation. The Highlander becomes an ideal object, the source of a norm. At about the same time Sir John Sinclair wrote of membership of the Highland Society of London that 'the true qualification is not so much the distinction of *"Highland Birth"* (though this is certainly desirable . . .) but the possession of a *"Highland Spirit"*'.[62] Thus institutionalised, the spirit was pedantically defended against adulteration, though not vigilantly enough for the egregious Macdonnell of Glengarry, whose Society of True Highlanders, formed in 1815, upstaged the London organisation in an orgy of bogus ethnic purity.[63]

In practice, inevitably, the sublunary home of the Highland essence was the army. Hierarchical, communal, resistant to change, labour-intensive and insulated from commercial rationality, the military establishment came closer than any other eighteenth-century British institution to replicating the conditions of production which the stereotype of the True Highlander both reflected and mystified. Although Anne Grant's own depictions of the Highlands are unusually pacific and domestic, they come to rest, in both the poem of 1803 and the essays of 1811, in the pseudo-clanship of the regiments; the recruiting officer is the *deus ex machina* who resolves her stalemate of economic sense and ethnic sensibility by offering the natives the only accommodation in commercial society which does not have the effect of 'extinguishing their high-toned enthusiasm, degrading their character, and effacing all [their] peculiar habits'.[64] The punctilios and icons of regimental tradition work to freeze the signs of Highland difference; and the amenability of warfare to the diction of Ossianic epic ensures that the poetical mountaineers don't simply descend into prose.

However, recruiting is once again an equivocal solution. In 1803 it chimed exactly with the political arguments in favour of Government action to resist emigration: a House of Commons committee, for example, recommended civil expenditure on Highland roads and canals in order 'to prevent that emigration which will deprive the country of its hardiest and bravest protectors, who have distinguished themselves most conspicuously by land and sea.'[65] In this typical instance the same Pittite rhetoric which lies behind Grant's separatist heroics is brought out to support just the kind of assimilationist development which she is opposing. Two years later the Earl of Selkirk, writing to promote emigration, faced the objection that his schemes would devastate the nursery of soldiers: the Highlanders' military distinction, he replied, had been founded in a social system which had to disappear if the region was to become economically dynamic enough to support its population; so that the hardy and intrepid defenders were bound to be lost, either through emigration or through the measures taken to forestall it.[66] The only escape from Selkirk's elegant bind was an appeal to the magic of race and place; this is in fact the line adopted by his critic 'Amicus', who looked for the sources of the Highland character 'in the climate, in the constitution, and in blood'.[67] Evidently that train of thought leads back to the dehistoricised True Highlander.

Wars, and especially those of 1793–1815, were pulling the concept of Highland particularity in two directions at once. On the one hand, they tied the Highlands more and more closely to the metropolis – through the raising of regiments and the attendant patronage, through intensified efforts to promote regional development, and through the high wartime demand for the area's natural produce. On the other hand, the overheated military rhetoric proposed a newly distinct and absolute Highland character, most crudely in the bellicose Highland laddies of the recruiting songs.[68] The combined effect was that, even as the local colour grew brighter, it was reduced to the function of tinting an imperial outline, just as regimental traditions, however particularist they might appear, are really nothing but idiomatic expressions of loyalty to the army as a whole. The Highlander became at once more vivid and less substantial: that's to say, he became theatrical.

Thus Highland dress, for example, having been first an ethnic peculiarity, then a proscribed symbol, and then a military uniform, becomes at last a form of fancy dress. The Prince of Wales made his first tartan appearance – foreshadowing the more famous extravaganza of 1822 – at a masquerade in 1789, in the character of 'the Royal Highland Laddie'.[69] Sinclair's account of the Highland Society of London describes how its members held ancient Caledonian feasts, with cakes, whisky and the Ossianic 'shell', as well as appropriate garb, 'transporting the spectator, as if it were by magic, among a new race of people':[70] this spectator, previously unmentioned in the text, is necessary to the description because of the theatricality of the observance. Nor is this a matter of Sinclair's eccentricity. In a very different kind of literature, a 'silver fork' novel of 1797, a nuptial boating party on the lake of a stately home is entertained with a very similar spectacle:

the music stopped, and from a little rock, at the end of the walk by the water side ... there sat two youths finely dressed in the highland dress, with a table before them, and bread and cheese, a clean wooden dish with milk in it, and at the far end of the board (a table it scarcely could be called) an old man with grey locks playing on a bagpipe, and a bottle of whiskey by him.[71]

In the story, these people turn out to be real tenants of the bridegroom's, but their ungrammatically picturesque 'discovery' makes them into the figures of a masque. The theatrical form is not drama but tableau vivant – a fashion that was moving from the stage to the drawing-room at just this point in its history. In another society novel, of 1788, a narrator arriving at a Highland castle is welcomed by the family:

I saw the old Lady attended by the two young ones, whose trains were borne by boys in Scotch bonnets and plaid dresses; and I really, as they did not stir, took them for figures in a piece of painting which was to represent some device emblematical of the present occasion. I was even going to express my admiration of the artist when the ladies began to curtsey.[72]

Here, extremely but typically, the feeling of unreality is part of the pleasure: like Sinclair's Fingalians in the Strand, the ladies appear to be illusory but charmingly turn out to be real. This antiquarian dressing up elusively but suggestively pervades the Highlands of the time, from Johnson's antics on Coll (in target and blue bonnet, 'he seemed much pleased to assume the appearance of an ancient Caledonian'[73]) to Robert Mylne's ingenuity in designing the great house at Inveraray, where civilised interiors were combined with a chieftainly external style by means of windows which were round-headed inside and Gothic outside.[74]

What is happening in all these performances is that the supposed characteristic appearances of Highland life are being made into a uniform – that is, a décor whose signification is fixed. Locked into an imperial sign-system by their new ideological function, Highland clothes and customs are freed from the shabby mutability of historical existence and become essential, with rigid forms and glossy colours — objects 'emblematical' of themselves. One paradoxical result of this fabrication is a growing anxiety about authenticity — hence the debate, launched in the *Edinburgh Magazine* in 1785 and later reopened by Sinclair himself, about whether the short kilt was 'genuine' national dress or whether, as some maintained, it was invented by an Englishman called Thomas Rawlinson in about 1720.[75] The unhistorical notion, evidently another back-derivation from regimental practice, that setts were appropriated to particular clans, was in circulation by 1810 and furnished matter for many more authenticity arguments. Standardised for a global market, Highland manners could no longer afford idiosyncrasy even in detail. Minutiae required authority, because they mediated, not any longer a way of life, but an order.

6 REACTION

In this abstract form, the Highland warrior becomes a superman, an uncomplicated phenomenon of hardiness and intrepidity. One of the breed appears in a pamphlet of 1791 entitled *Memoirs of the Life and Gallant Exploits of the old Highlander, Serjeant Donald Macleod*. Apparently written on Macleod's behalf by an anonymous hack, it tells how the sergeant has fought with astonishing success in every major conflict since Malplaquet. He enlisted under age in about 1702, having escaped from an uncongenial apprenticeship in Inverness by walking to Perth in the middle of winter at the age of eleven. After fighting in Marlborough's wars, he was at Sherriffmuir, where he defeated the champion of Mar's army in single combat. At Quebec, aged 70, he was hit twice, and it was in his plaid that the dying Wolfe was carried from the field. The following year, his shattered shin-bone completely healed, he was in action in Flanders. In the American war, reluctantly accepting that he was too old for combat, he served as a drill sergeant; and now, at the age of 103, he has walked from Inverness to London to claim a pension promised him by George III in person.

These are only the most notable adventures in a career packed with incident, and there are one or two phrases in the telling to suggest that even the narrator doesn't believe every word of it. But as fiction, the story is historically eloquent. Macleod is unmistakably a barbarian: his preferred weapon is the broadsword, and his use of it is bloody, indelicate and often almost motiveless. Yet he is presented in a wholly positive light: the ferocity is redeemed by its encyclopaedically Hanoverian orientation. Born in 1688, he seems a living allegory of the eighteenth-century constitution in arms, the fantastic length of his active service connoting not only the hardiness myth but also an ideal immunity to historical change.

In all this there is the Pittite conquering hero, but also something more — a specifically conservative emphasis which is directed against domestic opponents as well as foreign ones. Macleod's conception of Government is a naively royalist one: he has come to London to claim his due from the king just as he would claim it from a clan chief. He is thus acting unconsciously on the principle, enunciated in the same year by Mrs Grant, that monarchy is 'an institution, naturally growing out of that patriarchal sovereignty, which, in the primitive ages, the parent ... was wont to exercise over his numerous and obedient offspring'.[76] This patriarchal inflection of patriotism had not had any special point in 1756–63, when the enemy was an absolute monarchy. But the last war — that of 1776–82 — had been an attempt to suppress a democratic revolution, and by 1791 it was obvious that the next one would be too. Moreover, they were revolutions which spoke directly to political departures inside Britain. As deistic, libertarian and class-conscious ideas and practices took shape over the last quarter of the century, the Highland regimental image remained static, but the meaning of its stasis changed. Its fixity, increasingly, was just where its value lay: within the conventional bundle of military virtues, 'attachment' came to seem the most precious. If it could really be arranged that, through the clan spirit, a soldier's commitment to the King had the naturalness of a family tie, then, as an early pamphleteer observed, 'this gave great life and spirit to the friends of the present establishment',[77] founding sovereignty on a principle of loyalty which was, so to speak, prior to politics. This seemed the nub of Highland recruiting policy to Henry Dundas in the 1770s: he recommended that to arrest the decay of the clan ethos militias should be formed whose officers 'would recruit from their own [clans] and thereby renew that cement of connection which my opinion leads me to think ought now to be cherished, not to be checkt'.[78] 'Now' is the eve of the American Revolution; at the next crisis, in 1797, the same point is made in an anonymous state paper, which argues that the Highlanders are 'strangers to the levelling and dangerous principles of the present Age', and can therefore, unlike the populace in the rest of the country, be safely trusted with weapons.[79]

One mythic indicator of this specifically political incorporation is the idealisation of the chief. It appears rather startlingly in Thomas Pennant's 1772 *Tour*. On the whole Pennant concurs with the (then) prevailing metropolitan view that chieftainship is a dangerous and lawless anachronism: he writes in the same vein as Johnson about the 'vindictive severity' with which heritable jurisdictions were exercised, and retails island history of 'the great Mac-donald' with Great British derision.[80] At the end of his Hebridean voyage, however, he departs from his usual unpretentious diaristic manner and launches on a grandiose poetical dream.[81] An ancient warrior, with target and claymore, appears to the sleeping traveller and harangues him on the past and present state of the Highlands. In life, he explains, he was a patriarchal chief, the fierce despot, but also the protector, friend and father of his people, courting wounds for their sake as they for his. The relationship was at once hierarchical and reciprocal:

> The crowds of people that attended at a humble distance, partook of my bounty: their families were my care; for I beheld in their boys a future support for the greatness of my house: an hereditary race of warriors.

Saved from complete seriousness by the whimsical literary device, the image of clan fealty functions as a social ideal, explicitly set against the values of a market economy:

> The ties of affection among relations are now no more: no distinction is at present made between proximity of blood, and the most distant stranger. Interest alone creates the preference of man to man.

The spectre goes on, with a sanguine opportunism we have seen before, to exhort his degenerate descendants to 'restore ... the laudable part of the ancient manners; eradicate the bad', explaining periphrastically that this means using the remnants of patriarchal authority to lead the people to become fishermen, weavers, soldiers and sailors. The opportunity is there because 'they would submit to any restrictions; and think no restraints, founded on the safety of the whole, an infringement of liberty, or an invasion of property.' This last phrase situates the medieval Hebrides firmly in the 1770s. Potentially, the clansmen are not only productive workers, but also exemplary subjects, because their paternalistic traditions make them innocent of the Whiggish jealousy of civil rights which is unsettling England and ruining America. The Highland chief, whose arbitrary power was, only a generation earlier, a prime example of everything that was wrong and un-English about the region, is metamorphosed into an anti-democratic emblem.

This figure rapidly acquires the confidence of a cliché over the following decades. In 1786 it formed part of the picturesque Toryism of Boswell's Hebridean *Journal*; and two years later John O'Keeffe's comedy *The Highland Reel*, which drew most of its limited local colour from Boswell, included the character of the Laird of Coll, who feels his 'heart glow with all the regal pride of an ancient Scottish chieftain'[82] when he lands on his little principality. O'Keeffe uses the authority of this potentate to resolve the misunderstandings of the plot: in marked contrast with Joseph Mitchell's play of half a century earlier, the chieftain is not the object of comic justice, but its source. Comparably, *The Grampians Desolate*, an anti-emigration topographical poem of 1804, runs the older image of 'High minded chiefs/[Who] dealt their wide demesnes in servile fiefs', but also, inconsistently, the new monarchist idealisation:

> Behold a CHIEF! – at heart his kindred's weal,
> Dispensing justice due, with upright zeal;
> No discontents or murmurings are heard,
> All seem convinced that just is each award.
> Behold! – the hospitable board now spread,
> *The Father of his People* at its head.[83]

The absence of discontents and murmurings is oddly unmotivated: the fantasy reflects, all too obviously, its source in a society where the justice of each award is by no means universally convincing. The appeal is that of an authority whose legitimacy is unargued, immediate, personal. For this, though there was a second and more explicitly legitimist myth: sentimental Jacobitism.

It's not easy to fix the origins of this curious cult. Hostility to Cumberland, sympathy for Lochiel, admiration for the Highlanders' high-mindedness in disdaining the reward offered for the Chevalier's capture — these latently Jacobite sentiments were respectable among firm loyalists at an early stage; and tales of George III's playful indulgence of minor Jacobite indiscretions suggest that the Hanoverians themselves saw the advantages of a whimsical toleration as soon as the real opposition was crushed.[84] But Boswell, again, is near the source of the articulation. The *Journal* takes an extended break from Johnson to give an acount, collected from eyewitnesses and incorporating several romantic legends, of Prince Charles Edward's Hebridean wanderings. At the end of this sequence Boswell discloses the object of his enthusiastic researches:

> I am not satisfied with the cold sentiment which would confine the exertions of the subject within the strict line of duty. I would have every breast animated with the *fervour* of loyalty; with that generous attachment which delights in doing somewhat more than is required, and makes 'service perfect freedom' ... They are feelings which have ever actuated the inhabitants of the Highlands and the Hebrides. The plant of loyalty is there in full vigour, and the Brunswick graft now flourishes like a native shoot.[85]

Here Jacobitism is frankly situated at the level of affectivity: the dynastic question disappears, and what remains is the quality of sentiment it inspired. The divine-right piety of the allusion to the Collect, and the somewhat machiavellian grafting metaphor, make loyalty to the Stuarts into an emotive *style* of loyalty to George III. From the extravagant devotion which ran risks for hapless royalty, conservatism in a revolutionary age borrows the warmth to counter 'the querulous growlings of suspicious Whigs and discontented Republicans'. (Ibid.)

This deliberate revivalism is significant comment on the collected, revised or invented Jacobite lyrics whose vogue was gathering momentum when the *Journal* came out and peaked around George IV's 1822 extravaganza in Edinburgh with Hogg's *Jacobite Relics* (1819–21) and Baroness Nairne's adroitly lachrymose songs for the *Scotish Minstrel* (1821–4). In Hogg's songs, the Hanoverian takeover of Jacobite loyalism is blatantly enacted, whether this is done in prospect from the standpoint of 1746:

> O Cumberland! what mean'd ye then
> To ravage ilka Highland glen?

> Our crime was truth an' love to ane;
>   We had nae spite at thee, man.
> An' you or yours may yet be glad
> To trust the honest Highland lad;
> The bonnet blue an' belted plaid
>   Will stand the last o' three, man.[86]

or in retrospect from 1800, the year of the immensely successful broadside 'Donald McDonald':

> What though we befriendit young Charlie? —
> To tell it I dinna think shame;
> Poor lad, he came to us but barely,
> An' reckon'd our mountains his hame.
> 'Twas true that our reason forbade us,
> But tenderness carried the day; —
> Had Geordie come friendless amang us,
> Wi' him we had a' gane away.[87]

The *faux-naïf* subjectivism of these pieces loosens the sentiment from its occasion: the clans' Jacobitism becomes a 'truth an' love to ane' so strong in itself that, paradoxically, it can easily be transferred. The clownishly indiscriminate attachment professed in 'Donald McDonald' — civil war reduced to an over-enthusiastic expression of hospitality — is, exactly, 'a fervour of loyalty', a predisposition to fidelity as such. The Highlands are identified as an irrational source of pure loyalty, just as a slightly earlier military reading had made them a source of pure violence.

Together these mystifications give rise to a second, somewhat perverse paradox. The real condition of the Hanoverian assimilation of Jacobite mythology is of course the total failure of the rebellion itself. And the sentimental reconstructions sanitise the Highlanders' motives by reading that failure back into them. These clansmen, who are too good-natured to be hostile towards the enemy, support the Pretender not *despite* his disastrous unpreparedness but actually *because* of it: one feels that if the enterprise had held out the slightest chance of success they would have superbly refused to take part in it. A pedestrian but usefully schematic poem by Boswell's son confirms the impression:

> Fierce and untam'd, yet devoted to thee,
> Proud that their death should their loyalty seal

> In the torrent of battle, the block, or the tree;
> Though blind and mistaken, we honour their zeal.[88]

From this point of view, Culloden and its aftermath so eclipse the successes of 1745 that defeat appears as the object of the whole adventure. The piece ends, 'Exulting we'll think on Glenmorriston's cave.' The reference is to one of the legendary Highland locations where the Prince found safety after Culloden through the fidelity of his followers: it's the figure of the royal fugitive which carries the decisive value. Failure, dignified as the ultimate sacrifice, functions rhetorically as the apotheosis of 'attachment'.

It's at this level, too, that Burns's Highland militarism consents to the conservative myth of loyalty. Avoiding on the whole expressions of modern royalism – even exploiting, with sly radicalism, the opportunity to call down curses on England and 'Br—ns—ick'[89] – he nevertheless reproduces the excessive and vaguely erotic honour of legitimist emotionalism, popular –

> If I had twenty thousand lives,
> I'd die as aft for Charlie[90] –

or 'heroic' –

> In the field of proud honor, our swords in our hands,
> Our King and our Country to save,
> While victory shines on life's last ebbing sands,
> O, who would not die with the Brave![91]

These hyperboles mark a reversal in the whole construction of the Highland military essence. It is no longer a question of the rational utilisation of specific local military assets; these were in any case, as Selkirk pointed out, becoming increasingly abstract with the passing of the society which had produced them. It is much more like the attempt, adumbrated in Ferguson, to extract from Highland barbarism traditionary allegiances with which to retie the bands of society; but now, at the revolutionary close of the century, ideological polarisation and intense recruiting activity have combined to mystify that project, rendering it pious and reactionary. Against Improvement in its political form of liberal rationalism, the Highland image expounds a glamorous futility, a ritual of duty which ratifies authority even, or rather especially, at the expense of practical effectiveness. Reflecting, now, not really the tribal imperatives of a clan levy but the disciplinary ones of an imperial army, the devoted Jacobite soldier signifies the sublime of *compliance*.

7 THE PENINSULA

The symbolic liaison between the Highlands and the Army is the matter of a novel which appeared in the year of Waterloo: C. I. Johnstone's *Clan-Albin*.[92] A woman takes shelter in a Highland glen and dies in labour without being identified; the child, Norman, is then adopted by the old lady who is the last survivor of the glen's ruling family, Macalbin. Norman grows up, joins the army, and is with the British expedition that landed in Portugal in August 1808. After the disaster of the retreat to Coruña in January 1809, he finds himself at large in French-occupied Spain. Delighted with the country's scenic and cultural similarities to his native hills, he joins a band of wandering mountaineers who are harassing the French, and after various adventures meets the leader of the Catalan guerillas. This melancholy and aristocratic person turns out to be Norman's father, and also the long-lost son of the lady in Glen-Albin. Thus the broken moral and literal lineage of the clan is restored by recourse to a *parallel* Highland world — one, moreover, whose circumstances carry the patriarchal social forms and vivid small-scale wars of the pre-Forty-five Scottish Highlands forward into the present day.

In its mixture of topicality and fairy tale, the novel reads the history of Highland involvement in the Napoleonic wars as a myth of redemption. In the 1790s, while Norman is growing up and the rightful chief is absent, the glen is invaded by sheep and mercenary values; but then the stirring events of the Iberian campaign lead to the chief's rediscovery as a warleader and father. This patriarch then dying in action, Norman formally claims his heritage on Christmas Eve 1809, and the following year sees him using the moral authority he has gained from his Peninsular adventures to rebuild his community at home. The true Highlander has found himself in war.

The mythic narrative has a significant parallel in actual cultural production. During the period of Norman's wanderings, Spain was exercising the same fascination over Walter Scott. 'Gazettes dated from Oviedo,' he wrote in 1808, 'and gorges fortified in the Sierra Morena, sounds like history in the land of romance.'[93] Coruña gave him restless dreams of 'broken ranks, bleeding soldiers, dying horses — "and all the currents of a heady fight"';[94] and the whole enterprise so aroused his imagination that he contemplated visiting the theatre of war, not to write directly about Spain itself, but 'to collect from what I might witness there so just an idea of the feelings and sentiments of a people in a state of patriotic enthusiasm, as might hereafter be useful in any poetical work I might undertake'.[95]

The aesthetic gratifications of the Peninsular campaign had an essential political dimension. For Scott, it was a patriot war, needing 'a Wallace, Dundee, or Montrose' to lead a hardy and enthusiastic but disorganised peasantry against Napoleon in the name of the rightful royal family.[96] The combination of circumstances was irresistible; here was a cause at once popular and legitimist; it was the Jacobite Highlands brought to life in the present day, except that in this case the interests of the gallant mountaineers coincided with those of the British Government, the unattractive role of Cumberland having been happily reassigned to the French. The analogy led Scott to see commitment to the campaign as a test of *British* national will; and when he decided in 1808–9 to help launch the *Quarterly Review* as a conservative antidote to the Whiggish *Edinburgh Review*, the move directly reflected a passionate belief that the *Edinburgh*'s sceptical line on Spanish involvement was not only incorrect, but an evil influence, tending to corrupt patriotic feeling.[97] Just as in Johnstone's novel, the lost spirit of the native society must find itself, exotically, in the mountains of the Peninsula. At just this point — as the fictional Norman was discovering his paternity and the real periodical was getting off the ground — Scott was writing his Highland balladepic, *The Lady of the Lake*. The valiant warriors and flashing claymores of the romance have the fighting in Portugal as their unspoken referent.

The Highlanders of the poem, Clan-Alpine (the echo of that in Johnstone's title can hardly be fortuitous, given the *Lady's* phenomenal popularity[98]), make a spectacular appearance during a dialogue between their saturnine chief, Roderick Dhu, and the hero of the tale, Fitz-James. The latter, not realising who Roderick is, says he is eager to meet with the fabled Clan-Alpine. Roderick retorts, 'Have, then, thy wish!' and whistles, causing five hundred armed clansmen to rise up out of the heather of the apparently deserted hillside. They stand a moment and then, at a wave of the chief's hand, vanish:

> It seemed as if their mother Earth
> Had swallow'd up her warlike birth.[99]

This *coup de theâtre* — it's centrally featured as such in contemporary dramatisations[100] — is rather typical of the poem's technique in being *all but* magical. The hero's meeting with the clan *seems* like a numinous encounter with the fairy host, but at the same time it's clear that the warriors are ordinary mortals who have simply been hiding. This slightly fraudulent connotative enchantment serves to spirit away a historically crucial contradiction within the image.

Most obviously, the point of the uncanny camouflage is that Clan-Alpine are children of nature: they are 'Benledi's living side', as though the mountain itself has stirred to fight the Saxon. It's an idealisation of the guerilla, who wins against the odds through the strength of being *native*; and so reflects the eighteenth-century 'barbarian' stereotype of the Highland warrior as one whose soldiership and patriotism are both natural as opposed to the fatal artificiality of civilised troops. But then what the chief's gesture also demonstrates is his absolute authority. The moment when the warriors appear is the moment when Roderick reveals who he is; they illustrate his name; he is exhibiting his power to tell his people when they are to exist, and when to remain latent. This 'Asiatic' conception of his power is another eighteenth-century commonplace: the Highland chief as autocrat. As we saw earlier, the image of the historical clan was retrospectively overlaid by its modern militarisation; the old Highlands were imagined to be organised into something like a series of regiments; and one part of that model was the assumption that the leader of such a unit was its commander. Some evidence was in fact available to suggest a more complex power system, in which the hereditary rights of the chief were tempered by the corresponding hereditary privileges of the clansmen.[101] But this relatively alien concept barely dented the narrowly military image of a dictator 'at the head of followers who, counting that cause just and honourable which their chief approved, rushed into the field at his command'.[102] Thus if the armed men who suddenly 'garrison' the glen are a facet of their native hills, they are equally a facet of Roderick, terrifying in the completeness of their obedience, moving on the signal with a uniformity which effaces their individualities — the apotheosis, not only of naturalness, but also of discipline.

With characteristic adroitness, Scott is having it both ways: Clan-Alpine are both wild and regimented, spontaneous and docile. The double image of the Highlander in arms, as both the free warrior of a legendary past and the compliant private of a modern regiment, is magically, or rather theatrically, resolved. That resolution is precisely the ideological point of the Peninsular question. The war there — which at the moment of the poem's appearance had not yet reached its decisive phase — was both an indigenous guerilla struggle against French occupation and a moment in the contest between the highly organised forces of the two world powers. As such, it constituted both a demand and an opportunity for the identification of the disciplined national army with the archaic, 'natural' aggression of the mountain fighter.

Scott's biographer provides a text for that identification which is in its way as arresting as the apparition under Ben Ledi. In the lines at Torres Vedras in October 1810, a few months after the poem's publication, Sir Adam Fergusson knelt in a trench under fire and entertained his prone troops with a reading of 'The Battle of Beal' an Duine' from Canto VI.[103] The stirring stanzas were occasionally interrupted by the reader's needing to duck: few poets can have enjoyed so gratifying a context of reception. But what is the relation here, between the fictional battle and the real one?

One might simply say: the poem helped to pass the time. Torres Vedras was not exactly a battle, but a month-long struggle to hold the long, fortified lines round Lisbon and so preserve the British bridgehead on the European continent. The troops manned the fortifications at the beginning of October and were then required simply to stay there. What this demanded of the men was not spirited aggression but steadiness; what threatened it was not any liability to a sudden rout but the deterioration of morale and good order through boredom and constant danger. Fergusson's gesture is not as eccentric as it seems; any good officer would be on the look-out for useful distractions.

The poetic skirmish contains all the movement and passion which the constraints of the real situation frustrate. It is a fluid affair of charge and counter-charge through the appropriate scenery of the Trossachs. The rapid action is punctuated by wild cries and exhortations; the formations of men are forests and waves, cornfields, gusts of wind and darkening clouds. A sympathetic thunderstorm breaks over the loch, and literal and metaphorical torrents and whirlwinds collide. Everything is reduced to natural shocks and recoils; everyone is splendidly and barbarically immersed in what is happening. War is sentimentalised, not in the sense that the pain and death are glossed over — the 'fell havoc' is quite insisted on — but in the sense that there is no alienation. The combat is a total expression of the essence of the combatants; a need for distraction is inconceivable.

It goes with this self-completeness that the battle of Beal' an Duine is almost completely pointless. It ends, not with anyone's victory, but when a messenger brings word that the Highland leaders are already in custody; if the king had thought to communicate this fact sooner, the battle would not have occurred at all.[104] Again, there's an extreme contrast with the *raison d'être* of the listening troops in Portugal. By 1810 the war between Britain and France was primarily an economic one: neither side was in a position to mount a direct attack on the other, and each was attempting to strangle the other's trade. Lisbon had no particular strategic significance: it was just that its traditional British links, together with the Royal Navy's control of the Atlantic, made it a point where military pressure could realistically be sustained (in contrast with the previous year's failure on the Scheldt), and a long wasting of French resources begun.[105] In this context of interminably mediated global instrumentality, the gratuitousness of the poetic warfare is part of its value; its purity of action and sentiment is uncontaminated by any political consideration which would degrade it into a mere means to some ulterior end.

That contrast, between the organised competition of modern commercial states and the unconditioned aggression of a fabulous medievalism, finally restores the ideological forms of the Peninsular campaign to the themes of the whole history of Highland militarisation. Capitalist expansion entailed certain subjective qualities — prudence, competitiveness, individualism, enlightened self-interest, internationalism, sobriety, respect for law and order — which appeared, in the Highlands as elsewhere, as the moral face of Improvement. But at the same time, its necessary violence (necessary whether for extra-economic types of contest or to maintain hierarchical stability) made contrary ethical demands, eliciting audacity, subordination, patriarchal loyalty, sacrifice, chauvinism, enthusiasm, personal courage. One way of evading this contradiction was to compartmentalise it, assigning the latter set of values to marginal categories of archaism and ethnicity where it could be externalised as an exotic 'survival' from another world. It was for this reason that 'civilisation' would produce barbarisms wherever it conquered. As one such warlike and regressive Other, the closest to home, the Highlanders were to repeat their mythic role in the Peninsula across the face of the earth, the indispensable atavistic natives in the Victorian triumph of peace and progress.

4
The Land

1 THE PICTURESQUE

In the complex negotiation of assimilation and difference which accompanied the Highlands' integration into the national system, one factor was simply that the region *looked* different. This was by no means a marginal matter. Eighteenth-century Britain was a society governed by landowners — this was still more exclusively true of eighteenth-century Scotland[1] — and Adam Smith is in agreement with the common sense of the age in taking it for granted that a sustainable increase in rents is the only really solid measure of economic progress. Improvement *is* the improvement of the land. Moreover, the distinctive arts of the Georgian ruling class — architecture, landscape gardening, forestry, landscape painting, the planning of model parks and villages — all occupy a space where the aim of enhancing the capital value of the estate coincides with the aim of making it beautiful. From Pope to Austen and Peacock, what happens to the appearance of the landowner's physical environment can function as the literary measure of his taste, wisdom and even mortality, because of an underlying consensus which refers all cultural values back, in the last analysis, to that of the land itself. The unity, in the enlightened management of landed property, of aesthetic and economic criteria, is at the heart of the ideological coherence of Improvement. Pleasure and business, *dulce* and *utile*, are expressed in the same smiling landscape.

Within this harmony the land is a double sign. On the one hand, as an object of investment, it is something like a raw material, destined to be valorised by the ingenuity and enterprise of the owner. But the land is also the origin of value; from its natural virtue the landlord derives at once his material wealth, the legitimation of his power, and the standards of propriety by which his artificial works may be judged. To 'improve' it (the ambiguity is reflected in the semantic subdivisions of the word itself) is both to supplement its value by changing it and to elicit its immanent value by acting in accordance with its natural imperatives. A truly pleasing landscape, therefore, is one which reflects in a single prospect the success of the land's productive use and the extra-social integrity of its being. Ideally, a naturalised development programme becomes indistinguishable from a socialised nature. The science of these minute accommodations between the human and the natural in the harmony of the visible world is the system of the picturesque:[2] the symbolic medium in which the unity of the land is negotiated; the aesthetics of Improvement.

For this equivocally socialised scenic taste, the unamenable scale and barrenness of the Highlands had the attraction of a sort of limit-text. The presence of ruggedness and infertility stretched the picturesque synthesis, rendering its satisfactions more energetic and inclusive. Lord Kames – a notable Improving landlord as well as an aesthetician – theorises this turn in revealing terms:

> a flowing river, a spreading oak, a round hill, an extended plain, are delightful; and even a rugged rock or barren heath, though in themselves disagreeable, contribute by contrast to the beauty of the whole: joining to these, the verdure of the fields, the mixture of light and shade, and the sublime canopy spread over all; it will not appear wonderful that so extensive a group of splendid objects should swell the heart to its utmost bounds, and raise the strongest emotion of grandeur.[3]

Contrast, in Kames's thoroughly psychological system, offers a strenuous pleasure denied by the prospect of uniformly 'delightful' objects; the comprehension of such mighty differences in one view stimulates a corresponding expansiveness of feeling. But then, as his integrating use of colour and chiaroscuro intimates, the scale must not be so vast that the comprehension becomes impossible. He later speaks of the 'pain' of an unbounded prospect, which the eye strains in vain to take in.[4] Wilderness is there not to threaten but to validate the totalising successes of the eye; the rock and the heath, 'in themselves disagreeable', yield up a converse beauty once they are placed within a larger system of agreements.

The standard route for the 'picturesque tour' which became established as a fashionable amusement from about 1760 effectively protected that placing. Influentially laid down as the 'Short Tour' by Pennant,[5] it entered the Highlands at Dunkeld and left them via Luss, having taken in the trio of great aristocratic seats –

Atholl, Breadalbane at Taymouth, and Argyll at Inveraray. It was thus a very domesticated version of the country, excluding the highest and wildest mountains, the whole of the west coast, and everything north of the Great Glen; and concentrating on the places where large-scale plans of estate management were most in evidence. Its picturesque highlight, the accepted epitome of the Highland picturesque until the meteoric rise to fame of Loch Katrine in 1810, was Loch Lomond.[6]

A long line of admirers is headed by Sir William Burrell, who in 1758 made what seems to have been the first touristic ascent of Ben Lomond.[7] That, and his admiration for the views of 'that stupendous Mountain' from the road, suggest a taste for unaccommodated wildness. But a few miles on he passes through Glen Croe and Glen Kinglas, and sees these two purely wild and mountainous valleys as 'equally horrible, barbarous, & disagreeable': his pleasure at Ben Lomond was really conditional on the mountain's crowning a varied scene of woods, water and islands. That insistence on diversity is echoed in later eulogies: in *Humphry Clinker*, for example, Smollett presented his large readership with 'a sweet variety of woodland, cornfields, and pasture, with several agreeable villas emerging as it were out of the lake, till, at some distance, the prospect terminates in huge mountains covered with heath.'[8]

This satisfying accommodation of nature and society appeared in 1771; in the same year, Pennant's first Highland tour culminates in a systematic comparison of the principal lakes of Scotland, finally awarding the palm to Loch Lomond.[9] For Pennant, the key to Loch Lomond's distinction is the moment when the southbound traveller, accustomed to bleak mountainsides, surmounts a headland near Luss and commands a sudden prospect of the cultivated fields at the lower end of the lake. The point of this — the dramatic juxtaposition of extremes of barrenness and fertility — rapidly became a cliché; a naively schematic periodical verse of 1777 declares, whether 'the sublime delights thy roving eye' or, alternatively, 'the softer landscape please thee more',

> Know, trav'ller! LUSS, the contrast well displays,
> Here snows appear midst *Ben*'s untrodden ways,
> While zephyrs play along the fruitful plain.[10]

Travellers did know it, very well: the dissemination of travel books, topographical poems and, a little later, guide books[11] meant that visitors came to Luss specifically prepared to see a union of the sublime and the beautiful form 'an object both aweful and pleasing'.[12] The islands, too, supplemented the pleasures of contrast by their number, irregularity and differences. Loch Lomond was the exemplary inclusive prospect, the acme of the picturesque.

As a scenic text, then, it warns us against conflating the eighteenth-century taste for Scottish mountains too glibly with the contemporary cult of the sublime. It's true that the word, and its semantic associates such as 'lofty', 'grand' or 'magnificent', are freely applied to this kind of scenery. But the aesthetics of the sublime had a fairly coherent tradition,[13] and the pleasures Loch Lomond typifies cut across it in significant ways. Sublimity is associated by most writers, including Kames, with simplicity, whereas here the decisive virtue is variety; natural vastness sublimely intimates infinity, whereas here mountains provide a pictorially satisfying 'termination' which saves the prospect from indefinite extension;[14] sublime objects are somehow transcendent, awing the beholder with a power beyond the human, whereas here the point is to assimilate even the wild crags into a scenic ensemble which is fundamentally anthropocentric.

Gilpin, the most sophisticated exponent of picturesque tourism, relates this distinction to its intellectual origins in the controversy about the waste parts of the world which was provoked at the beginning of the century by Thomas Burnet's *Sacred Theory of the Earth* (1680–90). For Burnet, mountains were the debris of the Flood, not a primordial part of Creation but ruinous memorials of divine anger. This conception, as M. H. Nicolson has argued,[15] leads logically to a sublime of mountain scenery by associating it with religious dread. Gilpin, in considering the mountains of the Highlands, cites William Derham's *Physico-theology* (1711–12), one of the books that sought to vindicate the wisdom of God in Creation against Burnet by finding out uses – humanistically defined ones for the most part – for the ostensibly useless productions of nature. Derham argues that mountains provide shelter from the winds, habitat for a variety of flora and fauna, a screen to prevent the evagation of moisture, convenient national boundaries, and, above all, a site for the rise and conveyance of rivers, which distribute water through the plains and make them habitable.[16] This unapocalyptic theism accommodates mountains conceptually, just as the picturesque accommodates them visually, in a unity of contrasting but interdependent parts: sun, air, water and hills 'A social Commerce hold, and firm support/The full-adjusted Harmony of Things.'[17] Thomson's serene formulation returns us to the always latent context of political economy: nature has the intelligible diversity of commercial society, and by the same token society exhibits the harmony of nature.

A conscious imitator of Thomson, John Cririe, applies the idea directly to the Highlands in a poetical Short Tour of 1803. His optimism confronted by the unpicturesque (because uniform) hills around Tyndrum, he explains —

> Here mountains stand attracting wat'ry stores,
> To swell the limpid streams, that murm'ring flow,
> When undisturb'd, o'er rocks and silv'ry sands ...
> And, spreading, fertilize the distant vales.[18]

The streams take us literally back to Loch Lomond, which Cririe predictably hails as 'of Scotia's lakes fairest and first'. The loch is uniquely inspiring because, lying across the Highland line, it enacts the commerce of mountain and plain. Long and narrow enough to resemble an immense river, its continuous expanse leads the eye all the way from the barren crags to the cultivated vales, encompassing the whole meteorological harmony in one 'full-adjusted' view. It was a normal part of a visit to hire a boat and sail among the islands:[19] in purely visual terms, the surface of the water was not an ideal viewpoint,[20] but it afforded the sensation of being afloat on the very element of nature's unity.

Throughout the travel literature of the period, streams perform this pervasive reconciling role in the construction of Highland scenery. Gilpin singles out the rivers and estuaries of Scotland as her chief glory.[21] Water, the literal medium of communication between the contrasting components of the landscape, reassures the civilised beholder that everything he sees is comprehended in a single benign ensemble, and groups even the barren mountaintops round the smiling image of cultivation. Nowhere else did the latter appear so formidably attended, or so vividly and naturally itself.

2 TREES

The banks of the lochs and streams, by a universal touristic preference, ought to be wooded. Pennant finds 'a spot equalised by few in picturesque and magnificent scenery' at Dundonnell in Wester Ross:

> The banks of the river that rushes by the house is fringed with trees; and the course often interrupted by cascades. At a small distance the ground begins to rise: as we mount, the eye is entertained with new objects; the river rolling beneath the dark shade of alders, an extent of plain composed of fields bounded by groves; and as the walk advances, appears a deep and tremendous hollow, shagged with trees, and winding far amidst the hills.[22]

The praise of variety is familiar, but there's a certain uniformity within it: of the four objects in the rather itemising description, three are rivers, and all four are bounded by trees. The bare peaks of An Teallach to the west, by exactly the contrast we saw in Burrell, form 'a view where the aweful, or rather the horrible predominates'. It's the conjunction of wood and water which is instantly recognisable as picturesque; the same reflex is in play when Gilpin finds a cascade that 'graces the centre of a little woody theatre which nature seems to have made on purpose for it',[23] or Cordiner surveys a plain near Braemar 'finely divided by the windings of the river; enriched with variety of wood'.[24] Clearly the woods amplify the figure of the streams as a harmonising and fertilising agency: the meteorological cycle is ratified by their tangible (and moisture-retaining) presence. At the same time, though, they offer a further signification, adroitly celebrated by one of Burns's few Highland landscape poems, 'The Humble Petition of Bruar Water'.[25]

Burns's Highland tour consisted of a string of high-life invitations, and the poetry associated with it was 'the coin in which a poet pays his debts of honour and gratitude':[26] the fashionable guest left suitable compliments at each port of call. On the whole, this function produced couplets of glazed insincerity, full of pale personifications and conventional nature-loving poses. The Bruar Water poem, for the Atholl household, is more lively. The stream, respectful but vain (it claims, after some picturesque self-description, to be 'Worth gaun a mile to see'), and mortified by the dried-up state in which it was seen by the poet, petitions its noble proprietor for some trees to shade it, dwelling with persuasive sentiment on the collateral advantages of singing birds, shelter for 'coward maukin' and a congenial retreat for lovers and poets. This rhetorical pretext, precisely because of its self-conscious artificiality, clears a space in which the frigid postures of the prospect convention – the personifications, the solitary devotee of nature – are suddenly free to move. On the basis of the connection between the lowly but charming stream and its aristocratic protector (a connection wittily similar to literary patronage), the poem fills with relationship: the stream enjoys its own twistings among the rocks, the birds which the trees will attract will in turn cheer them in autumn, the 'birks extend their fragrant arms' to screen the lovers' embraces, the firs view themselves in the river's pools. As some of these conceits suggest, the underlying figure is amorous: trees, birds, stream and shepherds are all disposed in a mutual courtship, and the poems ends with a compliment to the Duke's sons and daughters which is almost epithalamic. True to the poetical house guest's status and reputation, the apprehension of nature is at once social and sexy.

Thus Burns's trees, so far from expressing nature's immanent productivity, are specifically the sign by which nature is assimilated to a cultural code of ownership and patronage. His emphasis on them is a personal compliment to the Duke, who was a famous planter and the pioneer of the larch in the Highlands;[27] Burns would know he was making the water address a patron who could (and apparently did[28]) carry out the whimsical suggestion in fact. Scotland's treelessness was after all a long-standing reproach, notoriously revived by Johnson:[29] planting was the privileged type of enlightened Highland estate management. Trees are the cultivated landlord's visible signature on the land, the means by which he at once acknowledges, enhances and appropriates – in a word, improves – its virtue. It's in just such Improving terms that Cririe compliments the same Duke of Atholl:

> Long may his presence bless his wide domains,
> To skirt, with sylvan scenes, the mountains wild;
> 'Mid rocks, to rear the high embow'ring shade.[30]

and Gilpin approaching Inveraray detects 'some powerful hand' (the Duke of Argyll's, as he knows) in 'the noble decorations of the scene'.[31]

But then the point which Burns's imagery encompasses, and which escapes the rhetoric of less talented tourists, is that forestry, a conspicuous and 'noble' intervention in the landscape, is nonetheless capable of assuming a unique air of naturalness. The imagined sylvan banks of the Bruar acquire unplanned denizens and self-sustaining reciprocities; the labour and investment the project entails are effaced by time; the Duke will, magically, have amended nature without its having ceased to be natural.

This happy outcome directly addresses Gilpin's concerns as a theorist of the Highland picturesque. 'Wherever man appears with his tools,' he declares at one point, 'deformity follows in his steps. His spade, and his plough, his hedge, and his furrow; make shocking encroachments on the simplicity, and elegance of landscape.'[32] But in fact, despite this apparent scenic primitivism, Gilpin is constantly praising or recommending subtle adjustments in the prospects he describes: very little, in his exacting critique of 'nature's workmanship',[33] is perfectly picturesque without some assistance from art. The point is rather that the necessary adjustments should be made invisibly: it's when man *appears* with his tools that deformity follows. The manager of the land, then, is to supplement nature and, in the same gesture, to naturalise the supplement, skilfully effacing the traces of skill which mark the disjunction between subject and object. Forestry, with its secular timescale and 'shagged' appearance, is the ideal medium for this slightly evasive *coup*. In the splendidly wooded glens of the Short Tour, Improvement achieved its most spectacular synthesis: it identified itself with the vital principle of that which was to be improved.

3 RULING THE WAVES

In Mountain-Waves and raging Wind,
Tell us, what couldst thou hope to find?
'Tis answer'd – These are Natures Schools
To teach the Power of Art and Rules.[34]

Outside the charmed circle of the Short Tour, the picturesque accommodation repeatedly broke down. The mountains of Lochaber or Assynt, the rocks of the west coast, and the treeless Hebrides, seemed to most eighteenth-century visitors to pose, directly and inescapably, a choice between abandoning the country to its hopeless sterility and intervening in vigorous and visible ways. It was not only that these places were poor in 'prospects' which satisfied the visual criteria of diversity, inclusiveness and anthropocentricity. It was also that the forms which Improvement could imaginably take in this context were necessarily more aggressive and innovative than they were in more amenable terrain. Nature and art were here decisively and visibly different.

The privileged form of the difference as far as the seaboard and the islands were concerned was herring fishing. James VI had attempted to settle Fife fishermen in Lewis as far back as 1598; the British Fisheries Society, formed in 1786 with the Hebrides especially in mind, was not wound up until 1893. The longevity of the idea did not simply reflect circumstances, which were steadily discouraging. Its economics were enriched by ideological considerations, most authoritatively expounded in 1730 by James Thomson, who, holding 'Caledonia in romantic view' as the muse hovers like a seagull over the Hebrides, calls for a patriot who will teach the labouring hand

>   with venturous Oar,
> How to dash wide the Billow; nor look on,
> Shamefully passive, while *Batavian* Fleets
> Defraud us of the glittering finny Swarms,
> That heave our Friths, and croud upon our Shores;
> How all-enlivening Trade to rouse, and wing
> The prosperous Sail, from every growing Port,
> Uninjur'd, round the sea-incircled Globe;
> And thus, in Soul united as in Name,
> Bid BRITAIN reign the Mistress of the Deep.[35]

Thomson's synthesising imagination executes, not only the political fulfilment of the Act of Union (fishing leads to trade, and trade leads to enhanced national unity and power), but also an assimilation of that power with the force of nature: 'dash', 'heave', 'croud' borrow for the fishing industry the dynamism of the waves it contends with, and 'rouse and wing' equates the trading ships with the swirling 'nations' of seabirds. It's consistent with this vigorous expansionism that the romantic view takes in, with unslackened pleasure, 'the naked melancholy Isles/ Of farthest *Thule*, and th'*Atlantic* Surge'. Thule is the remotest end of the earth in Virgil's compliment to Augustus — 'tibi serviat ultima Thule'[36] — and Thomson's allusion reproduces the hyperbole, with the difference that whereas the Romans only saw Thule, the British Empire is really going to be served by it.[37] The nakedness and melancholy are therefore not depressing, but euphoric on the basis that *even this extremity* can be made to contribute to the power of the State.

That assertion is another instance of the principle of plenitude: the faith that nature makes nothing – not even the wilderness – in vain. According to John Knox, founding member and publicist of the British Fisheries Society, herring 'seem to have been intended by the Author of nature as a compensation for the inclemency of the seasons, and the sterility of the soil'; they advance each spring 'from the northern ocean towards our highly favoured shores, to incite our industry, and to supply our wants'.[38] This providential political economy is perhaps an echo of Defoe's much-reprinted *Caledonia*, in which 'Nature's handmaid Instinct' is heard instructing the 'scaly Squadrons' to head for the nets of the Scots:

> *Be You Their Wealth* and plenteously supply
> What *Coldest Soil* and *Steril Climes* deny ...
> Present your selves to every Hungry Door,
> Employ *The Diligent*, and feed *The Poor*.[39]

The fish are a miraculous example of Nature's far-sighted attention to the interests of the United Kingdom, but at the same time, as both Defoe and Knox take care to point out, they demand investment and labour. The imperatives of capitalism are discovered literally in the sea. Knox's faith in this benign logic seems altogether indomitable: approaching Cape Wrath in autumn, he contemplates the savage coastline and proposes that a town be founded on the basis of a repair yard for the battered ships.[40] No extreme of nature can disconcert so resourceful a principle of utility: as Defoe says: '*Thus vanishes the Horrid* and the Wild,/And Nature's now with pleasant Eyes beheld.[41]

In other sectors, too, Improvement afforded similar reasons for beholding the Horrid and the Wild with complacency. The art of road-building, like that of navigation, directly confronted the resistance of nature; General Wade was praised in appropriately combative terms:

> Still shall his living greatness guard his name,
> And his works lift him to immortal fame.

> Then shall astonished armies, marching high,
> O'er causewayed mountains that invade the sky,
> Climb the raised arch, that sweeps its distant throw,
> Cross tumbling floods, which roar unheard below,
> Gaze, from the cliff's cut edge, through midway air,
> And, trembling, wonder at their safety there![42]

Wade is a hero of Improvement because he subdues the wildness of nature. But the wildness, rather than vanishing, is reproduced in the achievement: the soldiers of the future are seen climbing Wade's arch as well as nature's mountains; the abruptness of 'the cliff's cut edge', and the aggressive verbs of motion, reflect the boldness of the tactics which the terrain has forced from the engineer. The neat paradox in the last line almost unites problem and solution: do the soldiers tremble at the danger they would be in were it not for the road, or at the awesome human power which ensures their safety? Thus the mountains amplify Wade's reputation, substantiating with their real precipitous height the faint metaphor of his being raised up to immortality. The wilder they are, the more powerfully they express their conqueror's glory; for this reason the poet exaggerates their scale, and almost – but not quite – ends up, in about 1730, with a full-blown Romantic landscape.

The same reversal characterises the beginnings of Highland mountain climbing. As D.B. Horn points out, many of the earliest recorded ascents (that is, ascents by non-Highlanders) were made by botanists, geologists and astronomers; people to whom the wilderness offered very specific opportunities not available in more favoured regions.[43] By the 1790s these pioneers, like Wade, had inscribed their achievements on the rocks of the Highlands: the geographer Banks had delineated Fingal's Cave – 'E'en these lone scenes thy keen research proclaim;/Fix'd on Basaltic Columns stands thy Fame!'[44]; Maskelyne, the Astronomer Royal, had spent four months testing Newton's gravitational hypotheses 'On steep Schehallien's astronomic heights,/In sordid booth, by Science render'd cheer[45]; and Aikin, a mineralogist, had investigated 'Scotia's barren rocks, though not to thee/These rocks shall long prove barren, thou shalt gain/From Scotia's sons, the meed of fair renown.'[46]

In these tropes, science is purely contemplative; yet it still transforms the places with which it is associated, because its interest in them confers value on them. A use has been found for the apparently unusable: the empire of knowledge has driven its roads through them, making their former obscurity signify its illumination.

The pleasure of such appropriations is eloquently conveyed by Pennant, who came upon a fishing fleet in 'the wildest scene in nature' — Loch Hourn:

> So unexpected a prospect of the busy haunt of men and ships in this wild and romantic tract, afforded this agreeable reflection: that there is no part of our dominions so remote, so inhospitable and so unprofitable, as to deny employ and livelihood to thousands; and that there are no parts so polished, so improved, and so fertile, but which must stoop to receive advantage from the dreary spots they so affectedly despise; and must be obliged to acknowledge the mutual dependency of part on part, howsoever remotely placed, and howsoever different in modes or manner of living.[47]

It's a patriotic enjoyment: the sight of economic activity being carried on in a wild sea-loch inspires a warm sense of national interdependence. The place then derives a paradoxical centrality from its very remoteness: as in an imperialist adventure story, the periphery intimates the ideal of the whole as the metropolis, with its air of local self-sufficiency, never could. An engraving illustrates the scene,[48] and the test instructs the reader how to appreciate its picturesque gloom; the intransigence of the wilderness dramatises the converse power which enjoys 'dominion' over it. Read thus, dreariness can be delightful: on the reverse side of Improvement is written the scenic theme of the sublime.

4 THE SUBLIME

Within this conspicuous and transformative mode, the subject and object of Improvement come apart. Improvement registers as something which is being unilaterally *done to* the country; nature, conversely, appears as simply and blankly *unimproved*. Time and again in the specialist agrarian literature of the Highlands, 'land in a state of nature'[49] is angrily invoked as the type of idleness and neglect. Revd John Walker finds in the Hebrides of the 1760s that

'Their Soil remains, as it was left at the Creation'; in the 1790s, William Marshall's agricultural report on the Central Highlands compared the region's wildness to that of America, and spoke of the urgency of 'retrieving it from a state so disgraceful to a civilized nation'.[50] In these frameworks, the land is no longer the providential environment of Thomson or Gilpin, but an intransigent externality — 'matter', as Lochaber appeared to Johnson, 'incapable of form or usefulness, dismissed by nature from her care and disinherited of her favours, left in its original elemental state, or quickened only with one sullen power of useless vegetation'.[51] Here, hyperbolically, the hills are double unimproved, neglected not only by their inhabitants, but also by a personified nature. The Highlands appear as a dark, indigent sub-nature, different in kind from the bounteous inheritance of the south.

This negative version of the Scottish hills was eloquently and maliciously set out in 1763 by Charles Churchill:

> Far as the eye could reach, no tree was seen,
> Earth, clad in russet, scorn'd the lively green.
> The plague of Locusts they secure defy,
> For in three hours a grasshopper must die.
> No living thing, whate'er its food, feasts there,
> But the Cameleon, who can feast on air.
> No birds, except as birds of passage, flew,
> No bee was known to hum, no dove to coo.
> No streams as amber smooth, as amber clear,
> Were seen to glide, or heard to warble here.
> Rebellion's spring, which thro' the country ran,
> Furnish'd, with bitter draughts, the steady clan.
> No flow'rs embalm'd the air, but one white rose,
> Which, on the tenth of June, by instinct blows;
> By instinct blows at morn, and, when the shades
> Of drizly eve prevail, by instinct fades.[52]

As the slanderous references to Jacobitism indicate, Churchill's purpose is not simple landscape painting. The point of the scene's hyperbolic penury is to insinuate that Scots in general are snatching at the metropolitan fleshpots with a rapacity as extreme as their need. As a Scotophobic set piece, then, it draws on an older tradition than the picturesque tourists: it's in a line from James Howell's *Perfect Description of the People and Country of Scotland*

(1649), which Churchill had already used as *North Briton* XIII, and from John Cleveland's 'The Rebell Scot', with its unvarnished conclusion – 'Nature herselfe doth Scotch-men beasts confesse, / Making their Countrey such a wilderness.'[53] It's a tradition which owes nothing to the observation of nature: Churchill's bizarre speculative bestiary – 'There webs were spread of more than common size, / And half-starv'd spiders prey'd on half-starv'd flies'[54] – arguably owes more to the fantastic–satiric locations of the *Dunciad*.[55]

Still, the relationship between this harsh 'Scots Pastoral' and the land it purports to represent is not altogether arbitrary. The figures in the landscape are

> Shepherds of *Scottish* lineage, born and bred
> On the same bleak and barren mountain's head,
> By niggard nature doom'd on the same rocks
> To spin out life, and starve themselves and flocks.[56]

The tightly stated futility of this contains exactly the Improver's exasperation with the commercial uselessness of a subsistence economy. Churchill's 'niggard nature' is the same as the 'state of nature' of Pennant or Knox – the blank absence of Improvement, the agrarian zero.

Moreover, the rhetoric of the evocation declares a perverse enthusiasm for this wintry principle. 'Thou, Nature, art my goddess!' Churchill exclaims; and although the inauspicious allusion to *Lear* instantly defines the speaker as a satiric persona, the writing doesn't keep him very firmly at arm's length. The leading features which the Scottish scene lacks – verdure, doves, 'amber' streams and 'embalming' flowers – are witlessly conventional: the caricatured sterility is matched by an equally caricatured Theocritan muse which

> To flocks and rocks, to hills and rills proclaims,
> In simplest notes, and all unpolish'd strains,
> The loves of nymphs, and *eke* the loves of swains.[57]

Thus the 'good' nature against which the Scotch landscape could be placed as bad is itself presented in a manner which makes it impossible to take seriously. Meanwhile, on the other hand, the hopeless indigenous landscape 'scorns' greenery, 'defies' locusts, and rises with a sort of pride through its catalogue of negations to the glooming splendour of the short-lived rose: the description is, as it were, evocative in excess of polemical requirements. Behind its political unfairness, the poem marks out a surprising space in which the very bleakness of the land of Famine might appear as a value – an integrity, or a magnificence.

This value, marginal and probably inadvertent within the text, is nonetheless available to reception. In 1772 a tourist named Anthony Champion contrasted the valleys of Wales with the glens of the Highlands, emphasising the gloom and 'rudeness' of the latter, and adding:

> Claude's colours there, and Virgil's style are faint;
> Let Churchill's pen, and Rosa's pencil paint.[58]

Champion has no polemical purpose: he is simply using Churchill's politically inspired description to schematise a contrast of scenic tone. The opposition between the softness of Claude Lorrain and the savagery of Salvator Rosa was a cliché of eighteenth-century picturesque discourse,[59] and by fitting Churchill into it, Champion reads his abusiveness as a kind of sympathetic wildness, suited to the frowning scenery of the Highlands. Claude – Rosa, Virgil – Churchill; Wales – Scotland; beautiful – rude. *The Prophecy of Famine* is unexpectedly lined up as the Scottish sublime. It was read as such, certainly, by 'Lady L.S. aged 16' in 1775:

> Though 'tis declar'd, no herbage decks thy ground;
> Though rudest rocks thy barren heaths surround;
> Though, when transplanted to thy plains, 'tis said,
> The beeches wither, and the roses fade:
> E'en such descriptions more my soul emblaze,
> More transports waken, and more wishes raise;
> To hail sweet SCOTIA'S hospitable smile,
> And taste such joys, as know not to beguile.[60]

The verse is insipid, of course, compared with what provoked it. But 'emblaze' and 'transports' denote the unfulfilled intention of a matching intensity: what she calls, in exactly Champion's terms, 'the beauties of some southern vale' are being dismissed as faint and deceptive. The retort to the negative conclusions of Johnson or

Churchill is not to point out unsuspected positive features in the landscape, but to appeal to inward pleasures – the soul, 'wishes' – which reprove the enjoyment of merely beautiful countryside as shallow. This move leads to a sort of scenic unworldliness (Lady L.S.'s context is a conventional denunciation of metropolitan Pleasure) that cuts across the picturesque search for a *wealth* of visual impressions.

Gilpin, though he is mainly engaged in this search, is too active an observer to overlook the paradoxical appeal of visual paucity: the moorland above Killin seemed to him 'wide, waste and rude; totally naked; and yet in it's simplicity often sublime ... The ideas were grand, rather than pleasing. The imagination was interested, but not the eye.'[61] To explain this deviation from his usual aesthetic system, he has recourse to a somewhat lurid characterisation of Highland landscape by James Beattie:

> Long tracts of mountainous desert, covered with dark heath, and often obscured by misty weather; narrow vallies, thinly inhabited, and bounded by precipices resounding with the fall of torrents; a soil so rugged, and a climate so dreary, as in many parts to admit neither the amusements of pasturage, nor the labours of agriculture; ... a lonely region, full of echoes, and rocks, and caverns; the grotesque and ghastly appearance of such a landscape by the light of the moon.[62]

Beattie's reason for elaborating this picture is to explain how 'persons of lively imagination, immured in deep solitude, and surrounded with the stupendous scenery', end up believing that they possess Second Sight. Here again, projected this time on to the inhabitants, is the opposition of the eye and the imagination: whereas the picturesque, viewed psychologically, enlivens the beholder's reflections by means of a stimulating variety of ideas, these prospects of negativity provoke a different kind of mental life. Almost pathologically, the fancy is roused to feverish activity by the inhuman emptiness of the mountains.

In most eighteenth-century Highland tours there is an odd ambivalence about this sensation, which could be called the 'negative sublime'. Few were as frankly bewildered as the lady who found herself caught between conflicting fashions on a road near Crieff which 'was rather disagreeable, laying between immense "cloud-topt" hills, which strike with awe and wonder the astonished beholder'.[63] But many regularly use words like 'desert', 'desolate', 'gloomy', 'horrible', 'hideous' or 'melancholy' in phrases (such as 'wild and desolate beyond conception', or 'horrible grandeur'[64]) which leave it uncertain whether the dark epithets are meant to express admiration or distaste. The descriptive terms available to them are pulled two ways, by a humanistic preference for signs of productivity and use, and by a newer feeling for the untamed.

The latter taste is first expressed unambiguously by Elizabeth Montagu. She made a brief trip to the Highlands in 1766, and Glen Croe, abhorred eight years earlier by Sir William Burrell, was its high point:

> It is not within the compass of prose, hardly of poetry, to describe the sublime beauties that here opened upon us. We travelled down a glen encompassed by vast hoar mountains down whose wrinkled sides rushed impetuous streams which ended in the vale below. In a sort of proportion mountain rose above mountain, some from the steep declivity had had all the soil washed away and the rocks like the bones of a giant exhibited its strength without softness or mitigation, and made imagination tremble through all her powers.[65]

All regret for the *riant* in landscape is swept away by the sublime encounter of essences: the 'strength' of the land (revealed precisely by the absence of soil and vegetation) speaks directly to the 'powers' of the imagination. The governing analogy is not painting but personification: another letter describing the same scene evokes the sense of movement still more emotively, with the streams furrowing the mountain's cheeks, and a hanging rock waiting for a second earthquake to complete its journey.[66] The land is inert: rock, bone. But the tremulous imagination constructs the titanic struggles memorialised or latent in its mineral stasis.

This response is untypical in its time, and Montagu was exceptional in analogous ways. An independent woman of literary tastes, patronised as a bluestocking by contemporary literati and modern scholars alike, she financed a career as a literary patron from the collieries which she owned as a widow. Both as a woman and as an industrialist, she stands outside the categories of ownership, inheritance and use which underlie the picturesque construction of the land; accordingly, her version of the scenery breaks with the harmonies of organic nature and reads Glen Croe as a geological drama, an exciting intimation of the earth's violent energy. Like the professional lampoonist Churchill, she writes as a marginalised individual for whom the image – fundamentally an agrarian one – of continuity between the natural and the social is faint and abstract. Her language of the sublime is taken neither from classical rhetoric nor from the theodicy of Burnet, but from another figure as deracinated as herself: the 25-year-old literary adventurer James Macpherson.

Montagu, who secured Macpherson for her salon in advance of the publication of *Fingal* in 1761, seems to have confused Glen Croe with Ossian's official birthplace, Glencoe – hence, probably, the tear-stained ancient she makes of the rock face. But the scenic influence of Macpherson's peculiar rhapsodic prose runs deeper than that. Ossian was the definitive negative sublime: as his critical apologist Hugh Blair said, his paucity of imagery referred to 'the desert uncultivated state of his country, which suggested to him few images beyond natural inanimate objects in their rudest form'[67] – rivalling, in the absence of agriculture, industry, most animals and plants, and all but a few references to herding, the catalogue of vacancy of a Churchill. The emptiness is compounded by Macpherson's settings being, so to speak, topographically null: the place names are meaningless, and the scenic components – 'the tree', 'the rock', 'the lake of roes' – crop abruptly up out of the bardic flow in an abstract fashion which deprives them of spatial relationship, so that they remain arbitrary and inexplicit, wrapped in the mystique of translation. The Ossianic version of the Highlands, then, doesn't resist the Improver's view of its moors and rocks as scenic negations; on the contrary, it makes negation into a style. This election is then characteristically projected on to the dramatis personae: Fingal, refusing the rewards of victory in Book VI, declares, 'The desert is enough to me, with all its deer and woods'.[68] Quoted by Blair, and from him by many others, this line turns the absence of Improvement into a conscious refusal of it in the name of something higher. The bigger value, as we've already seen, is subjectivity. In Blair's account of Ossian, heath, misty mountain, torrent and scattered oak 'produce a solemn attention in the mind' which is the index of the poet's seriousness: 'We find not in Ossian, an imagination that sports itself, and dresses out gay trifles to please the fancy. His poetry ... deserves to be stiled, *The Poetry of the Heart.*'[69] This anti-sensuous height of taste, the theory of an aestheticised puritanism reflected in Blair's and Macpherson's respective Biblical cadences, commissions the Highlands — the more so the more barren — as the landscape of sensibility.

The Ossianic landscape is rarely a matter of sustained descriptive passages; the impression that the text is thronged with heath, deer, torrents and so on, is largely due to their recurrence as the bearers of tropical or associative personal meanings. Although these formulaic vehicles often get away, taking on a fantasy life which cuts across their ostensible function, the fact that they are deployed in this way has the effect of filling their sensuous inanity with feeling. In 'The War of Caros', to take an example at random, the disgraced Hidallan laments:

> Lamor will not feel my dogs, with his hands, glad at my arrival from the hill. He will not inquire of his mountains, or of the dark-brown deer of his deserts!

Lamor replies:

> I must fall like a leafless oak: it grew on a rock! it was overturned by the winds! My ghost will be seen on my hills.[70]

The hills, the mountains, the deserts and the rock are all almost obtrusively gratuitous; they neither define nor heighten the emotion, but simply absorb it; objects, lifeless and undifferentiated in themselves, soak up a ceaseless climate of moods which blow, rise, tremble, flicker, roll, pass. The coupling of the sterility of things and the emotional hyperactivity that plays over them is latently necrophiliac: the representative Ossianic locale is a visited grave. After one of Macpherson's many fatal triangles, for example

> By the brook of the hill their graves are laid; a birch's unequal shade covers their tomb. Often on their green earthen tombs the branchy sons of the mountain feed, when mid-day is all in flames, and silence is over all the hills.[71]

This rather potent mixture of peace and unrest — the unequal shade, the flaming silence, the troubling tangle of trees and antlers — is arrived at by permeating the secluded place with unappeased energies. As in Montagu's Glen Croe, the life of nature is not substance, but force.

The theoretical grounding of this revaluation is set out in Burke's *Philosophical Enquiry into the Origin of our Ideas of the Sublime and Beautiful*, which appeared in 1757, and is thus exactly contemporary both with the beginnings of scenic tourism in the Highlands and with the appearance of Macpherson's writings. As his title suggests, Burke confirms the tendencies I've traced in the Highland sublime, both in the schematic opposition of his two categories (which turns the sublime into a structural negation) and in his situating the whole argument in the mind of the beholder. In these psychological terms, what unites the various sources of visual sublimity — terror, obscurity, power, privation, vastness, infinity, uniformity, difficulty — is that they all draw on 'passions belonging to self-preservation',[72] which must logically be the strongest passions of all. In other words, the attraction of the mountains is rooted very firmly in their practical dangers; the affective power of the Highlands is located just where the Scotophobic convention directs its contempt — in the environment's inability to support life. In an extra section in the 1759 edition, Burke adds that sublime ideas attach only to strength we cannot use, since the useful is subservient to us and therefore devoid of awe. Even the wild ass is sublime as the plough-horse is not.[73] This distinction flies yet more specifically in the face of Improvement, which is, precisely, a programme for substituting plough-horses for wild asses.

It's an instance of a very broadly based redefinition of 'nature'. Instead of an inclusive principle which embraces the social productions of man, nature in its sublime form is the site of a pairing of complementary withdrawals from social concreteness — into the absolutely inhuman presence of the unused parts of the earth, and into the reflective consciousness of the solitary observer. Each of these places is conceived of as natural in opposition to the artificiality of human society, and each is heightened by its encounter with the other. This theme of alienation helps to make sense of the fact that, historically, sympathy for Highland barbarity and remoteness grew in proportion to the region's actual modernisation and accessibility. It wasn't only that more people could now get there; it was centrally that as the logic of commercial utilisation permeated the land, it gave to the remaining enclaves of commercial uselessness the radiance of a disappearing authenticity. In the shift from an agrarian to an industrial paradigm of progress — that is, from the piecemeal improvement of natural resources to their violent transformation — nature becomes detached from the totality of social practices and stands over against them as a darkly ruinous other, incommensurable, quasi-divine, fraught with the transcendence which a universal commodification exiles.

But if the negative sublime makes that radical gesture, it does so with an inescapable touch of frivolity. Some verses inscribed on a window at the inn near Ben Lomond in 1771 offered advice in case 'taste for grandeur and the dread sublime/ Prompt thee Ben-Lomond's fearful height to climb':[74] that mixture of magniloquence and facetiousness, still detectable in mountaineering description today, implicitly places such a taste as a kind of folly. This, the devotee is tacitly saying, is what I am perverse and quixotic enough to like. Thomas Gray's letter to Mason of 1765 is a stylish example of the register:

> the Lowlands are worth seeing once, but the Mountains are extatic, & ought to be visited in pilgrimage once a year. none but these monstrous creatures of God know how to join so much beauty with so much horror. a fig for your Poets, Painters, Gardiners, & Clergymen, that have not been among them: their imagination can be made up of nothing but bowling-greens, flowering shrubs, horse-ponds, Fleet-ditches, shell-grottoes, & Chinée-rails ... and this so sweetly contrasted with that perfection of nastiness, & total want of accommodation, that Scotland only can supply.[75]

Gray is teasing both Mason and himself, but the humour is not just personal. The contemptuously itemised sphere of mountainless landscape is a parody of English Improvement and the boasted discomfort a parody of Scotch backwardness. Nature and art are juxtaposed to their mutual discredit: the structure of feeling is really not very far from Churchill. It's not that Gray's excitement at what he has seen in the Highlands is insincere; rather, it's that the ideology of Improvement, so ramified and positive, leaves no clear diction for praising the unimprovable, the 'total want of accommodation'. So the enunciation of the negative sublime is unstable, slips sideways into burlesque, or attitudinising, or, in the extreme case of Macpherson, fraud.

Burke's formula helps to explain this pervasive insecurity of tone. The idea of the beautiful is linked to pleasure, that of the sublime to pain. The pleasure of the latter can't therefore be called pleasure; Burke makes a purely formal adjustment and calls it 'delight'.[76] This entailed, as S.H. Monk points out,[77] a sort of distinction of logical types. The sublime emotion was not literally the passion of self-preservation (calls upon which are *simply* painful) but a passion 'belonging' to it, a reflective derivation of it. John Dennis had said: not an 'ordinary' passion, but an 'enthusiastic' one. Burke's 'delight' is thus an *als ob* sensation, whose play depends on the distinction's being clearly apprehended. Johnson, for example, feels little enthusiasm for Lochaber because he is not prepared to draw the necessary line between practical and poetic considerations: when he thinks of 'want, and misery, and danger', he is thinking of the real thing; the imaginary rewards of remoteness he consigns, enfeebled, to 'the artifical solitude of parks'.[78]

Johnson's literalism reveals by contrast the basis of the active, Ossianic taste for scenes of desolation: it depends on the partial *aestheticisation* of the Highlands. Framed by a theoretical opposition, or literally by the window of a coach, the mountains could be experienced like dreams or works of art, not fully contingent in the practical world. The beholder's 'pilgrimage' to them is a half-conscious irresponsibility, a skittish refusal of the imperatives of civilisation which, however, also refuses to amount to a critique. This unacknowledged evasion underlies, I think, the universal popularity of Highland waterfalls.[79] The channelled violence of the cataract exhibits an essence of natural energy which, wholly undebased by usefulness, nevertheless is strictly contained and doesn't obstruct the progress of Improvement. It is thus unlimitedly terrific without being in the least inconvenient. That furtive accommodation is typical of the whole enthusiasm: the eighteenth-century Highland sublime both inverted and adapted to the real fate of the land, which was its aggressive and irreversible social appropriation.

5 BOUNTY

Cultivation or wilderness; Improvement or neglect; sylvan addition or original nakedness; pleasures of the senses or intensities of the heart – the polarity is so insistent in the literature that it comes to look natural. Amid so much repetition, it's easy to start talking as if the Highlands had simply been a desert, posing innocently and directly the choice between prudent transformation and romantic appreciation. This air of inevitability is effectively dispelled by the presence of a distinct alternative myth:

> This air ... notwithstanding its humidity, is so healthy, that the natives are scarce ever visited by any other disease than the small-pox ... Here are a great many living monuments of longævity; and among the rest a person, whom I treat with singular respect, as a venerable druid, who has lived near ninety years, without pain or sickness, among oaks of his own planting....
> Do you know how we fare in this Scottish paradise?...We have delicious salmon, pike, trout, perch, par, &c. at the door, for the taking. The Frith of Clyde, on the other side of the hill, supplies us with mullet, red and grey, cod, mackarel, whiting, and a variety of sea-fish, including the finest fresh herrings I ever tasted. We have sweet, juicy beef, and tolerable veal, with delicate bread from the little town of Dunbritton; and plenty of partridge, growse, heathcock, and other game in presents.[80]

This description by Smollett's Matthew Bramble, coming after the same correspondent's splenetic accounts of the polluted health resorts of England, has, designedly, an Arcadian freshness, cool and reviving. It draws partly on another influential book: Martin Martin's *Description of the Western Islands circa 1695*. Martin, who was read by every Highland enthusiast from Collins to Scott, projects a comparable image of intense local abundance — a stream where there are too many salmon to catch, an island where barley is so plentiful that it's given away, a rock in the ocean where cows are brought by boat to feed on the luxuriant grass. Martin also substantiates the curative theme of *Humphry Clinker*: medically trained like Smollett himself, he collects instances of wonderful longevity, and a whole herbal of natural remedies, such as ground shells, seaweed, wild sage, myrtle, plantain, limpet fat, and certain singular stones and springs.[81] There's an impression, not only of a diversely wholesome environment, but also of the minute familiarity with it which enables the inhabitants to lead frugally balanced lives. It's an apothecary's idyll, reproving the unhealthy excesses and iatrogenic disorders of metropolitan life.

Never as conspicuous as the motifs of the sublime, this countermyth of a healthy Highland world crops up occasionally throughout the century. Alexander Campbell's *The Grampians Desolate* includes a somewhat saccharine pastoral, one of whose characters is a young 'leach' who knows about

> Th'astringent *tormentil* that spreads the heath,
> The caustic *spearwort* of the lake beneath,
> The kindly *groundsel*, meet for healing sores,
> The precious *eye-bright* that lost sight restores...[82]

In a footnote, Campbell is sceptical about the last of these claims: the credulity of the verse reflects not medical naivety but a poetic image of nature's bounty; the idea of a quasi-natural 'lore' to which even the most negligible wild plant is full of goodness.

Other idylls, less particularly medicinal, exhibit the same sign of 'good' wildness. John Campbell in 1752 comments on the 'delightful Sight' of thousands of unbroken horses at a Highland fair, 'running and capering about like so many wild Deer';[83] for him the mountains, so far from being waste, are the source of this thronging vitality. And Anne Grant in 1773 characterises Knoydart (from hearsay) in comparable terms:

> inaccessible precipices, overhanging mountains, and glens narrow, abrupt, and cut through with deep ravines, combining with rapid streams, dark pools, and woods so intricate, that the deer can scarce find their way through them. Yet the natives are looked upon as happier than others. Redundant grass and luxuriant heath offer abundance to their cattle, who are never housed in winter. Deer, wild fowl, and fish, are in great plenty; salmon, in particular, crowd their rivers, and shell fish of all kinds abound on their rugged coasts. All this they enjoy without a rival or competitor, for who would go for it, or carry it away?[84]

The woods, the grass and heath, and the animals and fish, are not all merely adequate, but lavish; prodigality is the appropriate response to such Edenic superabundance. As in Smollett's Argyll, where wholesome food is 'at the door, for the taking', plenty is not the reward of industry but the spontaneous gift of nature. It's thus a quite distinct picture from that of even the most optimistic Improver (for whom, of course, the geographically determined absence of competition must appear as a fatal barrier to progress rather than the providential condition of a pastoral self-

1a. (*above*) The Scrubbing Post: Anti-Scottish Cartoon, from 1762.

1b. (*right*) 'God bless the Duke of Argyle for his Claw Post': Scots postcard *c*. 1914.

2a. Sir Henry Raeburn: 'Colonel Alastair Macdonell of Glengarry' (1771–1828).

2b. John Kay's etching 'W. Macdonald in the dress of an officer of the Highland Society of Scotland' (c. 1800).

3a. (*above*) Paul Sandby, 'View in Strathtay' (1747).

3b. (*below*) Engraving 'View of Strathtay' after Sandby (1780).

4a. (*above*) Engraving from Pennant, 'Lock Hourn' (1772).

4b. (*below*) Charles Cordiner, engraving of Loch Lomond (1795).

5a. Engraving by Bassing of Ossian by the Cascade near Carrill from Cordiner (1780).

5b. Fingal and Conban Cargla by Alexander Runciman (c. 1772–74) from a painting by Duncan Macmillan.

6. Inveraray in 1824, from the slopes of Duniquaich. Engraved after a drawing by John Clark. Courtesy of the British Museum.

sufficiency). This land calls for nothing from its proprietors but to be left in undisturbed felicity. Equally, its mountains and torrents are not sublime: grandeur and challenge in the landscape give way to friendliness and ease.

It's significant context for this dissenting version of the land that all the writers I've cited — Martin, Smollett, Grant, and both Campbells — were, or felt themselves to be, native Highlanders. The sublime is, in general, an expression read in the face of the land by outsiders: the historical encounter which is encoded in scenic awe is ultimately a colonial one, in which the initiative lies with the enterprising beholder, who attributes to the land the passivity, the menace and the pathos of a conquered province — the signification, in short, of nature *as opposed to* civilisation. In this respect, mountain sublimity is the trace, not only of the political subjection of the Gaeltacht, but, still more, of an extractive model of land use. In the course of the eighteenth century, the indigenous eco-system of the Highlands was exposed to a series of assaults: the distortion of the subsistence base by the introduction of the potato; the increased volume and efficiency of the export of black cattle; the commercial exploitation of natural woodland which was at least partly responsible for the catastrophic deforestation of wide areas; the environmentally destructive hegemony of sheep.[85] The sublime negativity of simplicity and barrenness was being produced by metropolitan intervention, not only ideologically, but ecologically as well. The contrary image of a Highland Arcadia, doubtless equally mythical, dissents from that negative typing and represents the region as a *habitat*, having its own centre and coherence and not simply waiting to be 'forced to flourish'[86] (with more or less compunction) by capital and methods imported from the south. Against that Improving aggression, which makes the native environment into its dark other, threatening and inspiring by turns, the myth of nature's bounty claims it as an independent locus of goodness and productivity.

This is latently a strongly anti-imperialist myth: it works as such, for example, in Neil Gunn's novel *Butchers Broom* (1934), where the figure of Dark Maire is another initiate of the mountain flora. But it received no such political articulation either in the eighteenth century or in the Napoleonic period in which Gunn's novel is set. It remained the faint trace of a rejected alternative. For what was in fact preoccupying the owners of the land in these years was not its native equilibrium, but on the contrary the need, for the sake of their own slender rentals, to maximise the cash income of its cultivators.[87] To see the land as an autonomous, even a secluded, habitat, was bound to be eccentric when the political economy of its management was integrating it more and more with a national and international market.

An effective dialogue between this commercial thrust and the indigenous patterns of land use would have entailed something like an ecological model of development; and this was by no means a flat impossibility in the agrarian debates of the time. A prize essay for the Highland Society, written in 1803, concedes that 'sheep are the true staple' of the Highlands, but adds:

> the country is also naturally laid out for every part of mixed husbandry ... all the necessary materials abounding; and every part, like the links of a golden chain, being connected with, and depending on one another. Cattle alone, are not, and cannot be a safe stock; sheep reared exclusively, turn all into a waste. The trees, if suffered to overspread the country, would convert it into a wilderness; and cropping on a large scale, is more than hazardous, it is impractical.[88]

The author calls this analysis of interdependent factors 'the true economy of the soil'. We can hardly judge, now, whether the piecemeal, locally sensitive policy which it implies would have been able to save the Highlands from the tale of decline and destitution which followed. It was not a political option; the landowning interest was, as it has remained, decisive; the graziers went ahead, and the assumption that the Highlands were in any case a 'waste' progressively confirmed itself.

What's striking, then, is the way the region's inherent productivity, ruthlessly effaced from the economic account, was equally written out of its aesthetics. Beside the aggressive monoculture of landlord capitalism flourished a correspondingly one-dimensional myth of nature − a landscape irreducibly bleak, obscure, vast and inhuman. As the country was emptied, its emptiness was mythologised as part of its aboriginal character. The sublime and the clearances were secretly paired: the golden chain's broken ends.

5

Ghosts

1 THE SUPERSTITIONS OF THE HIGHLANDS OF SCOTLAND, CONSIDERED AS THE SUBJECT OF POETRY

If the point about the negative sublime is its appeal to the imagination, then there exists a logical coincidence of interests between underdevelopment and poetry. The poet, it seems, is an incidental casualty of Improvement. Thomas Blackwell makes the point very clearly in his essay on Homer:

> It does not seem to be given to one and the same Kingdom, to be thoroughly civilized, and afford proper Subjects for Poetry. The *Marvellous* and *Wonderful* is the Nerve of the Epic Strain: But what marvellous Things happen in a well-ordered State? We can hardly be surprized; We know the Springs and Method of acting; Every thing happens in Order, and according to Custom or Law.[1]

He goes on to instance, as characteristic literary successes of a civilised state, *The Way of the World* and *The Rape of the Lock*. His choice is exact: both texts depict with conscious artifice an artificial life; a society permeated by knowingness, method, convention, is both reflected in them and inscribed in their form. Blackwell was writing in the 1730s, when in the Highlands the same ordering mechanisms were imposing themselves in the form of the first network of military roads.

To the self-conscious poet, the progress of such knowledge appears as an alienation: the marvellous and wonderful things which a scientific epistemology excludes are not abolished but withheld and then tantalisingly glimpsed:

> Thou, to whom the World unknown
> With all its shadowy Shapes is shown;
> Who see'st appall'd the unreal Scene,

> While Fancy lifts the Veil between:
> Ah *Fear*! Ah frantic *Fear*!
> I see, I see Thee near.[2]

Geoffrey Hartman remarks that this, the opening of Collins's 'Ode to Fear', 'invokes an emotion which is truly frantic: it wants to get at the poet, who wishes to be got at, but a historical fatality – the gentle mind, polite society – keeps them apart'.[3] This is characteristic of the 'Descriptive and Allegoric' odes: the speaker begs to see or feel what the great poets of more inspiring past ages experienced, and so to 'get at' a living object for his hectically self-imprisoned utterance. But the contradiction which inhibits him is written into the terms of his plea: the piled-up markers of the object's absence – 'shadowy', 'unreal', 'Fancy', and so on – are the same thing as the hyperbolical expression of its presence. It is *as* insubstantial and inaccessible that the scene beyond the veil exerts its power. 'The world unknown' is shut out, but also produced, by that 'well-ordered state' which is full of things we know. Where could the poet possibly go to encounter, in reality, poetic sources which define themselves by being unreal?

Collins's last, unfinished ode, 'To a Friend on his Return &c.', is programmatically the answer to this question. The impossible place, where the absent is present and the marvellous is quotidian, is Scotland. The poem is addressed to the Scottish writer John Home, as he leaves London for his native country:

> Fresh to that soil thou turn'st, whose ev'ry Vale
>   Shall prompt the Poet, and his Song demand;
> To Thee thy copious subjects ne'er shall fail
>   Thou need'st but take the Pencil to thy Hand
> And paint what all believe who own thy Genial Land.[4]

After the tortured obscurities of the allegorical odes, the simpleness of this gives it a tone of relief at the happy escape from solipsism which Scotland is taken to be offering. Instead of fitful images of the poet's own visionary world, here are subjects which are external, stable, and innocent of moods – simple *there*, like the landscape painter's chosen spot. The imagery amplifies the delightful materiality of the task: the enchanted country is nevertheless 'soil'; to paint it you take a pencil in hand; and a little later, with a literalism which is almost oxymoronic, Collins declares,' 'Tis Fancy's Land to which thou set'st thy Feet'. Scotland squares the circle, providing an imaginary space which can yet be reached, not by dreaming, but by walking there. The special condition of this miraculous resolution was the idea that the inhabitants of Highland Scotland, and of the Hebrides in particular, regularly saw, or believed that they saw, spirits, ghosts, and the phenomena of Second Sight. This was a fairly well established feature of the metropolitan knowledge of the Highlands by the mid-eighteenth century. Pepys, Aubrey and Robert Boyle had all made enquiries about paranormal vision in the islands in the late seventeenth century,[5] and it was discussed in a number of books appearing in the early eighteenth, most influentially Martin Martin's *Description of the Western Islands c. 1695*, first published in 1703.[6] Collins read Martin, as well as having conversations with Home, and it's easy to see how the information he derived from them seemed to promise deliverance from the imagination's disabling knowledge of its own falsity. It's not that brownies, familiar ghosts and so on could now be proved to exist. Such a demonstration, had it been achieved, would in any case have merely redrawn the boundaries of the known and understood, leaving the poet's predicament unchanged as the marvellous and the imaginary withdrew to the far side of the new frontier. What was valuable was precisely the indeterminacy of the question: the civilised poet continues to 'know' that the spirits are unreal, but he also acknowledges native traditions according to which they are real. The incompatibility produces scenes, as Collins says, 'which, daring to depart/From sober Truth, are still to Nature true' (ll 188–9). A special kind of truth is established, and on its basis 'superstition' becomes a privileged object of poetic knowledge.

But although the ode *describes* a breathtaking escape from the trap in which its predecessors struggled, it doesn't unproblematically *effect* such a move. If we look at the poem as a response to Martin's book, it soon becomes apparent that Collins, under pressure, has subtly tampered with the evidence.

The first problem concerns historical time. In a passage which Collins used, Martin reports that

> A spirit, by the country people called Browny, was frequently seen in all the most considerable families in the isles and north of Scotland, in the shape of a tall man; but within these twenty or thirty years he is seen but rarely.

> There were spirits also that appeared in the shape of women, horses, swine, cats, and some fiery balls, which would follow men in the field; but there has been but few instances of these for forty years past.[7]

'Forty years past', in 1695, situates these marvels in a period almost a century before Collins wrote the ode in 1750. This lapse of time Collins chooses to ignore, yet covertly reproduces in evasive markers of it:

> Where still, 'tis said, the Fairy People meet; (l. 20)

> Ev'n yet preserv'd how often may'st thou hear ... (l. 36)

> Fair Nature's Daughter Virtue yet Abides! (l. 157)

These muted admissions of the spirit world's decay are gestures of pathos rather than scholarly rigour: true to the conflictual nature of the poem's demands on the fugitive beliefs, it both wills them to be current and warms to the nostalgia of their passing. Between the two, an equivocation of tenses arrests Hebridean history in the attitude of Collins's own sophisticated and aestheticised supernaturalism.

The supernaturalist emphasis is itself a second significant deviation from the material Collins seized upon. Martin's record is the product of an itemising scientific curiosity, particularly about idiosyncrasies of medicine and diet. Since the beliefs and practices of the islanders in this sphere seem to be an undifferentiated mixture of local improvisation, herbal remedies and sympathetic magic, the writing often reproduces a notable indifference to the boundary between 'superstition' and natural history. For example:

> There are several springs and fountains of curious effects; such as that at Loch Carlvay, that never whitens Linen, which hath often been tried by the inhabitants. The well at St. Cowsten's Church never boils any kind of meat, though it be kept on fire a whole day. St. Andrew's Well, in the village Shader, is by the vulgar natives made a test to know if a sick person will die of the distemper he labours under. They send one with a wooden dish to bring some of the water to the patient, and if the dish, which is then laid softly upon the surface of the water, turn round sunways, they conclude that the patient will recover of that distemper; but if otherwise, that he will die.[8]

The first of these three cases looks fairly easily assimilable to the criteria of natural science; the second is more dubious; the third is clearly magical. But neither Martin nor the 'natives' show any interest in establishing that great divide. (Both are of course concerned to know which propositions are true, but that's not the same distinction.) Martin lists them together simply because they're all on the same island, and all to do with water. Collins on the other hand, has so consuming an interest in the moment of violation of the laws of nature that he can list elf-shot cows, runic bards and 'wizzards' in simple succession. They are phenomena which bear on the lives of the people in quite unrelated ways; but for Collins it's the twilit land of superstition as such that is the real source of fascination, and the diverse cats that prowl there are all grey. What he seeks is not the substantive belief but the shock of numinous disclosure which accompanies the account of it. Thus, in so far as the folk beliefs Martin catalogues are an integral and humdrum part of the life he is delineating, Collins can make no use of them. It's essential to his purposes that 'Such airy beings awe the untutored swain' (l. 30), and so, for example, the rather matter-of-fact routine of leaving out cream for the Brownie is adorned with the 'jocund notes' of unseen minstrels taken from elsewhere in Martin's book.[9] There must be an affective rupture with the ordinary world; the source material's easy intermingling of different kinds of knowledge is reorganised into a tense dichotomy.

This motivates a Hebrides of melancholy and fear strikingly unlike Martin's. The stanza about Second Sight is a good example. Home is to sing:

> How they whose Sight such dreary dreams engross
>   With their own Visions oft astonish'd droop
> When o'er the watry strath or quaggy Moss
>   They see the gliding Ghosts unbodied troop
> Or if in Sports or on the festive Green
>   Their   glance some fated Youth descry
> Who now perhaps in lusty Vigour seen
>   And rosy health shall soon lamented die
> For them the viewless Forms of Air obey
>   Their bidding heed, and at their beck repair
> They know what Spirit brews the storm full day
>   And heartless oft like moody Madness stare
> To see the Phantom train their secret work prepare![10]

Martin had described Second Sight, with many examples, as a faculty for seeing images which foretold future events. The event could be a marriage or the arrival of a stranger, but death was much the commonest, often taking the form of seeing the person who was to die in association with a shroud or a coffin. The visions were often distressing because of their meaning, but if the portent was happy or neutral, it doesn't appear that anyone was upset by the phenomenon itself. Collins, then, has altered the tone substantially. He has made the seers see ghosts and, by the end of the stanza, powerful superhuman spirits, rather than images of ordinary living people. And by making the visions 'dreary dreams' of 'secret work' whose apprehension is like madness, he has introduced suggestions of abnormal psychology at odds with the sources: Martin made it clear that the faculty was distributed at random, people who possessed it being linked by no other common characteristic; and a contemporary of his, Robert Kirk, insisted that the objects of the visions were not 'Creatures proceiding from ane affrighted Apprehensione, confused or crazed Sense, but Realities, appearing to a stable Man in his awaking Sense, and enduring a rationall Tryall of their Being'.[11] In other words, Collins has drastically *subjectivised* the whole phenomenon, both by relating it to the seer's mood and by enhancing its numinous emotional power. He has taken what was given as an unexplained medium of knowledge of the external world, and made it into yet another gateway to the inner world which was the overt preoccupation of the earlier odes.

These emendations are not only personal quirks of Collins's. In an odd little pamphlet of 1715, Defoe turned the Second Sight to account as the pretext for various more or less satirical prophecies having to do with European diplomacy. Their Highland setting is thus nothing more than rhetorical window-dressing; but then what's interesting is that this purpose, utterly different from that of the ode, leads to much the same type of distortion: Defoe's seer is the recipient, not of the prosaic communications of Martin's examples, but of a 'sublime Illumination' which opens upon him as he stands luridly silhouetted against the Northern lights atop a floating island on Loch Lomond, and which throws him into 'sacred Raptures'.

What Defoe most obviously has in common with Collins, despite their distinct viewpoints, is that both are assimilating the Hebridean tradition of Second Sight with versions of prophecy from their own culture: Shakespeare, Milton, the Old Testament. But equally, both are shaping the object to their use of it. For Defoe, one advantage of his colourful and confused prophetic persona is the chance it gives him to hedge his predictions: 'every one is at Liberty to take the above Account either for a real Prediction, or for a fictitious Fabulous Ramble of the Fancy; for we will impose nothing yet'.[12] This delightfully undisciplined area between reality and fancy is of course exactly where Collins wants to be too. 'We will impose nothing yet' – both writers need a space where empiricist distinctions between the actual and the imaginary can be suspended; both have adopted the Highlands as a refuge from the tyranny of the evidential. This is to be a recurring theme in the imaginary geography of the region.

Before we leave Collins's seers, there is one further appropriation to notice. At the beginning of the stanza, the vision seems to be something that happens to the seer, outside his control. But by the end, 'the viewless Forms of Air obey' him; he has become a sort of magician, summoning, or even creating, the phantoms he beholds. This ambiguity, wholly absent from the documentary sources, relates Collins's dreamers to what would shortly be theorised as poetic genius. William Duff's account of the latter, almost certainly uninfluenced by the ode, duplicates its terms exactly:

> By the vigorous effort of a creative Imagination, he calls shadowy substances and unreal objects into existence. They are present to his view, and glide, like spectres, before his astonished and intranced sight. In reading the descriptions of such apparitions, we partake of the Author's emotion; the blood runs chill in our veins, and our hair stiffens with horror.[13]

Duff is himself no less confused than Collins. At the start of this extract, he is talking about the poet's inner vision of *any* object he imagines, and the ghosts are only an analogy to show the vividness of the imagining. But as he goes on, the ghosts take over, and he ends up talking about poetry which literally has 'such apparitions' as its explicit subject matter. The distinction between imagination and superstition proves impossible to sustain: it's a striking instance of the importance of the latter in constructing the new supernature of poetic creativity, which has historically to be the effective escape route from Collins's dilemma.

This completes the logic of Collins's use of the Second Sight. The nostalgic and affective subjectivisation is the mark of an identification: the visionary faculty functions as a vehicle for imagining imagination itself. By the end of the century, seer and poet could be merged automatically: a closet drama of 1790, *Darthula*, features a 'Bard of the Second Sight'[14] and in 1811 Anne Grant adduces the phenomenon as evidence of the refined sensibility of Highlanders, arguing that only deep meditation and sensitive and fantastic feeling can nourish 'this creative faculty'.[15] What had happened in between, to turn Collins's suggestive cross-reference into a received identity, was Macpherson's Ossian.

2 THE WELL-TAUGHT HIND

Collins was not hoping to exploit the Highland vein of imagery himself. In a wistful gesture which like so much else in the text shadows and complicates its initial confidence, he entrusts the work to John Home:

> Proceed, in forceful sounds and Colours bold
> The Native Legends of thy land rehearse
> To such adapt thy Lyre, and suit thy pow'rfull Verse.

Although Home became something like the national poet of Scotland with the success of his tragedy *Douglas* in 1756, his response to this exhortation was rather limited. The play does have a Scottish setting, and occasional native spirits in the imagery; but other influences were more pressing. Against Collins's metropolitan primitivism Home could set the advice of a fellow Scot, David Hume: 'For God's sake, read Shakespeare, but get Racine and Sophocles by heart. It is reserved to you, and you alone, to redeem our stage from the reproach of barbarism'.[16] *Douglas* was allegedly based on the Scots ballad of Gil Morrice, but as Home's biographer points out, it is at least as dependent on Voltaire's *Mérope*, which was playing in London at the time of his visit.[17] Whatever the priority of sources, the dramatic convention – the confidante, the painstakingly plotted recognitions and reversals, the denouement by means of a sub-Sophoclean shepherd – is wholly neo-classical. There is one moment of slightly incongruous Gothic when the hero alludes to an old hermit, the instructor of his youth, who retired to a mountain cave after killing his brother by mistake:

> In the wild desert on a rock he sits,
> Or on some nameless stream's untrodden banks,
> And ruminates all day his dreadful fate.
> At times, alas! not in his perfect mind,
> Holds dialogues with his loved brother's ghost.[18]

But 'not in his perfect mind' is holding the uncanny very firmly at arm's length. Home clearly decided not to incur, on his own account, 'the reproach of barbarism'.

However, the role of writer was not the only one which Collins's poem had offered him. It also envisaged him as a listener: wandering in the northern hills, he may hear

> Strange lays, whose power had charmed a Spenser's ear.
> At Ev'ry Pause, before thy Mind possest,
>   Old Runic bards shall seem to rise around
> With uncouth Lyres, in many-colour'd Vest,
>   Their Matted Hair with boughs fantastic crown'd
> Whether Thou bidst the well-taught Hind repeat
>   The Choral Dirge that mourns some Chieftain brave
> When Ev'ry Shrieking Maid her bosom beat
>   And strew'd with choicest herbs his scented Grave
> Or whether sitting in the Shepherd's Shiel
>   Thou hear'st some Sounding Tale of War's alarms.
>   (11. 39–49)

The old bards are spectacular, but dizzyingly insubstantial. Collins is not suggesting that they exist, or even that they ever existed: they are the visions that will appear to Home's mind in the intervals of hearing the lay, so that what we have here is a poem which describes a poet imagining other poets while listening to a poem. The shrieking maids, who are mentioned because they accompanied the original performance of the dirge which is now repeated for the visitor, are almost as remote; and the action – the brave deeds of the Chieftain or the War's alarms – are still further removed, as if at the far end of a tunnel of mirrors. The whole society with its beliefs, historically actual in theory, dissolves in practice into patterns of poetic self-consciousness.

Despite, or because of, its vertically self-referring form, this is the recommendation of Collins's which Home, in a sense, really did carry out. On 2 October 1759, he wrote to a friend 'that he had at last found what he had been long wishing for, a person who could make him acquainted with ancient Highland poetry, of which he had heard so much'. This was James Macpherson, and Home was particularly pleased because he was not only 'a native of the remote Highlands', but also 'an exceeding good classical scholar'.[19] The problem posed by Home's own situation as a writer – that of reconciling the power of 'barbaric' superstition with the perspicuity of polite learning – was inscribed upon the strange cult of Ossian from its first day.

The story of what happened next has often been told,[20] and the barest outline will be enough here. Macpherson, a 23-year-old farmer's son from Badenoch who was working as a private tutor, provided Home with what he claimed were his own translations of ancient Gaelic poems in his possession; Home was impressed by them, and introduced him to Edinburgh literary society, and in particular to Hugh Blair, who took Macpherson under his protection, organised a subscription to finance further research, supervised the young translator's literary labours, and later contributed a *Critical Dissertation on the Poems of Ossian* which set the agenda for the poems' reception into the literary canon.[21] Three volumes of 'translations' appeared: *Fragments of Ancient Poetry, Collected in the Highlands of Scotland* (1760), *Fingal, an Ancient Epic Poem* (1761) and *Temora* (1763). The two latter volumes both contained shorter pieces as well as the title poems. All were written in high-flown poetic English prose, and except for a brief appendix to *Temora* no Gaelic text was published. All were certainly, in their essentials, made up by Macpherson.[22] Ossian, a third-century Gaelic bard and the son of Fingal himself, was supposed to be the author of the originals.

Macpherson produced no more translations, and embarked on an unspectacular but lucrative career in London and colonial politics and letters. Ossian's subsequent trajectory was more remarkable: he became an immense cult, hailed as the northern Homer by Herder, Goethe, Hazlitt, Pushkin, Thoreau, Mme de Stael, Napoleon and countless other celebrities, and at the same time the object of a vitriolic controversy over whether he was genuine.[23]

From the start, certainly, barbarism, with Macpherson as its representative, came more than half-way to meet politeness. The translation of ancient Highland poetry which Macpherson produced on the spot was the account of the death of Oscar, subsequently printed as the seventh of the *Fragments*.[24] In it, a lover contrives to be killed by his friend and rival, who then contrives to be killed by the beloved, who then dies. This geometrical murderousness directly reflects the formalism of neo-classical tragedies such as Home's; it's also typical of the 'fragments' that followed, in which, time after time, lovers, friends or siblings cause each other's deaths by accident or design, in symmetrical, grotesquely unlucky patterns of destruction. Many confirm their debt to the eighteenth-century stage by actually being dramatic in form – dialogues, or soliloquies, or else (like the death of Oscar) stories which include a narrative pretext, an interlocutor and grief-stricken narrator, and so resemble dramatic exposition. An effort of historical imagination is needed to see how these pallidly conventional miniature tragedies could have looked to their early readers like the excitingly alien productions of a third-century Gaelic bard. Did they not strike them as familiar?

One important answer is that the text of the *Fragments* teems with ghosts. Just as in Collins, evocations of the supernatural function as signs that one is entering the 'world unknown' – an absence equipped, this time, with a historical and cultural alibi. Here, vividly, is the intimation of poetic otherness which is missing from the form. At the same time, though, the ghosts are of a rhetorically peculiar kind:

> Yes, my fair, I return; but I alone of my race. Thou shalt see them no more: their graves I raised on the plain. But why art thou on the desert hill? why on the heath, alone?
> Alone I am, O Shilric! alone in the winter-house. With grief for thee I expired. Shilric, I am pale in the tomb.
> She fleets, she sails away; as grey mist before the wind![25]

Shilric, one gathers, is the last survivor of a shadowy and disastrous campaign; the girl, who died because of her love for him, appears in spectral form because of his love for her. Thus, while the *external* signification of the haunting is the primitive and therefore superstitious culture from which the text is supposed to come, its immediate motivation is the extreme emotions of the characters. The visions in Collins were, with dubious authenticity, accompanied by psychological disturbance; Macpherson boldly completes the subjectivising move and makes this one a *symptom* of psychological disturbance. It is wholly typical. In the following Fragment, for example, we get:

> But ah! what voice is that? Who rides on the meteor of fire! Green are his airy limbs. It is he, it is the ghost of Malcolm! Rest, lovely soul, rest on the rock; and let me hear thy voice. He is gone, like a dream of the night.[26]

The theatrical utterance, with its pedantically marked transitions from one passion to the next, effectively *produces* the apparition. These ghosts are condensations of the rhetoric in which they are addressed: as Hartman says, 'Their essence is vocative.'[27] We are back in the penumbra between a real contingency and a 'fictitious Fabulous Ramble of the Fancy': the elusive allegorical presences of Pindaric apostrophe have acquired personalities.

The broad rhetorical utility of this attenuated and sentimental supernaturalism is ingenuously revealed by Hugh Blair:

> It is a great advantage of Ossian's mythology, that it is not local and temporary, like that of most other ancient poets; which of course is apt to seem ridiculous, after the superstitions have passed away on which it was founded. Ossian's mythology is, to speak so, the mythology of human nature; for it is founded on what has been the popular belief, in all ages and countries, and under all forms of religion, concerning the appearances of departed spirits.[28]

This universality in Ossian's epic machinery is anything but an accident. Macpherson derided the spells and wizards he found in Fingalian material from Ireland,[29] and 'rejected wholly the works of the bards'[30] who, writing at a later date than Ossian, had, it appeared, marred their transmission of his work with vulgarity and idiosyncrasy. The Book of the Dean of Lismore, which Macpherson certainly handled,[31] includes, in Ossianic contexts, such marvels as a country under the sea, talking birds, and a magical cloak which detects adultery.[32] All these features are absent from Macpherson's productions: presumably they were the 'corruptions' which he excised in 'restoring' the Ossianic text 'to its original purity', an editorial principle later recalled by one of his collaborators.[33] This method, which of course led to wholesale falsification, was authorised by what almost amounts to an equivocation on the critical term 'nature'. Ossian, as a precivilised genius, was *ex hypothesi* a poet of nature. It follows that anything in the Ossianic texts which is 'unnatural' must be inauthentic. In this way, the ancient poetry is restored and reconstructed in the image of a humanist universalism: the simple and permanent passions which neo-classical aesthetics derived through an elaborate code of abstractions were in Ossian's case supposed to have been directly visible in real life because of the native simplicity of the age in which he lived.

The Ossianic, or rather the Macphersonic, supernatural world, which contains no divinity but only psychologised ghosts and portents, is the logical religious system of such a construction. Sensibility, that sign of the human so ideologically central that Blair and Macpherson imagine it to be transhistorical, literally gives rise to an immaterial pantheon which is precisely what Blair calls it, in a phrase which perhaps means more than it's intended to: the mythology of human nature. The 'Works of Ossian' aspired to be, and for half a century or so actually were, the sacred texts of pure subjectivity.

The priests of this cult of ghosts are, as one would expect, poets. Commenting on the exalted code of heroism which governs the behaviour of Fingal, Blair maintains that the poetry is in this respect a faithful reflection of ancient Gaelic manners, but then doubles back on himself to argue that the manners attained such heights of probity because of the social influence of poetry:

> For such songs as these, familiar to the Celtic warriors from their childhood, both in war and peace, their principal entertainment, must have had a very considerable influence in propagating among them real manners nearly approaching to the poetical; and in forming even such a hero as Fingal. Especially when we consider that among their limited objects of ambition ... the chief was Fame, and that Immortality which they expected to receive from their virtues and exploits, in the songs of bards.[34]

Here, in unconscious homage to the real origins of his text, the critic constructs a way of life literally governed by poetry. As if in premature parody of Matthew Arnold (a belated admirer of Macpherson), literature is seated on the throne vacated by dogma, and legislates directly for conduct. There are bards instead of priests, an institutionalised poetic tradition instead of doctrine, and instead of heaven, the prospect of immortality in song. The Fingalian heroes do in fact repeatedly allude to this prospect as they conduct their otherwise motiveless wars: in other words, the poems relate exploits which were carried out for no other reason than to provide appropriate exploits for the poems to relate. Take for example an incident in the fourth book of *Fingal*. The Caledonians are losing a battle, but Fingal delays coming to their aid at the request of one of his sons, who wants an opportunity to distinguish himself independently. Rather than injure the boy's 'fame' by effective intervention, Fingal sends a bard to encourage him.[35] David Hume, a sceptic in the Ossian controversy, asks, 'Are these the manners of barbarous nations, or even of people that have common sense?'[36] The answer is that the heroes do not have common sense; their motives are aesthetic; they *know* that they are fictional characters.

This circularity is greatly intensified by the narrative frame of most of Macpherson's pieces. Ossian, the only surviving son of Fingal, sits alone or in the company of his son's widow Malvina, and recalls the departed glory of the heroes. He is blind – a fact which links him via classical associations with visionary experience – and the memories that fall upon his inward eye are more real to him than his present bare and melancholy surroundings. That's to say: whatever ghosts may appear in the course of the story are secondary ones; before that, *all* the characters are ghosts, because their appearance in the poem is tantamount to their spectral appearance to the poet. The dramatis personae of Macpherson's poems are imagined beings – that is the information which is encoded in their presentation as ghosts – and the audacious editorial claim to authenticity is a bid, identical to that made by Collins, for a miraculous space in which the imaginary is real.

Expectably, then, the kaleidoscope of poetic self-reflections which characterised the ode is reproduced in Ossian: there are poems within poems like Chinese boxes, and a corresponding intratextual procession of surrogate readers, headed by the beautiful, tearful, and almost wholly anonymous Malvina, a mythologised flyleaf on which several generations of adolescent girls would write their names. One of these, Anne Grant, herself later wrote an Ossianic poem which makes explicit some of the elements in Macpherson's overheated reception. It was a versification of 'Morduth', a spurious heroic poem by one of the Highland writers who rode the Ossianic bandwagon in the 1770s and 80s,[37] but which Grant believed to be ancient. The tale has the familiar dramatised narrator:

> O you that pour'd the tempest on your foes,
> Look smiling from the clouds of your repose;
> And while your children hear your proud renown,
> See tears of transport silently steal down: –
> My soul grows bright while former years arise,
> With all their deeds of fame to glad my eyes:
> In long succession see the scenes unfold, –
> Hunter, attend! a tale of times of old![38]

The narrator is watching the scenes of former years. The Hunter is listening to the narrator. The 'children' are the narrator's secondary audience, virtually rather than literally present, rather like the readers of a published poem. And the ancestors who are the subject-matter of the story are watching the reactions of those who are listening to it. To read this kind of writing is to gain admittance to a fantastic mutuality which embraces the book's author, its characters, and its other purchasers, in a cat's-cradle of readings and responses. This baroque tableau draws attention to the fact that the key motif in the whole literary cult is neither an action nor a place, but the image of the poet (bard, hermit, seer), posed picturesquely among rocks and streams, mournfuly singing of what no longer exists. That is what recurs, in Collins, in Home,[39] in Macpherson and in his readers such as Anne Grant; often the events are little more than a pretext to substantiate the self-reflexive device. In these hands, the Highlands become a lavish *mise-en-scène* for the act of reading itself. Poet and public, having taken Collins's advice and set their feet to Fancy's Land, find it full of insubstantial images of themselves.

3 THE TALE OF OTHER TIMES

A further distinction of Ossian's epic machinery is its exclusive orientation towards the past. Whereas Homer's gods and Milton's angels imply parallel worlds which cut across historical time, and both biblical prophecy and Hebridean Second Sight refer to the future, Macpherson's supernatural manifestations almost always point back to a life that is already over. The Ossianic visionary typically encounters, not heaven or hell, and not portents of what is to come, but dead friends. Even the aged bard's lush apotheosis at the end of *Berrathon* is nothing but reunion with a disembodied Fingal in a Selma in the clouds: paradise consists simply of having everything just as it used to be. Moreover, the ghosts are impotent: they don't intervene, or exhort, or inform, but merely watch and are watched until they fade away. There is no revelation and no transcendence; there is only the ubiquitous and impalpable presence of the past, into whose illusive whirlings everything is constantly slipping.

This compulsive evanescence dominates every time-scale of the fiction: the moment, in the fleeting of ghosts or the darkening of the moon; the individual life, in the recurrent evocation of an old man's memories of youth; the epoch, in the equally insistent rhetoric of the last survivor; and the whole of history, in the editorial insistence on the immense age of the text. Thus (to pick out one example from dozens) to read of the death of Agandecca as related by the grey-haired bard Carril in *Fingal* – 'She fell, like a wreath of snow, which slides from the rocks of Ronan; when the woods are still, and echo deepens in the vale!'[40] – is to gaze into a receding series of surceases: that of the girl, that of the snow, that of the echo; that of Fingal's youth long ago when the deaths occurred, that of Carril's youth, that of Ossian's youth when Carril – now himself dead – was alive and telling stories, and that of the whole heroic age whose passing is the context for all the lesser ageings and losses. 'Lovely the tales of other times!' Cuthullin has exclaimed, generalising the sevenfold nostalgia in a phrase whose own syntactic archaism gratifies the taste it expresses. 'They are like the calm dew of the morning on the hill of roes, when the sun is faint on its side.' The chain of evaporations is endless, except that it, too, is on the point of disappearing. Nothing is more appropriate to these elaborately obsolescent performances than their subsequent critical history, a meteoric descent from hyperbolic fame into ridicule and neglect. 'The harp is not strung on Morven. The voice of music ascends not on Cona. Dead, with the mighty, is the bard':[41] the rhetoric of oblivion denotes, ironically, the handsome editions with their uncut pages that are to be found in libraries all over Europe. As Hazlitt remarked in 1818, cleverly catching the authenticity debate up into a critical perspective, 'If it were indeed possible to show that this writer was nothing, it would only be another instance of mutability, another blank made, another void left in the heart.'[42] Just as the inhabitants of the Fingalian world are essentially ghosts all along, at one with themselves only when they die, so the text as a whole is fulfilled by its falling historically into the state of cultural dilapidation which was always already its literary character.

Macpherson's readers testify to the pleasures of this perpetual bereavement. In 1780 Charles Cordiner, one of the picturesque tourists I discussed in Chapter 4, was excited to come upon a crag in Sutherland which was actually called Carril. Part of his rhapsodic reaction reads:

> Whether the memory of lapsed ages was preserved by the bards, or if only, like a morning-dream, the visions of *Ossian* came in later days, yet ... 'Lovely are the tales of other times;' they are faithful to the story, which deceives the winter evening among the hills. 'O *Carril,* raise again thy voice; let me hear the song of *Selma,* which was sung in the halls of joy, when *Fingal,* king of shields, was there, and glowed at the deeds of his fathers.'
>
> But the light and joy of the song are fled; the halls of the renowned are left desolate and solitary, amidst rocks that no more echo to the sound of the harp.[43]

Cordiner was a connoisseur of ruins, still more than of scenery, and what he's doing here is treating Ossian as the literary equivalent of a picturesquely derelict tower – having the same poignancy, offering the same stimulus to the reconstructive imagination, and tainted with the same margin of acknowledged inauthenticity. Indeed, the two contemporary cults intertwine: at least two ruined castles appeared in Runciman's Ossianic ceiling at Penicuik, perhaps cued by the popular description of the ruins of Balclutha in *Carthon;*[44] and the *Fragments of Ancient Poetry* themselves are misleadingly named, as Gray at once noticed[45] – the pieces are really complete, but the reader is invited to interpret their laconic emotionalism as a sign of antiquity and damage. Cordiner arrives at the same appreciative melancholy by way of another Ossianic receding series: Fingal 'glowed' at the memory of his ancestors; Ossian, recalling that, glows at the memory of Carril who sang about them; and now recalling *that,* Cordiner glows at the memory of Ossian. The response is so perfectly integrated with the text that it's quite difficult to disentangle the pastiche from the quotation. This proliferation of nostalgias makes sense of Cordiner's otherwise surprising indifference to the question of authenticity: if the sequence of lapses reproduces itself endlessly, it matters very little when the actual words were inserted to set it in motion. The question of whether Macpherson was lying or not, which seemed so important to a critic like Johnson,[46] is for the devotee only a matter of the difference between a memory that is like a dream and a dream that is like a memory. The people in the poem who glimpse and mourn the fleeting illusions of the night are teaching the reader to do the same for them. One could say that the phrase 'of other times', which Macpherson and his admirers attach tirelessly to nouns such as 'bard', 'tale' and 'song', owes its potency to a delightful and irreducible ambiguity in the 'of'.

What is the historical content of this obsession, not only with the past, but with pastness as such? A nationalist reading answers this question by recalling the 'national plight' of Macpherson's own time – the anglicising aftermath of 1707 and of 1745. M. P. McDiarmid, for example, assigns the *Poems of Ossian* to a class of 'politically inspired fantasies' whose most notable member is Allan Ramsay's 'A Vision', an imitation of the sixteenth-century makars, written in 1714 and lamenting, under its transparent disguise, the Union of Parliaments.[47] This comparison seems to me to flatter Macpherson for the sake of a myth of national continuity. Whereas Ramsay's language is a revival of literary Scots, cultivated for the sake of unmistakably political assertion, Macpherson's is a blandly unidiomatic English (which proved, as one might expect, effortlessly translatable). Whereas 'A Vision' points sharply and designedly at a particular event, the stories in Macpherson's Ossian offer no definite parallels with eighteenth-century history. And above all, whereas the status of Ramsay's poem as a fantasy is acknowledged in the appropriately late-medieval convention of the allegorical vision, Macpherson is demanding, implicitly and explicitly, that the society he depicts be accepted as historically actual; whatever the plausibility of this claim, the fact that it is advanced makes any clear reference to contemporary events impossible. So that when McDiarmid gamely concludes that '*Fingal* especially is indeed a heroic poem, celebrating in its national hero the vision and the values that an imaged past recommends to the present', he is attributing to the poem a historical and national consciousness which it not only fails to display, but is in fact prohibited from displaying by the terms of its production.

On the other hand, it seems absurd to maintain that the poems have nothing whatever to do with their historical situation.

Macpherson was from Ruthven, whose ancient castle, a barracks in Wade's time, was captured by the Jacobite army in the Forty-five and burnt down in the reprisals after Culloden, when Macpherson was ten. In the 1750s he was moving back and forth between a rapidly disintegrating Gaelic society and the Lowland seats of classical learning which were the gateway to a literary career.[48] A past of solidarity and fighting, a present of isolation and poetry: it's the dichotomy which is gloomily insistent in Ossian. And if we accept for a moment that Macpherson really was rescuing priceless relics of Gaelic tradition from the oncoming bulldozers of progress and anglicisation, then his chosen representative of the tradition – bereaved, decrepit, blind – has a historical pathos and irony which could conceivably amount to a protest.

Some of these connections can be traced by way of one of Macpherson's juvenilia, 'On the Death of Marshal Keith', which mourns, not only the Jacobite exile whose death in 1758 was its occasion, but also his house:

> But chief, as relics of a dying race,
> The Keiths command, in woe, the foremost place ...
> Now falling, dying, lost to all but fame,
> And only living in the hero's name.
>   See! the proud halls they once possessed, decayed,
> The spiral tow'rs depend the lofty head;
> Wild ivy creeps along the mould'ring walls,
> And with each gust of wind a fragment falls.[49]

As Laing points out, this is a sketch for Balclutha;[50] equally Ossianic is the structure's hypersensitivity to the wind. An emotional formula not essentially different from the Fingalian one is being applied to the heroism of 1745; elsewhere in the poem fervent appeals to 'Caledonia' place the gesture in just the context McDiarmid suggests for it.

But then that relationship, between the mourning bard and the historical defeat which is his modern situation, fails, or refuses, to meet the demands a nationalist reading places on it. So far from elaborating values which the past can recommend to the present, the fiction collapses back, as we've seen, through successive layers of historical absence, resigned to a present which is geriatric, futureless, exhausted by the multiple burden of ghosts. Moreover, if we attempt to reconstruct the lost Fingalian world from the bard's memories, it turns out to have been luridly dysfunctional.

The main action of *Fingal* is punctuated by what Macpherson calls episodes, usually sentimental tales performed by the king's bards in the intervals of the fighting. In Book I these tell of two separate fatal triangles, with one survivor out of the six participants. Book II ends with two stories about unintended killings. In Book III two damsels, in different episodes, are murdered while under Fingal's protection. In Book V there is another triangle, again fatal to all three lovers. All this on top of the hundreds who perish in the battles themselves. It's a level of destruction typical of the *Poems of Ossian* in general: an irresistible tendency is constantly increasing the already excessive spectral population. The point here is not just the sheer number of deaths; this is likely to be high in any military epic, real or fabricated. It's that love, the motive in all these tragedies, is the only serious business of the Fingalians apart from fighting, as Lord Kames observed.[51] (He added hunting, but this is normally an amusement, mentioned in the poems only if it is about to be interrupted by one of the other two.) The world of Ossian thus appears as one whose energies are all directed towards death. Macpherson several times asserts that the ancient Highlanders never killed themselves: this taboo is necessary because suicide is really, as Goethe immediately realised,[52] the underlying principle of the whole imagined culture. Those who don't die in battle fall victim to the misunderstandings and crimes of passion which inescapably accompany desire. Seen, as they always are, in retrospect, the friends of Ossian's youth seem like a monstrous species which has become extinct because its mating patterns were too destructive of life.

Whatever this abnormal closure may mean in the terms of individual psychology, it is *historically* decisive. These are epic poems with no births, no children, no mothers, and no sexual fulfilment; only virgins, longing, and death. Expressions of yearning abound, and white breasts are exposed at every crisis, but consummation is invariably withheld. Even when a 'dark' villain exerts his power over a hapless maiden, it is by stabbing her with a dagger. Perhaps much of the melancholy glamour of the poems came from this subtextual sense of desire denied; unlocalised sexual feeling permeates the action, sighing from caves and mountain streams, quivering in the foliage and darkening the sky. The endless duologues of Ossian and Malvina, the bereaved father and the widowed daughter-in-law, are typical of the whole structure in being at once erotically charged and sterile. Aroused by every association, the two of them wait for death. Thus what is missing from the Ossianic world is not sexuality in general but specifically generation; the nobility of the depicted society, its strained purity of motive and conduct, is bound up with its suppression of the genital; it is a historical nation which doesn't reproduce itself.

This comprehensive deadliness distinguishes Macpherson's work historically from later invented or reconstructed national epics such as *Pan Tadeusz* or the *Kalevala*, even though these were sometimes inspired by his example. In them, certainly, a more or less imagined past was offered, as tradition or exhortation, to the present and the future. But Macpherson himself, though he was officially proposing his 'Caledonians' as Scottish (not only Highland) progenitors, portrays the ancestral culture as totally incapable of transmission. In so far as the matter of Ossian is the erasure of regional or national identity by metropolitan cultural and economic power, the poems do not resist or even lament the process so much as form a part of it.

For what Macpherson had really produced, on the most charitable interpretation of his activities, was a drastic *Improvement* of the ancient poetry of the Highlands. The Highland Society's committee of investigation, which reported in 1805 in an attempt to settle the continuingly acrimonious debate about Macpherson's sources, formed the opinion that he had added

> what he conceived to be dignity and delicacy to the original composition, by striking out passages, by softening incidents, by refining the language, in short by changing what he considered as too simple or too rude for a modern ear, and elevating what in his opinion was below the standard of good poetry.[53]

Dignity, delicacy, softness, refinement, elevation – the criteria by which Ossian was prepared for the press are not merely 'modern' ones in general, but specifically those by which the Edinburgh lawyers and divines who were the project's patrons measured their own country's emergence from its native barbarism. The outcome, as Walter Scott put it, reviewing the report in language more vigorous than its own, was a primitive hero who resembled Sir Charles Grandison.[54] The third-century Highlands were rendered genteel.

This conclusion was a more damaging one than the report admits, because intellectual interest in Ossian had centred so much on just those features of his poetry which it now appeared Macpherson had supplied. It was the discovery of such 'civilised' aesthetic and moral qualities in the works of such a primitive age which constituted both their attraction and their scholarly value for a philosophic generation fascinated by the transitions between savagery, barbarism and civility. Ferguson, Gibbon and John Millar all allude to Ossian as an instance of high cultural achievement at a primitive stage of social development; all point to it in order to question what seems by contrast to be the formalism or the decadence of advanced civilisations.[55] Such comparisons turn more or less explicitly on the assumption that the primitive state of society reveals the true virtues and capacities of mankind more directly and innocently than the rule-governed literature of later stages: if, therefore, the 'artless song of the savage', as Ferguson calls it, had in fact been adapted to the categories of eighteenth-century 'art', this was far more than a detail of presentation – it made the evidence of the text inadmissible on the very question the literati wanted to ask it.

Indeed, they had effectively commissioned it. When Macpherson went to the Highlands in 1760, it was to look for what Blair was already calling 'our epic':[56] even if his researches had been carried out with more integrity than they apparently were, the whole project would still have been burdened with a wholly inapplicable set of Augustan assumptions about what literature could be. Macpherson had to find an integral text, in an identifiable genre, with an individual author; what he will have had to go on is a protean collective tradition in genres quite different from the Graeco-Roman ones he brought with him from Edinburgh. Consequently, he interpreted whatever songs, tales and reworkings were available as if they were scattered fragments of the unity he assumed to have existed, and set to work to reconstruct this thoroughly neo-classical ur-text. In short, his patrons got what they had asked for. Its 'refinement' was a turbid projection of their own.

Ossianic society, in other words, is an imaginary primitive world which is wholly structured and saturated by the categories of Improvement. This can be traced, not only in the incongruous gentility of the depicted *mores*, but still more in the negativity of the depiction: Fingal's world is *not* cultivated, *not* populous, *not* rational, *not* regulated – above all, *not* extant. An observer from a society which *is* all these things is implied in every stroke of the portrayal. But then this observer suppresses his modern identity with fanatical thoroughness in the visible text: as Blair says, 'from beginning to end all is consistent; no modern allusion drops from him; but every where the same face of rude nature appears'.[57] The civilised visitor, whose gaze makes all he sees in the wilderness appear exotically and poignantly doomed, is heavily disguised as a native. As a result, his presence is internalised by the characters he presents; their voices are disembodied and sepulchral, reduced to echoes by the suppressed awareness of their own irrevocable archaism. In an editorial gesture which is the acme of imperialist ideology, the *Poems of Ossian* idealise Highland culture by reading its extinction back into its very origins.

In this death-obsessed imaginary country, according to Blair, 'The greatest praise that can be given to the beauty of a living woman, is to say, "She is as fair as the ghost of the hill; when it moves in a sunbeam at noon, over the silence of Morven."'[58] It was as this beautiful ghost that Macpherson presented the Highlands to the literary public of the western world.

4 MEMORIALS

Setting their feet to Fancy's land, the early tourists established Ossianic classic ground at conveniently spaced points on their circuit of the Highlands. Passing the poet's grave north of Crieff, or his grotto in the Hermitage at Dunkeld, one visited Fingal's grave at Killin, Ossian's birthplace in Glencoe, and, after its naming by the geographer Sir Joseph Banks in 1772, Fingal's Cave on Staffa.[59] These external specifications, however, didn't really accord very well with the cloudy and self-reflexive experience of reading the texts themselves. The mapping of the tales of other times on to the landscapes of the present worked more effectively in a rather different form. Characteristically, there was already a space for the activity within the writing itself.

In the exceptionally mournful *Songs of Selma*, one of the laments ends: 'When night comes on the hill; when the loud winds arise; my ghost shall stand in the blast, and mourn the death of my friends. The hunter shall hear from his booth. He shall fear but love my voice!'[60] Over and over this hunter appears, never hunting, always musing over the mossy tombs of the protagonists or waylaid by their ghosts. He is one with the winds and hills because of the naturalness of his occupation, but at the same time he is one with the reader because of his solitary and random situation in the story. To the tourist, therefore, he offers a mythic identity inside the text.

Equally typically, the medium of the identification, the point of intersection between the devotee's experience and the imagery of the poems, is not a place, but the weather. What, in the passage just quoted, shall the hunter hear? The keening of the ghost, presumably – but this will be heard 'when the loud winds arise', and it's easy to see how the two sounds blend together on the ear of the enthusiastically fearful hunter. By a parallel visual equivocation, the ghosts, as a reviewer noted, 'are drawn exactly after phenomena that in Ossian's country are very common, local mists settling upon a hill'.[61] This adroit naturalisation of superstition fills the ordinary sights and sounds of Highland weather with numinous presence. In the 1790s, to take one example of hundreds, a traveller crossing Corrieyairick in cold cloud reflected:

> On those bleak and dreary mountains, how much are one's spirits in the power of the weather. Should the storm prevail, one is left utterly comfortless and forlorn. Were night to fall down with all its shades, the phantoms of the desert would be truly formidable: broken rocks and blasted pines, withered with age and moss, seen by the glimpse of the moon; while the roar of torrents, and unequal gales of wind howling around, would play some ghastly measures on the ear; – how easily could imagination hear, 'The spirit of the mountain shriek, and see the ghosts of the departed, becoming from the passing cloud.'[62]

The shrieking spirit of the mountain is a neat example of the involved literary relationships which are condensed in such responses. It's from the first edition of *Dar-thula*,[63] where it is understood as an omen. In a note, Macpherson explains that the phrase refers to 'that deep and melancholy sound which precedes a storm, well known to those who live in a high country'. He is perhaps thinking of the belief that Ben Doran emits a hollow sound twenty-four hours before heavy rain: Pennant and Gilpin both record this, Pennant illustrating the observation with Macpherson's line.[64] But the idea of 'the sad Genius of the coming Storm' which 'presageful, send[s] a hollow Moan' is, as the incredulous Laing points out, from Thomson's 'The Seasons'.[65] And in the background of Thomson's image there is clearly the warning sound – 'aridus altis/montibus audiri fragor'[66] – from the meteorological passage in the Georgics, which is cited as an interesting comparison by Pennant and Gilpin. To complicate matters a little further, Macpherson changed 'shrieked' to 'roared' in subsequent editions of *Dar-thula*, probably to avoid the echo of 'Red came the river down, and loud and oft/The angry spirit of the water shriek'd'[67] – which is a similarly classicised vernacular superstition from John Home's *Douglas*.

The traveller on Corrieyairick, then, brings to the concrete experience of bad weather in the central Highlands an elaborate supplement of interlocking literary associations. Their common theme is a sophisticated supernaturalism: they seize on meteorological obscurities – night, vistas hidden in cloud, sounds whose sources can't be seen – and use them as portals to an other-worldly presence which may be, but precisely because of the obscurity doesn't need to be, purely imaginary. Atmospheric dimness is the material mechanism of an enticingly vague suggestion, an indefinite postponement of closure through multiple texts and imaginings. Seen in this way, the Highlands become the privileged country of what Geoffrey Hartman appropriately calls 'surmise'.[68]

The most skilful hunter of this ambiguous transcendence is of course Wordsworth, and his clarity is a useful guide to the whole construction. On another wet day, in 1803, he was walking on the road by Loch Lomond with Dorothy and Coleridge:

> we stopped suddenly at the sound of a half-articulate Gaelic hooting from the field close to us. It came from a little boy, whom we could see on the hill between us and the lake, wrapped up in a grey plaid. He was probably calling home the cattle for the night. His appearance was in the highest degree moving to the imagination: mists were on the hillside, darkness shutting in upon the huge avenue of mountains, torrents roaring, no house in sight to which the child might belong; his dress, cry, and appearance all different from anything we had been accustomed to. It was a text, as William has since observed to me, containing in itself the whole history of the Highlander's life – his melancholy, his simplicity, his poverty, his superstition, and above all, that visionariness which results from a communion with the unwordliness of nature.[69]

In a way, this encounter is no less literary than the other: the setting sounds as if it draws on the description of 'long tracts of mountainous desert, covered with dark heath and often obscured by misty weather; narrow vallies, thinly inhabited, and bounded by precipices resounding with the fall of torrents'[70] by which James Beattie accounts for the visionary melancholy of the Highland character; and among the other poetic figures in play there seems to be Wordsworth's own Boy of Winander. What is distinctive in the account, though, is that it also provides a wholly prosaic explanation of the uncanny moment: the boy 'was probably calling home the cattle for the night'. Unlike Macpherson's, the 'text' is *not* projected on to the figure round whom it forms itelf, but appears explicitly as a function of the relationship between the scene and its beholders. It's for them that the boy's language and appearance are alien; it's to them that the mountains and torrents suggest 'the unworldliness of nature'; it's the estranging stillness created by their suddenly stopping on the road which shocks the elements of the moment into a significant unity. The text is shaped, moreover, not only by what they see, but equally by what is hidden from them – the mountains, the boy's home, the meaning of his 'half-articulate' cries: significance is determined quite as much by their remoteness from the boy as by their proximity to him. In short, they have *composed* this epitome of Highland life, and it's only when the act of composition is frozen, later, by a retrospective interpretation, that the interplay of land and fancy, vision and concealment, is reduced to the familiar myth of 'the Highlander's life'.

Among Wordsworth's 'Memorials' of the 1803 tour, the poem which relates most closely to this moment by Loch Lomond is 'The Solitary Reaper'. Again the traveller pauses on the road to listen to the Gaelic voice of a figure 'single in the field', and again the significance of the encounter is read in the silent spaces between the sound and the listener. But the lyric, by dramatising the reading, escapes the mythic closure of 'the Highlander's life'. Of the four stanzas, only the last does what Dorothy was doing throughout, that is, narrates the incident. The first fixes the point of apprehension with dramatising imperatives, and the middle two, side-stepping into questions and negatively phrased comparisons, avoid descriptive statement altogether while yet holding the reaper and the song at the centre of attention. So that when, six lines from the end, the narrative eventually defines itself as separate from the event – 'I saw her singing' – the effect is that *only now* is the listener sufficiently detached from the song to tell a story about it: until that disenchanting drop into the past tense, we now see, the poem was raptly *in* the 'Vale profound' which was filled with the singing; its exotic similitudes and guessed-at lyric themes were formed, as it were, inside the music. It's this sense of an unmediated intimacy which is unexpressed, or which is broken once it is expressed, that justifies the level tone of the summarising hyperbole: 'The music in my heart I bore'.

The condition of this extra-linguistic oneness, though, is distance. The first stanza's fourfold insistence that the girl is alone removes her from the company even of the beholder for whom she is so intensely present, and that strained feeling of remoteness is picked up by the Arabian sands and farthest Hebrides of the similes. Then the question 'Will no one tell me what she sings?' introduces a different kind of distantness, acknowledging that the girl speaks a language the poet doesn't understand; while at the same time it sets off a train of 'surmise' which carries the poem into its deepest interfusion with the song. Communion and separation are obverse sides of the same pattern, an identity which is confirmed at the close when the gap between singer and poet opens up to infinity, yet the song survives in silence.

That closing line – 'Long after it was heard no more' – resonates because of a specific ambiguity which was at least one of the poem's starting points (Wordsworth took it, and the incident, from the journal of another Highland traveller[71]). It makes it seem – inadvertently in the traveller's case, in Wordsworth's probably not – as if the girl had died. That note of elegy, once sounded, echoes back through the poem: the injunction 'Stop here, or gently pass!' is a convention of funeral inscription, and the Hebridean cuckoo is a portent of death from Martin Martin.[72] This is the term that resolves the play of communion and separation – the separateness is that of the dead, the comunity that of common mortality. Death is the invisible referent of the visible scene with its lively activities of working and walking; the secret source of the poet's emotion, carried lightly upon the surface of the text in the form of the melancholy of the tune.

It is thus an *ironically* Ossianic poem. Overhearing the Gaelic song in its self-enclosed solitude, the poet, like Macpherson, allows his reconstructive imagination to play over the irrecoverable text, which enters all the more deeply into his heart because an immense historical distance prevents him from appropriating its literal meanings. Like the voice of Ossian, the reaper's singing has the poignant sweetness of *lost speech*, whose reception is hushed and awed because it is full of the consciousness of death. Macpherson had both exploited that power, by referring his fictions to a source text which he never revealed,[73] and denied it by his pretence that translating this mysterious origin was an unproblematic business: as a result, the omnipresence of death in his writing was obsessive, perverse, symptomatic. Here, the acceptance that translation is impossible, that the lost speech is really lost, turns that same deadliness into a calm awareness of mortality which, paradoxically, functions as a human bond between the oblivious singer and the defeated interpreter. Wordsworth was firmly among the sceptics in the Ossianic controversy: he described the bard, with uncharacteristic ribaldry, as a phantom 'begotten by the snug embrace of an impudent Highlander upon a cloud of tradition'.[74] But though he is repelled by Macpherson's success, he identifies with his failure. The unread original which the translations travestied is for Wordsworth the *true* Highland text. The irony then is that, of course, this authentic source is itself really a product of the translations.

In its self-conscious exploitation of textual opacity, 'The Solitary Reaper' is the representative lyric of Wordsworth's Highland tour, as well as the most perfectly worked out. His characteristic activity as a tourist is pausing to decipher a wayside memorial, using its imperfect legibility as a point of entry for the surmising imagination, a break in the continuity of the understood which affords the necessary minimal occasion for a poetry of silence.[75] It was the ground on which a major form of his own (that of 'Michael' or 'The Ruined Cottage') coincided with the quite conventional touristic treatment of the Highlands as a gallery of monuments: most tourist guides noted graves and battlefields,[76] and even Johnson, in a famous passage, had come close to Wordsworth's transcendental sense of place when he identified the emotive power of the ruins on Iona with 'whatever withdraws us from the power of our senses; whatever makes the past, the distant or the future predominate over the present'.[77] Even for anti-Ossianists, the Highlands were full of ghosts; for Macpherson had done no more than give imposing (in every sense) expression to the attenuation and idealisation of Highland cultural identity which was determined by the logic of Improvement as a whole. What Wordsworth's meticulous rereadings show is that the Highland text was eloquent, not, as Collins and the Ossianists imagined, because it was still legible, but precisely because it had been erased.

6
Social Tribes

1   A STAY OF EXECUTION

Although it was an effect of various Highland stereotypes – the chief, the warrior, the seer – that they froze the region in archaic ethnic poses, it was also clear to all commentators in the second half of the eighteenth century that Highland society was changing. Improvement, which in 1746 had been spoken of as an urgent requirement, appeared by the 1770s, and still more by the time of Sir John Sinclair's detailed survey in the 1790s,[1] as something that was actually happening. In the 1780s Highland dress was legalised and the Forfeited Estates restored to their owners: the implication was that the region's integration into the polity and economy of Great Britain could now be left to proceed under its own steam.

What was happening, broadly speaking, was that the social structure of the Highlands, which had been a complex and largely conservative mixture of communal, tribal, feudal and commercial relations, was rather rapidly coming to be dominated by the agrarian capitalism which prevailed in (and was also revolutionising) the rest of British society. As James Hunter categorically says, 'The commercialisation of the agricultural structure in response to chieftains' financial necessitousness ... is the great fact of eighteenth century Highland history. From it all else follows.'[2] This process was not imposed on the Highlands by executive action from elsewhere; it was a social revolution initiated by those who directly controlled the land. They learned to think of themselves as individual proprietors rather than as the trustees of a collective inheritance; they doubled the rents in the third quarter of the century; they reset estates in such a way as to unpick the traditional hierarchies in the holding of land; they leased to the big sheep farmers who recast Highland husbandry along commercial lines between 1770 and 1815; they unconsciously called a new peasantry into being by their encouragement of subsistence potato culture and their labour-intensive exploitation of kelp; and when the combined effect of these departures proved incompatible with the existing patterns of population, they evicted the people.[3]

Had this programme produced the effects its more politically minded exponents had in view, the economy and society of the Highlands would indeed have become indistinguishable from those of the rest of Scotland, with medium-sized independent farmers employing landless labour, progressive urbanisation in commercial centres, the development of an indigenous middle class, and so on. There would perhaps in that case have been no Highland myth, or at any rate a very differently structured one. But in the upshot the programme met with selective success at best. The selection was dictated by the interests of British capitalism as a whole: where Highland developments serviced the requirements of the expanding metropolitan economy, they tended to thrive, but where they were in competition with that expansion, they failed.[4] The result was a client economy. The early nineteenth-century Highlands, with their sweated kelpers and vast sheep ranches side by side with an explosively increasing population of pauperised subsistence cultivators, present a startlingly recognisable picture of underdevelopment.

Within this 'internal colony'[5] of the British Empire, the old Highland ruling class was a historical Janus. On the one hand, the landowners participated as buyers and sellers of commodities in a dynamic capitalist economy; while on the other they presided over a system of primitive surplus extraction in which the primary producers scarcely used money at all except to pay the rent. The chiefs' discovery of themselves as landlords did not necessarily turn them into agrarian capitalists, as both political economy and Lowland experience might have predicted. Rather, it induced a phase of super-exploitation. As Malcolm Gray says:

> On the whole it seems clear that by 1815 landlords were taking a much larger proportion of the money income derived from husbandry than they had half a century before; indeed it had become the accepted policy so to set rents as to remove the whole cash income (of husbandry) in return for the tenants' right to use arable plots for subsistence production.[6]

The point about this response is that it was socially reactionary. The owners' insatiable claims on the agricultural surplus were not likely to erode their pre-capitalist authority, or to enhance the independence of the cultivators, who were of course frequently in arrears. Highland social relations were not liberalised by the advent of market forces: on the contrary, there are indications that they *became* archaic, tending towards a baronial caricature. Thus Eric Richards detects a 'feudal' recrudescence in the islands in the 1790s, and shows that during the Napoleonic wars several Highland landlords raised recruits by offering a family a plot of land in return for a son – a revival of military tenure in all but name.[7] Macdonnell of Glengarry, with his medieval pomp and ruthless evictions,[8] was the tip of an iceberg.

The great exceptions to the rule of this bastard feudalism were of course the commercial sheep farmers. They were entrepreneurs whose tenancies were based on a calculation of costs and profits and a normal commercial parity of status with the landowner. But they were almost always incomers from southern Scotland, and, as is very well known, their activities were not usually compatible with the existing native husbandry.[9] Often, they needed old tenants to be moved, and in delivering this requirement, the chiefs were making use of their traditional, extra-economic power. The land was reset, but the sclerosis of the indigenous society was confirmed.

This deeply contradictory situation turned out to be viable for a surprisingly long time. The Highland aristocracy was protected from its own obsolescence by a bizarre series of friendly circumstances, beginning with the potato, which, introduced into the Hebrides from Ireland in 1743, soon formed the indispensable subsistence base of the whole structure of exploitation.[10] The most important of these friendly circumstances was the favourable movement of prices. The region's basic export was and continued to be cattle on the hoof, the price of which rose fivefold between 1740 and 1810; kelp went up over the same period from under £3 to over £20 a ton; the revolutionary textile industry which undercut native manufactures nevertheless ensured a buoyant market for raw wool.[11] Wars, and the Napoleonic wars in particular, increased the demand for all these commodities and brought other benefits too: the raising of regiments offered the sons of the aristocracy respectable and lucrative careers, and the poor enlisted in such numbers that their pay and prize money made a significant contribution to the region's cash income, quite apart from the temporary easing of demographic pressures.[12]

Even under these freakishly friendly conditions, the tensions were acute. Kelp, while producing large short-term profits out of a system approximating to slave labour, also produced anomalous concentrations of tenants on barren coasts, vulnerable to the slightest hiccup in distant markets.[13] The sheep required the wholesale removal of communities, which in every part of the Highlands, though not in every case, was a bitter and sometimes violent process.[14] The wartime influx of cash produced little new working capital, because many of the big estates were already trapped in mortgages which devoured any increase in rent income.[15] These pressures combined were bringing landlords, at varying rates, to the stark choice between bankruptcy and eviction. Behind its anomalous prosperity, or even because of it, Highland society was breaking up.[16]

Nemesis came with peace. The troops returned and called the bluff of pseudo-military tenure: there was not enough land for all these men. Cattle and wool prices fell after 1815, and in 1825 a change in excise duty destroyed the kelp industry completely.[17] The extortionate rents immediately became unpayable; landlord and tenant plunged into debt together.[18] After that the collapse of the landed class was protracted but certain: around 1830 the population began to decline absolutely, and during the following 50 years two-thirds of the Highlands were sold.[19]

Seen in this context, the 70 years between Culloden and Waterloo have the character of a stay of execution. The Highlands were neutralised politically and militarily, but the economic collapse which eventually ensued was held off for a lifetime by a combination of adaptation and chance. It was during this period, which was one of far-reaching but in the end insufficiently radical change, that the myth of the Highlands was formed. Obviously, it doesn't constitute a direct representation of this history; in a sense, it's the whole point of myth that it *doesn't* do that; its mission, so to speak, is to dehistoricise its own making.[20] But neither is the myth reducible to a set of lies, an arbitrarily devised cover story. In the cultural constructions which are described in this chapter, the fate of the Highlands is neither shown nor concealed, but *displaced*.

2 POETRY AND EMIGRATION

The commercialisation of landed property in the Highlands is by no means the discovery of modern historians. Johnson and Pennant vigorously attacked rack-renting landlords in the 1770s;[21] a decade later, John Knox argued bitterly that the people were in misery not because the land was poor, 'But as the value of its natural produce, by sea and land, is almost wholly absorbed by the great landholders, and by many of them spent at Edinburgh, London, Bath, and elsewhere.'[22] J. L. Buchanan, a missionary in the Hebrides in the 1790s, uncompromisingly portrayed the condition of the people on absentees' estates as slavery.[23] Many of these denunciations were extracted, reviewed and paraphrased in the press and in subsequent books. By the end of the century the proposition that the Highland lairds had disgraced their ancestors by preferring sheep to men was as familiar, though also as contentious, as it is today.

The universal epigraph, quoted again and again, was from Goldsmith:

> Ill fares the land, to hastening ills a prey,
> Where wealth accumulates and men decay:
> Princes and lords may flourish or may fade;
> A breath can make them, as a breath has made;
> But a bold peasantry, their country's pride,
> When once destroyed, can never be supplied.[24]

So influential were these beautifully chiselled antitheses that in 1824 the political economist J. R. McCulloch wished they had never been introduced into a debate which, in his view, they had muddled with pretty irrelevances.[25]

Certainly the poem was timely: it appeared in 1770, and the first flurry of literary and journalistic anxiety about Highland emigration came in the period 1771–6. On the other hand, it had little to offer sociologically; its prelapsarian Auburn, a society of independent peasants, could hardly be equated with the old Highlands, which were understood to have been clannish and hierarchical. What counted was its powerful ethical linkage of emigration and luxury. This was rapidly applied to the Highlands by Goldsmith's scarcely less influential friend, Johnson.

The *Journey to the Western Islands*, published in 1775, noted an 'epidemick desire of wandering, which spreads its contagion from valley to valley', and followed 'the general opinion' in attributing it to excessive rent rises.[26] Not content, however, with the idea of an arbitrary outbreak of landlord greed, Johnson offers a historical explanation. The Laird, he argues, was deprived by the legislative aftermath of the Forty-five of his social and judicial power:

> When the power of birth and station ceases, no hope remains but from the prevalence of money. Power and wealth supply the place of each other.

The tenant, however, gained no power from the changes whereby the Laird lost his, and so has no corresponding motive for the substitution:

> He refuses to pay the demand, and is ejected; the ground is then let to a stranger, who perhaps brings a larger stock, but who, taking the land at its full price, treats with the laird upon equal terms, and considers him not as a Chief, but as a trafficker in land. Thus the estate perhaps is improved, but the clan is broken.

Johnson has been told about some irrationally high demands, but he doesn't put the burden of his analysis on individual errors. The notional new rent, in his account, is the 'full price' of the land – that is, all it will yield, but not more. So the quantitative increase turns out to contain a qualitative change in social relations; the hereditary subordination of 'ancient dependent' to chief gives way to the impersonal equality of buyer and seller; it is now the land, rather than the people, that is considered to be producing the rent.

Suppressed within this reading of events by its trenchant abstraction of manner is a question of moral values. In rejecting the 'multifarious and extensive obligation' of the old filial dependency in favour of the simple issue of the return on landed capital, the landlord, it's implied, is choosing money rather than humanity. Emigration then appears as an unanswerable comment on his priorities: take the money, and the humanity literally departs. Although Johnson is far from making a pastoral out of the 'muddy mixture of pride and ignorance'[27] which he supposes the clan ethos to have been, his verdict on the depopulation reproduces Goldsmith's dichotomy with scathing urbanity:

> to make a country plentiful by diminishing the people, is an expeditious mode of husbandry; but that abundance, which there is nobody to enjoy, contributes little to human happiness.[28]

At this point, evidently, the argument gives on to wider perspectives than just the Highlands. The particular local history – the literal patriarchs in the recent past, the literal exodus in the present – offers a vivid exemplary image of wealth accumulating while men decay. However, the image isn't an innocent one. In a contemporary poetic account of the same change, 'The Emigrant. An Eclogue', its implications are extended through a large access of sentiment. Standing on a heath-clad hill, looking down at the ship which will carry him from his native land, the grey-haired Caledonian recalls the living his family's 'niggard lands' once afforded:

> Scant as it was, no more our hearts desir'd,
> Nor more from us our gen'rous lord requir'd.
> But ah, sad change! those blessed days are o'er,
> And peace, content, and safety, charm no more;
> Another lord now rules these wide domains,
> The avaricious tyrant of the plains;
> Far, far from hence, *he* revels life away,
> In guilty pleasures *our* poor means must pay.[29]

The guiltiness of the pleasures taints by association the rent rises that pay for them: the choice of cash values instead of human ones is not so much condemned as exorcised by the reassurance that is the preference only of bad men. That the 'gen'rous lord' has not changed his policy, but has arbitrarily been replaced by a Lowlander, seals the political insulation. Conversely, the speaker's assertion of human values as opposed to cash is *unworldly*:

> I am contented here; I've never seen
> A vale more fertile, or a hill more green;
> Nor would I leave this sweet, tho' humble cot,
> To share the richest monarch's envied lot.

The old man's contentment directly reflects the narrowness of his experience, and it appears that his tranquil relationship with the old lord was based on a threadbare minimum of demands on both sides. Movement is a symmetrical disaster: it's because the landlord is 'far, far from hence' that the tenant is compelled to emigrate. In 'those blessed days', one gathers, everybody stayed still. Highlanders were deferential, disinterested and poor, dominated by unquestioned custom and hereditary overlords. Thus, although the poem perhaps had some effect in drawing attention to what was happening,[30] its polemic is negated by the paralytic nature of its social ideal. Typically, the opposition of 'wealth' and 'men' doesn't hold up as a real choice: the latter option turns antique and nostalgic.[31]

The politics of this wan protest can be seen by contrast with a far more energetic emigration poem, Burns's 'Address of Beelzebub'. Written in 1786, it was provoked by a report that the Highland Society of London had agreed to co-operate with government to frustrate the design of 500 tenants of Glengarry who were planning to go to America. The Prince of Hell congratulates the aristocrats of the Society on their determination to deny their vassals 'that fantastic thing – LIBERTY', exclaiming sympathetically:

> THEY! an' be d – mn'd! what right hae they
> To Meat, or Sleep, or light o' day,
> Far less to riches, pow'r or freedom
> But what your lordships PLEASE TO GIE THEM?[32]

The satire is directed at the same target – self-seeking lairds – as the critiques which take their cue from Goldsmith. But the angle of attack is completely different. So far from lamenting or resisting the decay of the kindly bond between chief and clansman, the poem accepts it, even drawing a sort of genial swagger from the openness of class hostility: these Highlanders are not meek and faithful, but wild and free (Beelzebub offers advice on how to curb their 'stubborn Highlan spirit'). Thus, ironically, the strength of the polemic comes from its *not* seeking humanist values in some traditional Highland way of life. It's the Society, attempting to reassert paternal authority in the face of a new social mobility, which is implicitly taking up the imperatives of the opposition between wealth and men. Burns brushes aside that conservative problematic, and judges actions, with scant regard to cultural identity or organicist regret, by the universal criterion of the rights of man. That hard radical light reveals the other face of clan nostalgia to be social repression.[33]

When the Highland emigration debate was renewed in the opening years of the nineteenth century, there was general agreement within it that the patriarchal relation was as dead as Burns assumed. For Selkirk, the extinction of a residual 'feudal' sentiment is an accomplished fact: new heritors, educated away from home,

> and feeling more remotely, the influence of antient connexions with their dependants, were not inclined to sacrifice for a shadow the substantial advantage of a productive property. The more necessitous, or the less generous, set the example; and one gradually followed another, till at length all scruple seems to be removed, and the proprietors in the Highlands have no more hesitation than in any other part of the kingdom, in turning their estates to the best advantage.[34]

But then what is striking about this passage is that while it portrays the transition from social to economic values as natural (the change from 'shadow' to 'substance'), it doesn't at the same time discard the moral content of the 1770s debate. It's still an abandonment of 'scruple' which is in question, shamefully led by the needy or the grasping; the landlords are still depicted as acting badly, except that now they no longer have the option of acting well.[35] The picture is thus darkened by an unusually local and referential sense of human virtues that are denied a home in reality at all – of a good fatally exiled. An ethical attitude to the social structuring of the Highlands has moved across into a romantic one.

The shift expectably produces a different kind of verse. In 'The Emigrant's Lament', published in 1803, the dramatic situation is the same as that of the 'Eclogue', but the tone has changed:

> Ye wilds and ye mountains, farewell!
> Ye springs, and ye murmuring streams!
> Though forc'd to forsake you by day,
> We'll visit you oft in our dreams....
>
> Though dimm'd by our tears as they flow,
> Their image becomes more obscure,
> We wish that the ship might sail slow,
> And the picture for ever endure.[36]

The things the emigrant is losing have dissolved in the prettiness of the metre and the insubstantiality of the representation. Home is a dream or a picture; the desire to stay there is only the consciously vain wish to linger indefinitely over a tear-dimmed image. It's not only that the 'wilds' are subjectively preferred: they connote subjective preference as such, as opposed to the real contingencies encountered 'by day'. From appearing disinterested and unworldly, the refusal of the economic logic of market rents has taken a further step back and become explicitly imaginary.

In other words, what has happened, during the last quarter of the eighteenth century, is that the representation of the indigenous Highland society has *internalised* the imperatives that lead to emigration. Hymns to the homeland include their own withdrawal; it is by deferring to the reality of clearance that the *status quo ante* can attain such ideal heights. The condition of this defeated apotheosis, in the relevant period, was the coming of the sheep. The stocking of Highland farms with Lintons and Cheviots was an uneven but sustained movement north and west, crossing into Argyll around the mid-century, Perthshire and Inverness in the 1760s and 70s, Ross in the 1790s and Sutherland in the 1800s.[37] As they established themselves, they changed the terms of estate management for everyone. Previously, it had been possible for individual landowners to sustain the common-sense view that the more tenants one had, the more rents one would get: this was presumably the assumption of the grandees assailed by Burns. Now, as Eric Richards puts it, the sheep 'provided a precise calculation of the opportunity cost of the human presence in the glens'.[38] Possessing this information, a landlord was still free to refuse the ranchers' offers, as many did. But he could not wish away the criteria by which his family and neighbours, his factors and creditors, and even he himself, would judge the refusal to be an act of folly.

So it was to the discourse of folly – of vain repining and unrealisable dreams – that the 'human presence' migrated. The human beings themselves – the dispossessed tenants – may well have had values by which the rationality of profits and costs continued to appear as criminal and delusive, though this code seems to have been weakened in the crisis by its traditionary assumptions about landlord paternalism.[39] But they and their anglophone sympathisers stood on opposite sides of a widening gap of culture, language, class and history, which was itself an outcome of 50 years of Improvement. This mutual alienation prevented any common oppositional formation: neither the moral regrets of the romanticisers nor the ill-directed resistance of the Gaelic poor[40] showed any capacity to challenge the Improver's frame of reference – that is, to amount to an effective *political* ideology. The tasteful monument which was erected on the site of that decisive absence was Poetry.

3 SACRED RETREATS

The election of Poetry itself as an ideology *against Improvement* was another possibility suggested by 'The Deserted Village'. There, by what Raymond Williams calls a 'negative identification',[41] 'sweet Poetry, thou loveliest maid, / Still first to fly where sensual joys invade',[42] shows her purity by sharing the exile of the rural virtues. In the Highlands, the most ambitious exponent of this ambiguous identification is Anne Grant. In her writings, and particularly in her long discursive poem *The Highlanders*, published in 1803, the poetic values which she attributes to the tradition of communal farming lead her into quite direct confrontations with the prevailing rationality of Improvement. A Highland minister's wife, and so the supervisor of a glebe farm, she nevertheless enjoys as an aesthetic success – 'Here all is open as the ambient sky, / Nor fence, nor wall, obstructs the wandering eye'[43] – the state of agriculture which her husband, writing for the *Statistical Account*, sees as agrarian failure: 'Farmers have at last found out the advantages of enclosures.'[44]

That enclosure was the necessary precondition of agricultural progress was not seriously questionable: Improvers had been urging it on the Highlands since about 1760.[45] But Anne Grant's mild dissent represents more than the touristic pleasures of the 'wandering eye'. The couplet leads into a sequence enlarging on the pleasures of the open rig:

> Each hamlet's flocks and herds, a mutual charge,
> That wander up the mountain's side at large;
> Alternate claim the rustic's daily care;
> And thus each various rural toil they share.[46]

The point this detail is making is that the inefficient method of herding it describes involves a sharing of work and responsibility: unlike a shepherd on a deserted ranch, the people are carrying on their social and their economic activities at the same time. The sequel details the interaction:

> The lesser *Children* guide the bleating lambs,
> When wean'd and forc'd to quit their tim'rous dams;

> The more advanc'd the sportive kidlings guide,
> Where rocks o'erhang the torrent's dashing pride.
> The little *Maiden*, whose unsteady hand
> Can scarce the distaff's yielding weight command ...
> Her flowing tresses decks with garlands gay,
> Then spins beside her playful calves the day.
> The *Youth*, whose cheek the manly down o'er spreads
> Wide o'er the hills the stronger cattle leads.[47]

Despite its somewhat tawdry poetic diction, this description is not simply fantasy. Its evocation of communal husbandry matches, ironically, the accounts of disapproving agricultural writers. William Marshall points out the disadvantages of the 'Youth's' ramblings with the cattle: 'the drift of the stock; the driving across intermediate grazings; the inconveniencies and dangers of having stock at a distance; the never-ceasing disputes with the occupiers of the surrounding lands'[48] – and it's easy to imagine, too, how the specialist sheep farmers formed the view that the old sheep economy was 'a sort of slovenly domestic petting'.[49]

By the more general criteria of political economy, Grant's hamlets are no less deplorable. The playful maiden who spins as she tends the calves is the type of 'various rural toil'; a few lines later her father 'forms the hamlet's fold,/Or else with patient labour turns the mould.' Much of the appeal of the scene lies in this impression of leisurely variety: it seems that not only the flocks and the poet's eye, but all the different members of the family, are 'wandering'. Just this rural dilettantism is one of the reasons for identifying the separation of occupations as the master key to the wealth of nations:

> The habit of sauntering and of indolent careless application, which is naturally, or rather necessarily acquired by every country workman who is obliged to change his work and his tools every half hour, and to apply his hand in twenty different ways almost every day of his life; renders him almost always slothful and lazy, and incapable of any vigorous application.[50]

This is Adam Smith, with a characteristic conflict of valuations: the country workman is 'lazy', although he is doing his work in the only way it can be done, because of the available comparison of more highly developed organisational forms. As in the case of the sheep, Grant's easygoing pastoral is burdened with a newly discovered opportunity cost which renders it uneconomic. As another Improving writer puts it, with marginal ambivalence, communal farming 'is one of the most ancient customs in our country. It is a relic of the pastoral age, or feudal system. But it is ruinous to the interest of the landlord, the tenant, and the public, in the present enlightened state of agriculture.'[51]

In implicit opposition to this paradoxical enlightenment which renders ruinous what was viable before its advent, Grant's model of rural toil is informed by values which are ultimately, and characteristically, educational. The hamlet's children all have tasks suited to their age and sex, calculated to make them independent, brave, responsible and physically fit. Considered as a productive unit, the farm is clearly typical of the eighteenth-century Highlands in being overstocked, overmanned and undercapitalised; however, Grant is rather considering it as a school of useful virtue. In one of her essays, published in 1811 and dealing polemically with many of the same issues as the poem, she takes up directly, albeit in a slightly romanticised historical context, the point about changing one's work every half-hour:

> Among these hunters, warriors and graziers, who were continually varying their occupation, as well as occasionally changing their abode, a constant exercise of sagacity was required, both in those that governed and those who obeyed, from the mutability of outward circumstances, and the permanence of individual characters and motives.[52]

The variety is bad for productivity – that is not contested. But it is good for the people who work in this way, because of the mental exertion their mode of life calls forth. Smith wouldn't disagree: he makes a comparable point in a later passage.[53] But what for him is a concession is for Grant the nub of the whole question. What is ultimately a religious imperative in her text consistently subordinates material interests to those of 'immortal mind'.[54]

Later in the poem's description of the joint-farm, she explains that the people build their own houses:

> For here scarce known the sordid arts of trade,
> They seek no gross mechanic's frigid aid:
> Tho' mean the dwelling thus uncouthly rear'd,
> 'Tis still by kindly gratitude endear'd.[55]

Grant is still conducting her unconscious dialogue with Smith: although there's no evidence that she read him, it's as if his ideas were so influential in the period as to stand for economic rationality as such. Her observation here confirms his mention of the Scottish Highlands as an example of an area too sparsely populated to admit of much specialisation or exchange.[56] But she gives the same information a sharply different sense. Smith had observed:

> It is not from the benevolence of the butcher, the brewer, or the baker, that we expect our dinner, but from their regard to their own interest. We address ourselves, not to their humanity but to their self-love, and never talk to them of our own necessities but of their advantages. Nobody but a beggar chuses to depend chiefly upon the benevolence of his fellow-citizens.[57]

This is precisely the 'gross mechanic's frigid aid'. Grant is resorting from its internally irresistible logic to the Highlands as a place where everyone *has* made the beggar's choice, and 'humanity' does, routinely, figure as a practical motive in the satisfaction of needs.

It's at about this point that we confront the limitations of the idyll. Grant accepts, in a neat hostile summary of *The Wealth of Nations*, that in the commercialised south, 'grovelling interest draws each sordid plan, / And all things feel improvement's aid but man.'[58] But the Highlands are, or at least were, different. Here, in a straight inversion, *nothing* feels improvement's aid but man: the house is 'mean' and 'uncouthly rear'd', but no one minds this because of the immaterial qualities of fellow-feeling invested in it. The Highlanders, who were being evicted from these dwellings by the insistent pressure of others' material interests, are reactively conceived of as having no material interests of their own at all. Quixotically disdaining the arts of trade, they devote themselves to a frugal life of the mind. Even the production of food and clothes appears to be secondary to the aesthetic and educational values which Grant traced in the rhythms of communal farming. In other words, Poetry, Goldsmith's 'loveliest maid', with her elevated sentiment and innocence of sensuality, is being projected on to the whole social formation. The Highlanders are not simply being written about by a poet – they *are poetical*.

This emerges very clearly in the poem's explicit summary of the communal ideal:

Thus while they sow and reap the *mutual* field,
And each to each by turns is wont to yield;
With one consent they trace the general plan,
And blended interests form the social man:
Hence gradual ties of kind endearment flow,
Hence bland address and courteous actions grow;
And hence th'unstudied manners of the swain
The graces of a gentler mind explain.[59]

The prize of this mild climax, through 'mutual', 'social', 'kind' and 'courteous', is the wholly conventional poeticism 'swain'. Throughout eighteenth-century rural poetry, the word has been used to denote a real peasant or agricultural labourer on the one hand, and on the other, the genteel lay figure of neo-classical pastoral. Here the two meanings are conflated, and real-life rustic gentility is offered as a local fact, attributable to a definite type of land tenure. The poetic and the literal merge.

One key to this equivalence is the special connotation of the word 'social'. Grant typically uses it in constructions like 'social joys', 'social tribes', or, as here, 'the social man', which imply the distinctively subjective sense which the word has, for example, in Thomson:

The social Tear would rise, the social Sigh;
And into clear Perfection, gradual Bliss,
Refining still, the social Passions work.[60]

Society here appears as a sort of psychological principle – not a contingent organisation, but the love of humankind in general. An expression like 'social tribes' implies that universal humanism, but it is also meant to indicate a sociological fact about the Highlands (that the people grouped themselves in clans). Elsewhere in the poem, a line about 'the social hamlet's mutual plough'[61] has the same dual reference: the pleonastic epithets are an emotive assertion of the universal principle of sociality, but at the same time, as a footnote points out, the line is a piece of information (joint-farms often shared the ownership of ploughs among several families). The word thus both invokes an ideal way of life and points literally at a *particular* 'society'. The metonymic doubling makes the individual community into a poetic image of community as such.

Elsewhere, it's understood, in the artificial culture of the south, 'social' sentiment is only a mediated and distorted principle which remotely underlies actual society. But here in the Highlands, the empirical society and the society of sentiment are one.

This immediately poetic way of life, despite the wealth of detailed social observation which substantiates it, is essentially a conservative Utopia, deprived of historical substance by the contradictions of its form. On the one hand, it mounts a complex and combative opposition to a reductively utilitarian Improvement: by talking about work in fully ethical and aesthetic terms, Grant powerfully asserts its value as human self-production against the alienating and instrumental categories of political economy. But on the other hand, these propositions are contained within picturesque glens whose mythic topography, secluded from lowland corruption by mountains that point to the sky, is a naturalised allegory of unworldliness. Their inhabitants are credited with a subjective refusal of the 'sordid' values of Improvement, but the insecurity of this attribution is felt in the repeated insistence on their geographical seclusion. The massively material 'barriers of holy freedom' [62] which keep materialism at bay are an oxymoronic acknowledgment of the repressed possibility that the poetical Highlanders would be self-interested Smithian citizens if they were free to choose. Their concrete necessity, by an overdetermination which is finally colonial in structure, is made the visible form of the poet's imaginative freedom: they are compelled to *be* the ideal she *is pleased* to entertain. The critique of Improvement is then constantly liable to slide into a fear of modernity in general: 'It grieves me to think the iron age of calculation approaches fast towards the sacred retreats of nature and of sentiment'.[63] At that point of easy nostalgia, the construction of the social tribes is at once reactionary and depoliticised; and the counter-ideology of Poetry subsides into the self-ironic mode of folly.

Saddled with this anti-materialist role, Highland culture is a privileged term within national and imperial discourse, not despite its inability to engage with the practical issues of Improvement but because of it. Its very vulnerability connotes a high-minded indifference to the base considerations which govern the rest of us. In this spirit, a collection of Highland music of the 1780s notes that while pipers were traditionally required to serve a long apprenticeship, mechanical trades were free: typically, the Highlanders 'were satisfied with bungling artificers, but required a degree of excellence in their musicians'.[64] Comparably, Grant herself, praising the richness of Highland traditional lore, admits – or claims – that:

> In respect to general knowledge, useful arts, and profound or elegant science, this volume of tradition was very scanty, or entirely silent. Not so with regard to the heroic, the tender, the ludicrous, the moral, and the decorous.[65]

This is to absorb into the myth of the traditional Highlands the utilitarian verdict on their uselessness. The territory of positive knowledge is ceded to the *Statistical Account*, and the natives must be content with an expertise of sentiment. In a single move, Highlanders are condemned to be poetical, and poetry to be impractical.

4 THE LANGUAGE OF NATURE

One source of the immaterial society of sentiment is the exercise, a characteristic one in the philosophic historiography of the Scottish Enlightenment, of comparing 'rude and cultivated ages'. We have already seen two examples of the genre, in Adam Ferguson's *Essay on the History of Civil Society* and Hugh Blair's *Critical Dissertation* on Ossian. For both these writers, in different ways, primitive ages are interesting because of the possibility that, being closer to the *origin* of society, they will reveal something about its general principles. This assumption is explicitly argued by James Dunbar in his essay 'On the Primeval Form of Society', which appeared in 1780.[66] For him, civilisation is a process of escalating artificiality in which human nature has become so altered and disguised that 'its independent character has become dark and problematical'. The true nature of man is directly observable, not in the absence of society – for Dunbar contends that the qualities we regard as human are social ones – but precisely in the moment of its origin. Of this imaginary crux, Dunbar's view is optimistic: he regards it as an immediate expression of fellow-feeling, so that, against Hobbes for example, society is 'not the sickly daughter of calamity, nor even the production of an aspiring understanding, but the free and legitimate offspring of the human heart'.[67]

Dunbar's original society is thus clearly akin to Grant's Highland hamlet: in both, people associate, not in order to further their interests, but for the immediate human pleasure of it; in both, the immaterial principle of sociality is directly realised in the visible forms of society. Among these forms is language. His primeval state is characterised by pure feelings of sociability which we can't now recover — 'nor, if the feelings remained, could artificial language, in this respect, supply the language of nature'.[68] The language of nature, as he explains in the next essay, is that first universal expression which was neither arbitrary nor chosen, but knit by inevitable harmonies to sentiment — a uniquely forceful and natural language of the heart. In other words, the proposition here is an impossible language of pure presence, that originial speech which is innocent of writing.

Dunbar doesn't identify the language of nature with any actually existing tongue. Others were less cautious. Lord Monboddo apparently nominated Gaelic as the Adamic language,[69] and although this was an uncommon position,[70] the pro-Ossianists came close to it. For one, Gaelic is naturally onomatopoeic: 'soft and tender objects are expressed by words which bear some analogy to them in sound'.[71] And Macpherson himself goes further in explaining how it was possible for the extended poems he claimed to have unearthed to be transmitted orally:

> Each verse was so connected with those that preceded or followed it, that if one line had been remembered in a stanza, it was almost impossible to forget the rest. The cadences followed in so natural a gradation, and the words were so adapted to the common turn of the voice, after it has been raised to a certain key, that it was thought almost impossible, from a similarity of sound, to substitute one word for another. This excellence is peculiar to the Celtic language, and is perhaps to be met with in no other.[72]

This seems to mean that Gaelic poetry was so suited to the nature of the language, and the language in turn so adapted to the nature of vocalisation, that it was physically easier to recite a poem correctly than to get it wrong. As the last sentence assures us, with its fraudulently judicious air, other languages may articulate and abstract, but Gaelic is organic. The Ossianic canon dramatised this idea: by laying claim to the status of translations, the English poems posed as maimed linguistic exiles, gesturing pathetically in the direction of the home language where they were once whole.

In Grant's own writing, this myth of origin is typically transposed from a world-historical to a personal mode; it becomes a myth of education. In a letter of 1785 she declares:

> I am determined my children shall all drink 'from the pure wells of Celtic undefiled.' They shall taste the animated and energetic conversation of the natives; and an early acquaintance with the poetry of nature shall guard them against false taste and affectation. I never desire to hear an English word out of their mouths till they are four or five years old. How I should delight in grafting elegant sentiments and just notions on simple manners and primitive ideas![73]

Here the Scottish primitivism of origins shifts easily into a Rousseauistic primitivism of childhood: the natural (self-present) child develops by a micro-historical fatality which is both loss and gain into the civilised (alienated) adult. Gaelic is, so to speak, the native tongue of the Imaginary; English bears the paternal prohibition which initiates the order of the Symbolic.

Many of Grant's ideas about the Highlands are exhibited in extended and somewhat vulgarised form by a number of women novelists, mostly Scots, who were writing between the 1790s and the 1820s; the best known now are Susan Ferrier and Mary Brunton.[74] The idyllic bilingual curriculum is a good example. In Elizabeth Helme's *Duncan and Peggy* it happens by accident: after ten years in the care of an old peasant woman who imparts traditional ballads and 'unassuming virtue', Peggy is noticed and adopted by an anglicised landowner under whose supervision she receives a secondary education based on books and ideas.[75] Similarly, though by design, the hero of Christian Isobel Johnstone's *Clan-Albin* learns Gaelic as his first language and imbibes folklore from the oldest woman in the glen, before progressing to a classically based curriculum with a presbyterian clergyman who, though his pedantry and sectarianism are mildly satirised by the standard of the easygoing oral culture around him, can apparently be trusted with the boy's mental development.[76]

Both of these pedagogic idylls carry out Grant's grafting metaphor. Gaelic is the wild stock, the source of simplicity and emotional vigour, English the gentler scion which mends it with elegance and judgement. Perhaps significantly, too, in both the fictional cases, the handover from one language to the other is also a transfer of pedagogic responsibility from a woman to a man. English, to pursue the Lacanian analogy, is the language of the father.

From a sociolinguistic point of view, the context of this asymmetry is the attack on Gaelic as a living tongue. Its replacement by English was part and parcel of the missionary drive in the eighteenth-century Highlands and Islands: in 1772 a report to the General Assembly of the Kirk could say that 'To spread the English language over the Highlands, has always been a laudable endeavour of the church, as it is at once the most effectual means for the religious instruction of the inhabitants, and the improvement of the country.'[77] It's true that as the century advanced, practical needs and pro-Celtic sympathies combined to moderate the anti-Gaelic thrust of religious policy.[78] But then increasingly, the socioeconomic logic of internal colonialism took up where conscious ideological intention left off. The anglophone education of the ruling class, the influence of the army, the construction of administrative and communication networks, the involvement of lowland entrepreneurs in new ventures, the coming of tourists and returned emigrants – everything conspired to make English the language of social competence and upward mobility. Gaelic was in the classic predicament of a peripheral language under multiple pressures from the core.

Moreover, many of these pressures, such as formal education or employment opportunities, bore much the more powerfully on men. Displaced from its public and economic functions, Gaelic tended to fall back on the hearthside, to become the speech of the very old, the very young, and those who looked after them; this sphere, meanwhile, was being redefined by the same anglicising hegemony as the proper place for women.[79] Grant's separation of responsibilities between the two languages corresponds to a literal division of labour along the line of gender. Gaelic comes to occupy a 'feminine' space, each category working to seal the desocialisation of the other.

The Gaelic idyll does not resist this process but complements it. The proposition that English is the language of Improvement, and Gaelic the reverse, is precisely endorsed by its model of language development. Just as Grant's poetic version of runrig farming internalises the Improver's contempt for it in the form of unworldliness, so the originary status of Gaelic accepts as an immanent characteristic of the language the historical trap in which external circumstances have confined it. The resulting idealisation is specifically disabling. For the corollary of Gaelic's pre-articulate truth of sentiment is that it is *not* the language of conscious thought. It contains no ideas, only feelings; it can represent the speaker, but not itself; it is only under the metalinguistic supervision of English that it discharges its animating function.

If we look again at the group of gaelicising women's novels, we can see the same myth of upbringing worked out in narrative terms. Whether in the invariant foundling plots of historical romance,[80] or the moralistic domestic novels in contemporary settings, the region figures routinely as the appropriate environment for the production of healthy, high-principled juvenile leads. In Elizabeth Helme's *Albert*, for example, 'the wilds of Strathnavern' confer virtue on their offspring, the hero and his sister, so schematically that the man who wants to marry the latter is made to rusticate there for three years while his character and credit recover from a profligacy which is, in turn, the result of a misconceived upbringing in London.[81] Comparably, native heroines in novels by Helme, Brunton and Ferrier, more or less beleaguered in the egotistical and deceitful society of Town, all owe their successful negotiation of its moral dangers to their keeping faith with their Highland childhoods. 'As I hope soon to return to the Highlands,' Helme's Peggy retorts when offered a diamond necklace by a libidinous peer, 'so elegant an ornament would be useless, for a wreath of roses there would be more estimated.'[82]

As that sentiment fairly suggests, the region's educative value is expressible by negatives: children grow up there unaffected, unavaricious, unsuspicious and serious-minded because of the absence, respectively, of etiquette, wealth, malice and trivial amusements – the absence in short of The World, the tyranny of whose ill-founded opinions is an explicit and intense preoccupation of Susan Ferrier's. What there is, where The World is not, is nature, which in this context has a range of linked associations, including the taste for mountain scenery, but also denoting, in heroines especially, a simplicity of life that embraces forthright manners, unsophisticated clothes and hairstyles, sensible bedtimes and practical ability around the house. (Town-bred ladies, by the contrast which is never far away, are coquettish, take hours to dress, rise and retire late, and would expire without constant attention from their servants.) All these definitions, it's clear, are constitutively relational: it's as opposed to the novels' metropolitan settings that the environment exhibits its qualities. In Ferrier's *Marriage*, for example, a Highland home which was represented as having very definite geographical and social drawbacks so long as the heroine was in it starts turning into a paradise as soon as she is on the coach for Edinburgh.[83] Almost never the setting for an entire story, the Highlands repeatedly appear as the nursery annexe of British society.

Accordingly, Highland life itself, in so far as it's positively represented in the fiction, is comprehensively domesticated. At its simplest, this means that Highland remoteness serves to motivate the seclusion of the perfect family: this is the pattern, for example, of the Douglas household in *Marriage*, and of the estate of Clathen in Mary Johnston's *The Lairds of Glenfern*.[84] It appears at its most extreme in Elizabeth Helme's medieval romance *St. Clair of the Isles; or, the Outlaws of Barra*. The eponymous outlaws are a wholly innocent and law-abiding family whose exile, in plot terms the result of some mistake, is really nothing but the arbitrary condition of its innocence (one member, venturing to the mainland for the first time, found 'the country was mountainous, dreary and unpeopled; but, unaccustomed to villainy, he knew no fear'). The romance of the establishment is based on a genteel home life – 'In fine weather, our morning entertainment on the water; our afternoon walks; and our evening's music, when thy voice mixed with mine' – and a demurely expressed sexual contentment:

> The proud dames of the fertile south, stretched on silken beds by their listless lords, would envy the wife of Monteith, amidst the barren rocks of Barra, defended by the arms of a hero.[85]

The anti-aristocratic touch completes the implications of the seclusion, the home-made entertainment, the married love: Barra is the apotheosis of bourgeois private life; the ultimate detached villa.

By an alternative which is ideologically both less transparent and more ambitious, the construction of domesticity can draw on the understanding that the whole organisation of the traditional Highlands was based on kinship. In this case, rather than belonging to a nuclear family in a landscape where there is nobody else, the protagonists are placed in a miraculous community where they are related to everybody.

In the clearest examples of this genre – for example Glen Albin in C.I. Johnstone's *Clan-Albin* and Glen Eredine in Mary Brunton's *Discipline* — the most conspicuous sign of this universal kinship is, perhaps surprisingly, good manners. In The World, politeness is always suspect: polite people are falsifying their feelings, either for a reason (in which case they are *designing*) or else for no reason (in which case it's *affectation*). But an equally characteristic hostile type, in many of these novels, is the rich tradesman whose insensitivity to social tone is registered, with pain, as *vulgarity*.[86] The fiction's system of values seems to have its characters in a double bind: if they aren't condemned for being polite, they're pilloried for being impolite. The impasse is more serious than it might seem, since these novelists, like their contemporary Jane Austen, often use the minutiae of propriety as indicators of larger social values. Manners matter, which means that good characters — the ones who articulate authorial values — cannot themselves be allowed to speak either politely or rudely. If, then, there is no proper and acceptable code of speech and behaviour in which positive values can be enunciated, what that has to be saying is that goodness can't find expression at all in the depicted society. Goodness and social realism are driven apart, so that the one becomes frustrated and misanthropic, and the other languid and incurious.

The Highland glen is able to redeem politeness and so rescue the unity of the narrative through a number of related features. The most important is that whereas in the metropolis good manners (tact, delicacy, refinement, appropriately formal address) are associated with the upper class and therefore tainted by privilege, here gentility is common to all. Innkeepers and footmen are gentlemen; intricate considerations of protocol govern visits to huts as well as to drawing-rooms; illiterate smallholders incur quixotic amounts of inconvenience for the sake of etiquette.[87] The effect of this general social diffusion, the documentary evidence for which is mostly taken from Anne Grant,[88] is that courtesy is naturalised. 'Humble', or 'uneducated', these people can't be thought to behave as they do out of mechanical conformity to an external set of rules. Their code is taken to be woven into the whole texture of their lives: it is 'instinctive politeness'[89] — that is, the precise behavioural equivalent of the language of nature. The effect of *that* is to naturalise, in turn, the social hierarchy within which the politeness operates. In adopting upper-class manners, the tenantry assert a kind of egalitarianism which makes snobbery and class conflict impossible, while at the same time the *content* of the etiquette turns on the minutest gradations of rank, and so places the superiority of the landowner at the top of a tirelessly maintained pyramid of deference. Class distinctions don't need to be enforced because they are spontaneously accorded; politeness is not the badge of an élite but the immanent principle of a total structure of subordination.

Whatever the accuracy of this as a description of Highland society at any period, its attraction as a conservative myth for British society in a revolutionary age is understandable. For the enabling term in the whole lush naturalisation is the family: it is because the poor are cousins to the rich that they share their social *mores*, and it is for the same reason that they accept their superiority. It's the family which redeems the code of manners from the anxiety of artificiality, because it is a rigorously hierarchical and rule-governed social institution which is nevertheless, in the same breath, supposed to be the home of natural feeling: projected on to the picturesque screen of a Highland glen, this powerful but circumscribed ideological resolution is enlarged until it appears to embrace a complete way of life. When the heroine of *Discipline* looks back from her Highland retreat at the tribulations of her metropolitan career, she sees that the latter disciplined her will but did not engage her heart: 'My affections and my imagination were yet to receive their culture in the native land of strong attachment.'[90] 'Attachment' — the concept reconciles the conflict of duty and impulse by representing family ties as both. The Highlands are the homeland of this principle; Ellen has been received into a sort of moral *unité d'habitation* where the whole world is domestic.

The problem with this miraculous code, whether it's realised as the language of nature, or as instinctive good breeding, or as the organic society of the family, is that it has the structurally determined character of an *object language*. Highland signs, being by definition immediate and present, are all of the order of naivety. The last thing they could do is represent themselves; it is their blessing that they are not self-aware. There must be a metalanguage to expound their value. But then, since this value is always produced within an opposition between the Highlands and metropolitan British society, the indispensable *raisonneur* can't be a non-Gaelic figure either. What's needed is a discursive authority which is rooted in the Highlands but not reducible to them, a speech which is somehow idiomatic and national at the same time.

All the novels have this difficulty, and nearly all of them come up with the same solution: the army. Over and over again, the wise supervisor of the Highland idyll is a half-pay officer, whose native stock has been improved yet not falsified by service in a Highland regiment.[91] The new generation travel from enthusiastic youth to mature understanding by the same route: the man the heroine eventually marries is first saved from natural unconsciousness, but also from metropolitan corruption, by character-seasoning war.[92] In the lives of the domestic kingdoms of the glens, the army has the function of delivering a worthy sovereign.

Its fitness for this role is conditioned by the whole pattern of Highland militarisation which was the subject of Chapter 3. On the one hand, the regiments can work as a kind of extension of the Highlands themselves, securing continuity with the region's warrior past through the vestigial clan basis of the levies and the adventurousness, traditionalism and economic innocence of military life. On the other hand, the service entails the study of engineering, cartography, and so on; social contact with men from all regions and classes in Britain; and, above all, iron conformity to a discipline whose explicit reference is to the king – in short, it is a brief but compendious initiation in the life and learning of the Empire.

It is also, importantly, a male institution – not only in the sense that women don't enlist, but also in the sense that its professional demands (neatness, efficiency, cool-headedness, command) are constituents of a mode of power which is both Improving and masculinist. The wholly natural society of the tribes is underwritten by the wholly artificial order which is represented by military discipline. This touch completes the pattern of repressive idealisation which organises the domestic image of the Highlands. The social tribes cultivate a repertoire of feminine virtues – naturalness, sentiment, refinement, the innocence of childhood – under the protection of a male British authority which controls the applications of their language and polices the boundaries of their secluded glens.

Thus what might be called a 'women's Highlands' is constructed – the myth whose writers are Joanna Baillie, Jane Porter, the novelists I've been reviewing here, and, of course, Anne Grant herself. They were all writing, it's true, in the lengthening shadow of Scott, but as a Highland romancer he is almost alone among the women. And even in his work, a related bias is noticeable: in the

Waverley novels, for example, the purest articulation of Highland identity regularly comes from a woman, so that Flora MacIvor reproves the Lowland compromises of her brother, Helen Macgregor those of her husband, and Elspat, the Highland Widow, those of her son.[93] The basis of this feminising move is an identification. The Highlands provide documentary authentication and splendid décor for making a local world in the image of the bourgeois family, with its depoliticised domesticity, its gentility, its consciously cultivated artlessness, and its ultimate reference to patriarchal authority. The Highlanders in their glen, and the matron in her suburban villa, are drawn together by a system which charges both with cherishing, as it were in reserve, the deepest humanity of a social order which deforms and marginalises them.[94]

5 CALEDONIA

Clan-Alpine, the Highlanders of Scott's *The Lady of the Lake* who appeared in Chapter 3 as a romanticised regiment, are also another organic community. Their emblem, in contrast with the deciduous vegetation picturesquely associated with the characters who are merely visiting the Highlands, is the pine:

> Ours is no sapling, chance-sown by the fountain,
>   Blooming at Beltane, in winter to fade;
> When the whirlwind has stripp'd every leaf on the mountain,
>   The more shall Clan-Alpine exult in her shade.
>   Moor'd in the rifted rock,
>   Proof to the tempest's shock,
> Firmer he roots him the ruder it blow...[95]

As the combativeness of that metre and imagery suggests, the clan's native rootedness defines itself, like the naturalness of the domesticated 'social tribes', against the artificiality of what is here called 'the Saxon'. Clan-Alpine's chief, Roderick Dhu, disdains the rule-bound life of the Lowlands, defends his lawlessness in the terms of 'the birthright of the Gael', and even warns that if the centralising power of the Crown is not resisted, the Highlands will become, as the Borders already have, 'one sheep-walk, waste and wide'.[96]

This highly poetical people is both similar to the other versions I've examined in this chapter and distinct from them. What's recognisable is the formula by which they assert an originary integrity against Improvement, but do so with a quixotic unworldliness which silently ratifies the superior rationality of what they resist: their nobility is colourful because it is bathed in the sunset light of their impending historical extinction.[97] The distinction of Scott's construction, then, is that instead of resolving the opposing forces into a hopeful complementarity, as the domestic projection seeks to do, he produces them as the dramatic conflict of an adventure story. The anglicising order is present in the poem as the legal and military power of the monarch who is, as it transpires, its main character; and the indigenous community, fully aware of the intention to suppress it, is militantly geared up to resist. The Trossachs are central to the action, not only because of their value as scenery, but also because they're a gateway between Highland and Lowland. The dichotomy of rude and cultivated ages is inserted in a historical and geographical narrative.

At the centre of this narrative, as the title suggests, is the predicament of the lady herself, Ellen Douglas, who is wooed by both Roderick and the disguised King. Her maidenly situation at the meeting-point of the poem's antithetic worlds — she is detached from the Highlands by her birth and from the Lowlands by her exile on Loch Katrine — establishes her as historically innocent, a pre-cultural criterion for the claims of the rival valuesystems. As far as Roderick is concerned, this criterion turns out to be that of the eighteenth-century British establishment: just like Pennant or Johnson, Ellen finds the chief brave but wild, generous but cruel, true in friendship but a vindictive enemy, and so on.[98] Moreover, when she feels a momentary impulse to accept her Highland suitor for her father's sake, it is described, in an extended simile, as the subconscious urge to throw oneself off an exposed height (Canto II, stanza xxxi). This appropriately Alpine image seals the text's commitment, underlying its flamboyant romantic gestures, to the values of Improvement. The clan is powerful, natural, even fascinating, but its appeal is to the anarchic and self-destructive elements of personality and society.

As Scott was completing *The Lady of the Lake*, he was also involved in arranging the Edinburgh première of a Highland melodrama, Joanna Baillie's *The Family Legend*. The play, which was received as the first notable native tragedy since *Douglas*,[99] strikingly duplicates the poem's historical construction of the heroine's plight. Helen, daughter to the Duke of Argyll, is really in love with a thoroughly anglicised figure called Sir Hubert de Grey, but has selflessly married the chief of the Macleans in an attempt to patch up a Campbell–Maclean feud. Fundamentalist Macleans sabotage this arrangement by pressurising their weak-willed chief into marooning her on a rock, from which she is rescued in the nick of time by her lover and her brother, who take her back to Inveraray. A final confrontation between the two clans leads to a skirmish in which Maclean dies repentant, leaving Helen free to marry Sir Hubert and her father to dictate terms to the discredited and leaderless opposition.

Baillie uses the well-known pro-Government alignment of Clan Campbell to construct the Argyll–Mull polarity, not as an antagonism between two indistinguishable tribes, but as a conflict between civilisation and wildness, reason and enthusiasm, which is essentially the same as that between the King and Roderick in *The Lady of the Lake*. So that Helen's story is the same as Ellen's: she is carried into a temporary alliance with the dark and lawless Highlands; the error leads to oneiric extremes of danger (the sea-girt rock encodes the same Gothic terror as the vertigo) before she is saved by enlightened metropolitanising forces and united with the fair and modest character she really loves. The Highland side of the conflict is much less seductive in Baillie than it is in Scott, because of the latter's skill as a *romancer*, but it doesn't finally matter how seductive it is, because it's the centralising forces which have it in their gift, all along, to make the heroine heart-whole. The poetical Highlands are placed, within the melodramatic formula, in the role of the villain.

Helen's true love is part of the centralist establishment: the denouement simply excludes the Highland end of the structure altogether. Scott is subtler. Ellen doesn't accept her royal suitor, but instead marries her lover Malcolm Graeme, who is a Highlander. This complication means that the satisfactory resolution of the romance depends on Graeme's being kept separate from the dark, anarchic signification which his ethnic origin points out for him. His extreme youth, his flaxen hair, and his modesty all contribute to this precaution, but its real guarantee is the moment at the end when the King playfully throws over him a golden chain which denotes both a royal blessing on the match and the state's apprehension of a Highland outlaw. The political meaning of the marriage itself is the bridegroom's incorporation in a national synthesis. Despite this ingenuity, Graeme's character remains seriously underformed, as Scott observed: 'my lover spite of my best exertions is like to turn out what the players call a *walking gentleman*. It is incredible the pains it has cost me to give him a little dignity'.[100] The reason for the difficulty is that the figure is necessarily a compromise. If Scott strengthens his 'Highland' character — that is, moves him in the direction of gloom, lawlessness, rugged independence, clan fealty — he will subvert the closing harmony for which he is destined. If, on the other hand, Scott makes that easy by enhancing Graeme's good nature, tolerance, gentlemanly style — in short, by *improving* him — then he'll detach him from the Highlands altogether. He is stuck with him — and the impasse is a mark of the *national* imperative which is constraining Scott's tale-telling. Highland and Lowland, wild tenderness and reason of state, *must* be reconciled in the end, and the hybrid lover is the unsatisfactory but indispensable means to it.

The interesting question then is: why is it necessary that the sentimental-cum-political resolution of the story should embrace the Highlands? The answer is directly suggested by a third Scottish romance which appeared in the same year as *The Lady of the Lake* and *The Family Legend* — Jane Porter's *The Scottish Chiefs*.

This, certainly the most successful Scottish historical novel to appear before *Waverley*,[101] is a hagiographical fictionalisation of the life of Wallace. Its patriotic romanticism seems to have earned it a nationalist readership in Europe; in one of its editions it claims to have been banned by Napoleon.[102] And its use of Highland imagery explicitly serves this political purpose. The first gathering of Wallace's patriot band takes place in *The Lady of the Lake*'s territory, among the crags and torrents of Glenfinlas:

> The awful entrance to this sublime valley, struck the whole party with a feeling that made them pause. It seemed as if to these sacred solitudes, hidden in the very bosom of Scotland, no hostile foot dared intrude. Murray looked at Ker: 'We go, my friend, to arouse the genius of these wilds. Here are the native fastnesses of Scotland, and from this pass the spirit will issue that is to bid her groaning sons and daughters be free!'[103]

Here, programmatically, the Highlands are the essence of Scotland

– her bosom, genius, native fastness, spirit. This simple idea, which recurs several times at crises of Porter's story, cuts ironically across the unifying mission of the King in *The Lady of the Lake*: the wilds which he is seeking to subdue to a national imperative are now declared to be that same imperative's sacred source.

The rhetoric of *The Scottish Chiefs* is drawing on an odd but long-established convention whereby Highland insignia, scenic, cultural, and especially sartorial, have the capacity to represent the Scottish nation as a whole. The zenith of this identification was the celebrated pageant which Scott himself organised for George IV's visit to Scotland in 1822, when real and imaginary Highland clansmen paraded through the streets of Edinburgh in a sort of collective 'hallucination'[104] which temporarily effaced the actual lives and traditions of the overwhelming majority of Scots, to say nothing of the real contemporary breakup of Highland society itself. Scott's biographer Lockhart attributes this delusion to the mythmaking genius of his hero, and the two-edged compliment is often reproduced in modern accounts of 'tartanry'.[105] But the 1822 extravaganza was new only in its scale and the thoroughness of its vulgarity. It had been anticipated exactly a century before, in Allan Ramsay's 'Tartana', a poem written to promote native textiles and reduce imports. Ramsay elaborates a consciously fanciful Scottish past 'When ev'ry Youth and ev'ry lovely Maid/Deem'd it a *Deshabille* to want their Plaid',[106] and, with just the 1822 mixture of patriotism and silliness, rigs out the warriors and shepherds of 'Caledonian' rhetoric in tartan. At around the same period, tartan also appears as a patriotic emblem in a ballad in praise of the second Duke of Argyll, who is shown putting on plaid and bonnet by way of proving that his involvement in London politics has not sapped his loyalty to bannocks of barley meal and Paisley Fair.[107] It was presumably the same unhistorical image of a pan-tartan medieval Scotland which in 1773 initiated the stage tradition of dressing Macbeth in a plaid.[108]

I've already noted in another context the boost that was given to the prestige of Highland dress by the reputation of the regiments who wore it; and during the hyperpatriotic phase of the Napoleonic war many of the volunteer corps, paramilitary clubs and short-lived Fencible regiments which sprang up all over Scotland adopted kilts as their costume.[109] This had a national as well as a picturesque content. In 1804, when the Highland Society of London voted to wear tartan at its meetings in order to recall 'the high character of our ancestors', its decision was certainly a response to the resumption of war and its demands on British morale. But Sir John Sinclair, who wrote the resolution, also alluded to the need to assert *Scottish* identity before 'Scotland becomes completely confounded in England'.[110] As Lowland Scotland becomes more and more like England, it turns to the Highlands for symbols to maximise its difference.

The scholarly basis of this tenacious fancy was the view that the very difference between Lowland and Highland reflected the latter's character as a sort of Scottish lost world — a place which had preserved, down to the recent past, the social system, the language and the manners which had prevailed throughout the country in remoter times.[111] The common poetic name, 'Caledonia', helped to keep the resulting ambiguities in play: it could mean sometimes the whole of Scotland, sometimes just the Highlands, and sometimes a blur which gave either definition access to the privileges of the other. The claim, endlessly repeated in the praise of Scottish arms, that from the borders of Caledonia the Romans were repulsed, makes happy use of this flexibility: one could be thinking of Hadrian's Wall, or of the Antonine Wall, or of Agricola's *ne plus ultra* on the edge of the Grampians, so that it's uncertain whether the Lowlands are being accorded the cachet of invincibility or not. Macpherson was doubly influential in cementing these associations: as an antiquarian he gave succour to the 'pro-Celts' who maintained, against both 'pro-Scythians' and Irish scholars, that the Scottish Gael were the 'original' Caledonians;[112] and as a popular poet, he set all his classic ground in the Highlands while at the same time producing a national mythology (an early staging of the poems in Edinburgh huffed that

> the author of this piece
> Had fix'd on Caledonia, not on Greece;
> That he had scorn'd tow'rds *foreign* climes to roam,
> When he'ad such fair examples *here at home*.)[113]

Such vague iconographic and ancestral associations certainly played around the romances of 1810. Porter's homage to Wallace was acted out in the same year when the Wallace monument was dedicated by 'a great concourse of people, carrying Scots thistles in their hands, and accompanied by a drum, and a pair of Highland bagpipes'.[114] The success of *The Family Legend* must, as Scott suggested, have owed something to the same feeling in 'a national audience'.[115] And Scott himself, having first dedicated his muse to 'Caledonia! stern and wild' in the famous patriotic lines in *The Lay of the Last Minstrel*, and then extended his unofficial laureateship to the Highlands by solemnly taking down the 'Harp of the North' at the beginning of *The Lady of the Lake*,[116] could not possibly exclude the Highlands from the national consensus of his ending. It would have been to exclude the nation's very spirit.

Even so, it's a curious nationalism which seeks its heart in an impoverished margin of the nation which it also defines as anarchic, uncivilised and ripe for domination by an anglicising centre. Of *what* Scotland did the Highlands harbour the spirit?

Scott's own national role was shrewdly described by the young Lockhart in 1819. It lay, he argued, not so much in his literary gifts as in 'the extent and importance of the class of ideas to which he has drawn the public attention': that's to say that in

> re-awakening the sympathies of his countrymen for the more energetic characters and passions of their forefathers ... he employed, indeed, with the skill and power of a true master, and a true philosopher, what constitutes the only means of neutralising that barren spirit of lethargy into which the progress of civilization is in all countries so apt to lull the feelings and imaginations of mankind.[117]

This assessment starts out by sounding nationalistic, but by the end the 'important ideas' seem to have less to do with nationality than with the familiar opposition of primitive feeling and civilised languor. At this point, Scott's project is less remote from Anne Grant's than it has seemed. It raises the matter of Scotland as hers does not, but its nationalism is one of memory, dealing in past energies rather than future struggles, counteracting social organisation as such rather than envisaging new ways of organising society, and seeking to produce a change, not of government, but of imagination.

This emphasis is confirmed by the prologue which Scott wrote for *The Family Legend*. Addressing his 'national audience', he naturally recommends the play as the vernacular offering of a daughter of Scotland. But the main thrust of the rhetoric that develops this idea is, unmistakably, nostalgia:

Chief, thy wild tales, romantic Caledon,
Wake keen remembrance in each hardy son.
Whether on India's burning coasts he toil,
Or till Acadia's winter-fetter'd soil,
He hears with throbbing heart . . .[118]

Admittedly, Baillie herself was living in London. All the same, it's a strange way for a Scottish poet to talk to a Scottish audience in Scotland. The inflection of nationality is insistently elegiac, as if 'romantic Caledon' is a country from which all Scots are exiled, whether they live in India or Edinburgh. Connecting this displacement with the empty 'fastnesses' to which Porter's Wallace appeals, and the archaic and impractical attitudes of Clan-Alpine, we can see a whole structure of national feeling in love with self-defeat. The poetical Highlands function as the lost spirit of Scotland; spiritual *because* lost.

This melancholy paradox can be demystified by considering Scotland's position within the British Empire. By 1810 it was obvious that the Union with England was, in social and economic terms, working. Dependence on the more powerful economy to the south, which up until the mid-eighteenth century had been an obstruction to Scotland's growth, fairly suddenly turned into an advantage; Scotland ceased to be a victim of 'British' imperial and commercial expansion and became instead a partner in it. The Scottish agricultural and industrial 'take-off' in the late eighteenth century was, as Immanuel Wallerstein says, a case of 'development by invitation', as England, on the brink of world hegemony, broadened its domestic socioeconomic base.[119] In this situation, the attitude of the indigenous ruling class towards its own Scottishness was inevitably a contradictory one. It needed to assert a national identity, if its junior partnership was not to collapse in a simple English take-over of its intra-Scottish functions. But such assertions could not afford to have any serious economic or political content which might threaten the smooth and increasingly profitable running of the partnership itself. The solution was a depoliticised nationalism: what Nicholas Phillipson has neatly called 'an ideology of noisy inaction'.[120]

The Highlands had a special place in this accommodation because they were excluded from its material base. As is indicated by the quasi-colonial patterns of underdevelopment described at the beginning of this chapter, the far north and **west were not** co-opted into the British core state along with the rest of the country, but continued to be invested, in an increasingly sharp and total way, in the client role of 'periphery'. Thus the processes which promoted capital accumulation in the Lowlands through economic integration with England simultaneously exaggerated Highland difference: the Highlands were of course dominated, but not assimilated, by the incalculably more powerful British state. For the Scottish bourgeoisie, therefore, the Highlands had the aspect of a residual historical nation – a reminder, certainly, of an economic stagnation they were relieved to have left behind, but also an accreditation, held in reserve, of the national identity which was both required and eroded by their participation in the imperial adventure. This is why the Highlands acquired the role of representing Scotland *for the English*; it's also what prevented the ideology of the social tribes, innocent, communal, unbusinesslike, from achieving either power or oblivion.

7
Holidays

1 MAKE-BELIEVE

In July 1771, an English tourist called Anthony Champion found himself in a remote Highland valley. The farmer who occupied it was away, and his wife, anxious to be suitably hospitable, sent a boy to the hill to fetch 'a lamb and a kid'. Charmed by this pastoral injunction, and clearly a little titillated by his sudden intimacy with the pretty mistress of the isolated holding, Champion recorded the whole encounter in the style of the Authorised Version.[1] For example, it appears that the woman was puzzled by Champion's touristic enthusiasm for the scenery. The account makes her express her reaction in these terms:

> the country from which thou comest ... is a rich and plentiful country, and the people thereof live in fair dwellings, and eat of the fat of the land; but this country, thou seest, is poor and barren, and the manners thereof are rude and ignorant; thou canst not surely be pleased with such things.

The narrator's comment is:

> The very wildness of the country is pleasing to me, and for the manners thereof, this kindness to the traveller must indeed seem strange to those who come from afar.

It isn't altogether barren in any case: there is a stream, and good pasture, with trees — 'And he cast his eyes around, and the place seemed to him as a portion of Eden.'

The thought here — the contrast between the material assets of the south and the immaterial assets of the poor Highlands — is familiar from Anne Grant; as is the poetic literalism which ties an aesthetic pleasure down to a well-documented Highland fact (the laws of hospitality). These values are gravely, even touchingly enforced. But the biblical pastiche undermines their seriousness in a peculiar way: despite its aptness − or rather, precisely because its aptness is so neat − it has the effect of facetiousness. It's like fancy dress: Champion is playing at being Abraham's servant meeting Rebekah at the well, and it's that tone of make-believe, of walking into literature, that makes everything so delightful. This wilful frivolity affects the treatment of history as well. Champion is aware that the absent husband is a Lowland sheep farmer whose 'flocks multiplied exceedingly, and fed upon a thousand hills' − that is, the pastoralism actually reflects contemporary change. But he chooses to see it as timeless, exclaiming, 'Surely this is the ancient world, and the manners of the times of old'. He is able to indulge in this interpretation because he is a visitor, with no commitments or connections in the neighbourhood − at the end, he looks back, sighs, and bends his way into the hills. In other words, his eccentric form is a stylistic production of a historically new relationship with place, crucial to the Highlands: *going on holiday*.

Although going on holiday is a practice which is clearly related to the Tours and Journeys I've drawn on extensively throughout this book, the similarity of the activities conceals a significant retextualisation. The 'describer of distant regions', as Johnson put it in 1760, 'is always welcomed as a man who has laboured for the pleasure of others, and who is able to enlarge our knowledge and rectify our opinions':[2] that is, travelling comes under the sign of information; it is rather like reading works of history or agronomy or aesthetics, with the added advantage that one is seeing the antiquities, fields, paintings, for oneself. This is the notional status of the Grand Tour which is the model for the lesser tours − it's a part of the tourist's education. A holiday, on the other hand, is a gesture, not of inquiry into the world, but of playful refusal of it; not an extension of one's practical experience but a licensed truancy from it. The literary analogy is not information but fiction (a critical opposition which is exactly contemporary with the invention of holidaying as a social practice[3]); the travelling, to invoke a greater eccentricity from the same moment as Champion's Highland trip, is not so much a Grand Tour as a sentimental journey.[4] In this, the holiday directly picks up the readings, which we have already seen, of Highland scenery and society as literally poetic, and seeks to enact them. Adopting the region as the setting for a pleasurable and circumscribed narrative, one constructs a personal text, a literarisation of a few weeks of one's own real life.

The shift of models is intriguingly visible in Johnson's own journey, which happened two years after Champion's. Johnson's account of it conforms wholly to his own principles for such works, being informative, philosophic and only rarely and uneasily anecdotal. But then it is shadowed, so to speak, by Boswell's *Journal*, whose preoccupation with Johnson as a personality has the unmistakable effect of rewriting the itinerary of the *Journey* as a holiday. The biographical emphasis recurrently turns the Highlands into *décor*: the piquant vignettes – Ursa Major on a horse, the Rambler practising stoicism at a poor inn, the English Tory in a bed once slept in by Prince Charlie, the famous Scot-baiter posing with Caledonian broadsword and blue bonnet, the editor of Shakespeare walking upon the locations of *Macbeth*[5] – have exactly the character of an album of snapshots.

This light-heartedness also retextualises the issue of the patriarchal past: against Johnson's sombre analysis, Boswell sets a curious hilarity:

> My endeavours to rouse the English-bred Chieftain, in whose house we were, to the feudal and patriarchal feelings, Dr Johnson this morning tried to bring him to our way of thinking. – *Johnson*. 'Were I in your place, sir, in seven years I would make this an independent island. I would roast oxen whole and hang out a flag as a signal to the Macdonalds to come and get beef and whisky.' (p. 256)

Whatever the tone of Boswell's endeavours, Johnson's are parodic: the picturesque vision of rude hospitality is a fantasy which delights in its own absurdity. At Dunvegan, he reacts with the same high spirits to the playful offer of an island:

> Dr Johnson was highly amused with the fancy ... He talked a great deal of this island; – how he would build a house there, – how he would fortify it, – how he would have cannon, – how he would plant, – how he would sally out, and *take* the isle of Muck; – and then he laughed with uncommon glee, and could hardly leave off. (p. 327)

The attraction and the absurdity have the same source: the small, interpersonal scale of the imagined polity. It's not only that Johnson knows his plans aren't real; the plans themselves, with their lilliputian principalities and naively direct power relations, have a playacting quality; he is imagining *being* an imaginary king. So that when he exclaims, on Raasay, 'This is truly the patriarchal life: this is what we came to find' (p. 268), his delight is partly that of the philosophic traveller, pleased at the chance to learn about a society different from his own; but it is also the pleasure of make-believe, of playing the role of Ulysses among Homeric islets (p. 59).

Another doubled tour, that of William and Dorothy Wordsworth, records the same 'uncommon glee'. Wanting to see the Trossachs, they and Coleridge left their horse and car at Tarbet, crossed Loch Lomond and walked east to Glengyle with no idea of where they would stay. They ended up in the house of the ferryman who took them on Loch Katrine. Their night there thus represented the success of a mildly adventurous departure from the ordinary tourist route from Dumbarton to Inveraray: it was as it were an exclusion from their excursion, a double truancy. Their response is full of that pleasant irresponsibility:

> We caroused our cups of coffee, laughing like children at the strange atmosphere in which we were: the smoke came in gusts, and spread along the walls and above our heads in the chimney, where the hens were roosting like light clouds in the sky. We laughed and laughed again, in spite of the smarting of our eyes.[6]

It's not altogether clear what they were laughing at, until later on, when Dorothy describes herself going to sleep thinking 'of the Fairyland of Spenser, and what I had read in romance at other times, and then, what a feast would it be for a London pantomime-maker, could he but translate it to Drury Lane, with all its beautiful colours!' This is again, intensely, the sense of being on holiday. To be really here, in a sort of pantomime woodcutter's cottage, with smoke, and criss-cross beams, and hens! – the childlike laughter is not so much amusement as *merriment*; a suspension of normal prudence.

Later in their tour, the Wordsworths revisited the same hut by deviating westward from their route south towards Stirling, this time leaving the horse at Callander.[7] This second piece of touristic inventiveness is the context for William's poem 'Stepping Westward': they heard the suggestive phrase in a civil greeting from a woman on the road by Loch Katrine. The incident is a variant of those we looked at in a different context: again, it is an evening encounter on the road, with a native speaker in a lonely place furnishing the mind with an enigmatic text that carries it beyond itself and beyond the material world. But this time, although the intimation of mortality is still felt in the implicit allegory of the westbound road as the course of life, the tone is markedly less elegiac:

> And stepping westward seemed to be
> A kind of *heavenly* destiny:
> I liked the greeting; 'twas a sound
> Of something without place or bound;
> And seemed to give me spiritual right
> To travel through that region bright.[8]

The difference is that the moment of transcendence is not founded on the intense feeling of separation which characterised 'The Solitary Reaper' or the Ossian poem. Instead of the indecipherable Gaelic text, there is just a slightly idiosyncratic English; and the poem's expansive construction of the phrase is consciously and waywardly *chosen* – that is, the imagination is self-delightingly at play. Hence the relaxed tone – 'seemed', 'liked', 'something'. What motivates this pleasant easing up is that by returning to the 'pantomime' hut from a different direction – by knowing that it is waiting for them in 'that region bright' towards the sunset – the travellers have made it into an imaginary home. The 'something without place or bound' is as it were the freedom of the country: it is eternity as mediated, not by any theological category, but by the holiday game of staying somewhere a few days and acting as if one lives there always, always retaining the fresh impressions and uncommitted liberty of the chance visitor.

It was on the same loch, a few years later, that Scott established the shrine of this holiday-cottage Elysium. In a lavish costume dramatisation of Champion's homestay, the lost traveller, who is the King in disguise, is welcomed into the island retreat of the mysterious Lady of the Lake who might be an enchantress and who will not divulge her parentage. The King is wandering in dangerous country for reasons in which political finesse and whimsical pleasure are obscurely mixed; the Lady is hiding on the island because her noble father has been outlawed. Their first meeting, before the determinacies of the plot cut short its possibilities, is thus the encounter of two Shakespearean holiday myths — Prince Hal and Rosalind. For both, to be in the Highlands is to leave behind one's constricting official identity and assume a playful and temporary innocence. The island refuge, then, with its ready music, its rich adornment of trees and flowers, and its weightless 'shallop' the delightfully fragile link with the shore, is a retreat, not just from specific dangers, but from 'life's uncertain main' in general. The lyrics, such as 'Soldier, rest!', 'The lonely isle', 'Ave Maria!',[9] which undercut the rather philistine comedy of the main narrative, reflect in their self-absorbed melancholy the transitory perfection of that withdrawal. Real life is a scene of brutality and self-interest, but before long one must leave the island and go back to work.

2 THE TOURIST IN THE TEXT

In the most incompetent literary fictions of the Highland romance, the analogy with going on holiday is naively visible. For example, in *The Romance of the Highlands*, a deservedly forgotten publication of that *'annus mirabilis* of romance',[10] 1810, the hero, Kenneth, is wandering in the mountains one day when he is impressed by a portent we've encountered before, the hollow sound of the wind among the rocks: 'He looked around, expecting to see the majestic form of some ancient bard, seated upon a high rock, musing upon the scene, and now and then striking the strings of his harp.'[11] It's an expectable fancy in an Ossianised tourist. But Kenneth is a medieval Highlander; he plays the harp himself, and a few chapters earlier, in another rugged setting, he really did meet with a majestic form — that of an ancient hermit rather than an ancient bard — who told him the secret of his birth. The author has forgotten that his hero is part of the romance, and incongruously made him part of the romanticism too. Something similar is happening in other costume fictions of the Highlands when heroines about to be ravished, and generals marching into battle, nevertheless continue to admire the cataracts and woods around them.[12]

In all these cases it's inadequate to say that the reader is being invited to identify with the character. Rather, the character is identifying with the reader; the romantic associations of the story have won a pyrrhic victory over its practical details; we are reading about lives which are imaginary, not only for us, but also for the people who are supposed to be leading them. What many of these novels need is a preface explaining that the story is really set, not in the fourteenth century, but in the 1790s, and that the characters are all guests at an elaborate fancy-dress weekend party.[13] On such a basis the narrative becomes fairly intelligible.

More sophisticated romancers integrate the holiday-maker in the fiction by the device of *wandering*. By being homeless, or losing his way, the protagonist approximates naturally to the designedly 'truant' condition of the visitor for pleasure exemplified by the Wordsworths. In Ann Radcliffe's first book, for instance — *The Castles of Athlin and Dunbayne* — the noble heir to one of the castles is an enthusiast in the mould of Beattie's 'Minstrel'[14] who goes for long walks amid 'the wild variety of nature'. The story begins when, straying too far in one of his poetic reveries, he finds he is lost.

> He remained for some time in a silent dread not wholly unpleasing, but which was soon heightened to a degree of terror not to be endured ... His memory gave him back no image of the past; and having wandered some time, he came to a narrow pass ....[15]

Through the pass he comes upon a lushly wooded valley where, in a romantically situated cottage, he encounters a peasant of inexplicably noble mien who eventually turns out to be the lost heir of the other castle. The aesthetics of holiday scenery have passed seamlessly over into the mechanics of narrative. But then it's clear from this transition that Radcliffe is really interested, not in the places, which are only differentiated to the extent needed to separate out the romantic, the terrible and the beautiful, and not in the plot, which is a cliché, but in sensibility. The hero's emotional responses to his changing situation are traced with a subtlety that stands out from the crudity of the rest; the narrative is essentially a pretext for the subjectivisation of the landscape, as the mystery which is the plot provides a formula for the *sense* of mystery which is the desired effect of the mountainous setting.

For the definitive version of this formulation, we must return once more to *The Lady of the Lake*. As is well known, the poem was received as a literal invitation to visit its locations. It made the Trossachs into the prime Highland tourist site overnight, spreading prosperity along the banks of the Teith and redundancy along those of Loch Lomond.[16] Sir John Sinclair's carriage in the autumn of 1810 was the 297th of the season; since the previous maximum was about a hundred, he concluded with appropriately statistical wit 'that the effect of praise in verse compared to praise in prose is as 3 to 1'.[17] Scott's appropriation of the place continues to be acknowledged by the Ordnance Survey, which marks 'Ellen's Isle' in the current series.

One result of this extraordinary instance of literary effectiveness is an impression that Loch Katrine was actually discovered by Scott. As is suggested by Sinclair's control figure, itself quite high, the impression is false. As early as 1800, John Stoddart could say that the celebrity of Loch Katrine made him anxious to visit it;[18] this may reflect rhapsodic descriptions in Mrs Murray's *Companion to Scotland* (1799) and, earlier still, in the Callander entry for the *Statistical Account*, which was written by the minister, James Robertson, in 1791. Robertson records that 'the Trosacks are often visited by persons of taste';[19] so even he was not the pioneer. Scott himself generously drew on (and acknowledged) a local guide book produced in 1806 by the minister at Aberfoyle, Patrick Graham. In short, he chose for his Highland poem a setting which was already well known for its scenery. The poem did not create a tourist attraction inadvertently, as *Hamlet* has done at Helsigør, for example. Its holiday connection with place was part of its making.

At the opening of the poem, when the 'antler'd monarch of the waste' pauses on the slopes of Uamh Mhor to decide whether to make for Loch Ard or Loch Achray, it is surveying the alternative approaches to the Trossachs which make up the two sections of the Revd Graham's booklet — the west road from Callander and the south road by Aberfoyle from Gartmore. The animal chooses the more popular Callander route, and so leads the hunt up the valley of the Teith through a litany of place names and thumbnail descriptions — Cambusmore, Ben Ledi, Loch Vennachar, Loch Achray, Ben Venue — which exactly rehearses the notable features of the road as they would appear to a user of the guide book.[20] So the ride which occupies the first eight stanzas is like a day trip to the Trossachs, delightfully transformed into a breathless and antique adventure.

As in Radcliffe, the destination of this journey is a pass, on the far side of which the story is waiting. Scott specifies that vague sense of inadvertent admission to an alien world by linking it to the romantic topos of the wild rider who, like Sir Walter in Wordsworth's 'Hart-Leap Well' (1800) or Bürger's 'Wilde Jäger' (1778),[21] is separated from his companions and led by his quarry into an encounter with the supernatural. So that by the time the stag reaches the 'darksome glen' of the Trossachs, the place is already charged with magical expectations; and these are fulfilled in literal fashion when it transpires later that the huntsman is expected, his arrival having been foreseen by a second-sighted bard. But the real enchantment is not supernatural: it is scenic.

The noisy vigour of the chase is abruptly cut off by the death of the huntsman's horse. In the strange stillness he sets off on foot to find his 'comrades of the day': clearly that should mean that he follows his own tracks eastwards in the direction of Brig o' Turk. At this point, however, the landscape takes over, in four stanzas of virtuoso natural description which refract all the accumulated energy of the ride, so that now it's the path that finds its way, the rocks that shoot up, nature that scatters the flowers and trees which themselves mingle, find their bowers, group, weep, cast anchor and fling their boughs across the sky.[22] The huntsman, now the 'wanderer', loses the initiative: first his eyes and then his steps are passively drawn upward and westward by the brilliant and balletic scenery. His subsequent discovery of Loch Katrine itself is displaced in the same way:

> Onward, amid the copse 'gan peep
> A narrow inlet, still and deep....
> Lost for a space, through thickets veering,
> But broader when again appearing,
> Tall rocks and tufted knolls their face
> Could on the dark-blue mirror trace.

The movement denoted by 'onward' and 'veering', and the seeing suggested by 'trace', must literally be the wanderer's, but the syntax avoids having him as subject, and misrelates its participles confusingly in order to keep the objects of his gaze in motion. The effect is like subjective camera: the person vanishes and the text records only the retinal image swaying and scintillating. So one hardly notices that he is walking in exactly the wrong direction. He is unresisting: the picturesque leads him to its mistress like a fairy herald.

Thus, as in the romantic novels but with incomparably greater power, the hero's adventure provides a formula for the affectivity of the setting. The sublimity of the Trossachs contributes directly to his destiny, by half-stealing him from himself and drawing him into the presence of the mystery. Burke's conceptual link between mountain aesthetics and the 'passions belonging to self-preservation', which underpins the whole theory of the sublime, is made dramatic by literally concealing in the precipitous scenery the perils which the plot holds in store. So readers of the poem who then go to Loch Katrine see it, not only highlighted for them by a minute picturesque description, but also bathed in the glow of a narrative aura. In a letter of August 1810, Elizabeth Spence, one of Sinclair's 296 predecessors, describes the locality in terms which are ecstatically soaked in the poem's imagery, but also declares that even Scott's description is inadequate to the beauty of the real thing.[23] This is the poem's unconscious accolade: the readers see its romance, not printed on the page, but inhering in the land.

This triumphant naturalisation, however, is marked by an operating contradiction. Scott's huntsman is an *ideal* picturesque tourist in the precise sense that the ideas suggested by the scenery – solitude, danger, wonder – are practical aspects of his situation. The holiday-makers imitate his extreme experience, but their own practice is in fact organised by considerations – convenience, safety, planning – which specifically negate the terms of the original. The huntsman, after all, finds Loch Katrine by accident: one could hardly arrange to do that. This is the ironic force of Sinclair's calculations: the glamour of the image is measurable by the number of people who come to contemplate it and so render it commonplace. The brighter the aura, the faster it is dispelled. Like the search, in our own time, for 'unspoiled' Mediterranean resorts, the project of actualising the Highland romance is caught in a self-defeating circularity.

3 THE HUNTSMAN

Scott was offering one beguiling chance of squaring the circle. The activity which precipitates his hero into the enchanted Highland world is itself a kind of game. Hunting, of the kind pursued by James V, has the same kind of doubleness as holiday-making. Like tourism, it *denotes* a relationship with the land which is more primitive and immediate than its own: the civilised sportsman, who could go to the butcher's if he preferred to, is in a sense imitating the pre-pastoral hunter for whom it is a matter of survival. But at the same time, hunting as an amusement is not reducible to the category of make-believe: it is a real institution, with a tradition whose length and cultural richness renders it effectively independent of its inherent reference to food-gathering. Besides, the animal really dies. In short, here is one social practice in which the imagined and the actual, romance and materiality, seem to suspend their mutal contradictions and form a single object. A strategy for realising the 'literally poetic' Highlands in practice is afforded by the special fictiveness of sport.

The condition of this reconciliation is of course one which is threatened by Improvement. There must be wild creatures available to hunt, and a sufficiently spacious habitat in which to hunt them without destroying the crops and herds of husbandry. Consequently, as agricultural revolution proceeds and land use approaches totality, hunting tends to be pushed into the margins[24] – geographical margins, certainly, in the sense that the peripheral wilderness, whether it is a primeval relic or an ecological casualty, continues to harbour 'game'; but also cultural margins, as the activity becomes more and more remote from the socioeconomic concerns of actual rural society and makes new connections with myths of wildness and pastness. It's unsurprising, then, that the Highlands should have begun to attract the attention of sportsmen as the region's own agrarian and cultural marginality became more and more pronounced.

The English pioneer was Col. Thomas Thornton, a wealthy Yorkshire landowner and fanatic of gun and rod, whose love affair with the Highlands began in 1784. That summer, he established a camp on Speyside on a military scale, bringing (by two baggage wagons and a sea-going sloop) equipment including boats, fishing-tackle, guns, ammunition, hawks, horses, dogs, furniture, hay and corn, materials for stables and gardens, and a gargantuan quantity of provisions for himself, his retinue, and his numerous guests.[25] Throughout the season he supplemented these resources with a steady haul of fresh fish and game. Thus, interestingly, his overall plan of campaign treated the Highlands as if they were uninhabited: he lived on what he had brought and what he killed. He knew very well that this wasn't necessary: he socialised with the local gentry and made use of local sporting knowledge. His preparations, with their massively practical air, thus have something irreducibly imaginary about them. He appears to be co-ordinating an ambitious expedition; what he is actually doing is substantiating a fiction. The aim is not only to bag a quantity of game, but also to invent a certain primitive and princely style of life — a holiday.

His enjoyment of the result comes freshly off the pages. Sitting on top of the Cairngorms, eating soup made from newly killed ptarmigan and drinking champagne which has been chilled in a nearby snowdrift, he reflects somewhat sententiously that this meal

> was relished with a keenness of appetite that none but those that have been at Glen Ennoch can experience; an appetite, far, very far superior to the palled one, with which the gentlemen at Weltgie's or Lethellier's eat their sumptuous and costly meals.[26]

He is also a partisan of wild scenery, with a contempt for 'beautiful, highly-finished landscapes' which suggests the natural sublime; but this taste is wholly innocent of 'horror'. It is not a question of the spiritual rewards of negativity: Thornton simply likes his views, as he likes his establishment, to be rough and lavish, connoting the adventures of the chase rather than the successes of cultivation. At this point it's clear that the enterprise includes a familiar animus against Improvement: refusing, like Anne Grant's Highlanders, the 'frigid aid' of the butcher and the baker, or rather of the waiter and the landscape gardener, Thornton pours his immense energy into a simulacrum of unalienated and undivided labour. His exertions produce, not exchange value within an abstracting system, but, directly and physically, food and the appetite to enjoy it. Glen Ennoch is his escape from the reifying relations of commodity production — that is, of the sources of his own wealth — 'back' to a means of satisfying needs which is cumbersome, certainly, but feels natural and wholesome.

As the champagne reminds us, though, the escape is a playful one. Thornton is perhaps recreating the enormous hunts and royal hospitality of the old lords of the Highlands, such as the famous stag drive of the Earl of Mar described by an English visitor in 1618.[27] But whereas, historically, such occasions had an intelligible function in the life of the nobility, Thornton's hunting and fishing summer is a private extravaganza, requiring personal inventiveness and disposable income acquired elsewhere. In such a context, the real cost of dining in rude splendour on top of a mountain is much greater than the price of a meal at Lethellier's. Barbarism is more of a luxury than luxury.

In other words Thornton, despite his gentlemanly philistinism, is really an aesthete, going to extraordinary lengths to arrange his life in accordance with a literary conception of beauty. The covert priority of the aesthetic motive is, as we have seen, an Ossianic structure; and Thornton resembles Macpherson's heroes of sensibility, not only by the unconvincing alternation in his behaviour between the earliest and the latest stage of civil society, but also in his devotion to activities which seem functional but aren't. His unremitting pursuit of food *looks* like a productive activity, but actually the product is the pretext for the pursuit. Like the ancient Caledonians, he fights only for fame, disdaining plunder.

In all this he foreshadows the Victorian and Edwardian cult of the Highland stag, which would take his own playacting to extreme heights in the artificiality of its naturalism and the mingled facetiousness and kitsch of its artefacts. He might even be called the father of the sporting Highlands were it not for one omission: as Scott pointed out in a review of his book,[28] Thornton failed to discover deer-stalking. He was a little too early: in his time, the only forms of deer-hunting which were well known in the south were the big traditional drive with hundreds of beaters, and the wild mounted chase using deer hounds, both of which were impractical in modern conditions. Stalking – pursuing the deer alone and on foot by stealth – had been a task or amusement of young Highland men for generations; but it was not until a decade or so after the publication of Thornton's book that it was discovered by Englishmen, such as the Duke of Bedford, who tried it in 1818, and William Scrope, who started stalking at Bruar Lodge on the Atholl estate in 1822, and in 1838 published *The Art of Deerstalking*, thus launching the upper-class English craze which peaked only in 1914.[29]

As the dates strongly suggest, Scott is decisively present at the very beginning of this development. His use of the word 'deerstalking' in the Thornton review is probably its first appearance in this sense;[30] moreover, the hunt in the *Lady* adumbrates the emotional logic of the whole subsequent enthusiasm. Although the poem's hero doesn't stalk his stag – like Thornton, he doesn't know how to pursue deer in the Highlands, and the quarry escapes once it has crossed the Line – the chase is what leads him to his encounter with the Highland romance. For landscape, as James Holloway and Lindsay Errington have pointed out,[31] the point about deer-stalking is that it makes it impossible to plan your route; it is dictated as you go along by the direction of the wind and the wanderings of the quarry. Attached to the animal as if by a spell, you are led irresistibly into unknown scenes, vast solitudes, immediate and exhausting and possibly dangerous contact with the wilderness. That is, you remake for yourself – disdaining imitation – the predicament of the royal huntsman carried beyond the limits of conventional hunting, standing alone, dismounted, nameless and entranced amid 'the scenery of a fairy dream'.

According to the conventions of the game, then, the pursuit of the deer is the means of entry to a primeval, extra-social world of direct sensations – in short, to nature. Of course, it cannot really produce the transition: rather, the sport is a text which *signifies* it. And in this case, the difference between signified and signifier amounts to a direct incompatibility. Game was in practice a minor issue of Improvement. Alexander Irvine, for instance, a Highland minister and Improving writer, noted in 1802 that

> Some things in the Highlands were not considered by the peasants property till very lately. It was necessary to change their ideas, and teach them to respect the rights of their superiors to game, fish and wood.
>
> The old notions are yet strongly retained in some districts, and not infrequently put into practice; for it is not easy to convince a Highlander, that a landlord has a better right to a deer, a moorfowl, or a salmon, than he has himself, because he considers them the unconfined bounty of Heaven.[32]

According to this, the Highlander shares the romantic view that hunting is a natural activity, and draws from it the logical but inconvenient conclusion that it cannot therefore be private property. Although this 'savage' attitude is one that must appeal to the aesthetics of a Thornton – the last phrase suggests that Irvine himself is not wholly unsympathetic – it's nevertheless out of the question to concede anything to it; for it's the sportsman, precisely, who makes it so necessary to enforce shooting and fishing rights, because of the commercial value his interest confers on the game. By coincidence, it was in Thornton's first season, 1784–5, that a system of game certificates was first introduced in the Highlands,[33] thus formalising the complex struggle between sport and poaching which is still in progress in the region today. The new hunters were hastening the actual extinction of the way of life to which they did imaginary homage. Although the sportsman has succeeded, with great ingenuity, in circumventing the law of diminishing imaginative returns which undermines the satisfactions of the tourist, he is caught in what is essentially the same trap. Its underlying form is now clearly visible: it is that the holiday escape from commodification is itself a commodity.

4 LEISURE AND INDUSTRY

The Highland holiday, in other words, is one trace of the complex process which, around the end of the eighteenth century, was making leisure into a form of private property.[34] The hunts, fairs and holydays of traditional British society, both rural and urban, were forms of recreation which were definingly public in their orientation and presence:[35] they were things which extended communities did, and since they often included various kinds of production and trading, they represented a sort of 'leisure' which was not wholly separated from work. The new type of holiday is quite different. By leaving his home area and going to somewhere he has selected as a holiday place, the holiday-maker detaches himself completely from his normal social environment and from the ways in which he makes a living. Instead of being an expression of society, the holiday becomes a turning away from it, towards solitude, fantasy, nature, domesticity; we have already seen how closely adapted the Highland image was to the orchestration of exactly these themes.

This new practice is associated with the growing strength and universality of commodity production, not only in the sense, exemplified by Thornton, that the holiday is itself a commodity, privately purchased and consumed, but also in that it projects an absolute separation of leisure and work, constituting the two states as mutually exclusive opposites. That's to say, the identification of one's holiday as a finite time which is 'all one's own' is a reflex of the identification of working time as belonging entirely to someone else. The logic of political economy, which requires for its calculation of the costs and productivity of labour a clear distinction between working and not working, throws out as the converse and compensation of work the theoretically unconditioned category of 'spare time'.

For the activists of Improvement, the absence of any such clarity was one of the main causes of Highland underdevelopment. The two decades between Thornton's first visit to Speyside and the publication of his book were dominated by the search for what one influential pamphlet called 'the means of exciting a spirit of national industry'.[36] The Highland Society of Scotland and the British Fisheries Society were both founded with the fostering of such a spirit as one of their explicit social aims; the 'General View' series of agricultural reports on Scottish counties and Sinclair's *Statistical Account* pursued the same goal in countless local observations.[37] In 1803, the year of the Wordsworths' holiday and of Anne Grant's leisurely pastoral, the Caledonian Canal was begun, partly in the hope of 'improving the Habits of the Country by Teaching Lessons of systematic Industry'.[38] Thus the discovery of the Highlands as a regular location for leisure pursuits went in step with a systematic attempt to control and reduce the irregular leisure of the natives.

Conversely, the pre-capitalist Highlands, considered as a place devoid of the blessings of industry, could also be read as a place free of its pains:

> At two seasons of the year, they were busy; the one in the end of spring and beginning of summer, when they put the plough into the little land they had capable of receiving it ... the other just before winter, when they reaped their harvest; The rest of the year was all their own, for amusement or for war. If not engaged in war, they indulged themselves in summer in the most delicious of all pleasures to men in a cold climate and romantic country, the enjoyment of the sun, and of the summer-views of nature; never in the house during the day, even sleeping often at night in the open air, among the mountains and woods. They spent the winter in the chase, while the sun was up; and in the evening, assembling round a common fire, they entertained themselves with the song, the tale, and the dance.[39]

Unimproved Highlanders, as here described by Sir John Dalrymple in 1771, do very little work because their primitive husbandry and barren country leave very little work that can be done. Thus, ironically, they derive from their poverty what members of the privileged class in Dalrymple's own society derive from their wealth: the leisure to cultivate their sensibility . Their lives are an undemanding mixture of poetry, scenery and field sports; whatever its accuracy as an account of the Highland past, this was a fairly exact programme for the near future. The original state of society which is projected as the *absence* of Improvement is reproduced as a *holiday* from it. The heir of the carefree savage is the Victorian plutocrat, seeking temporary refuge from his rational and profitable mode of life in a sort of anthropological quixotism. But then the inheritance is inescapably also a falsification: the primitive unity of work and play within a single natural necessity is commemorated in a totally gratuitous form of play which deliberately places itself hundreds of miles away from the scenes of work; and the 'common fire' of the primitive collective is rekindled in a private hearth.

In holiday-making, that is, the aesthetic refusal of Improvement finds a form which is essentially a phase of what it refuses. It was even perhaps the decisive phase. By the time the Caledonian Canal was finished, the sheep were coming under pressure from the spread of sporting estates; the Highlands were attaining new dignity as the summer homeland of royalty; and tourism, rather than trade, was proving to be the beneficiary of the new forms of transport such as steamships and railways.[40] The meagre rewards of crofting were, and are, eked out not by any new dynamic in the real Highland economy but by the expenditure of the consumers of the myth. It had been Thornton and Scott rather than Sinclair or Telford who spoke for the practical future. 'Fancy's Land' imposed itself on the literal territory.

8
The Structure of the Myth

1 PERIPHERALISATION

The Highlands, then, are imaginary. It follows that the non-Highlands (the Scottish Lowlands, or the metropolis, or anglophone Britain generally) are real. The consumer of the myth partakes of 'the pleasing enthusiasm which these wilds impart' and then quits them 'with regret':[1] to move back across the Highland line is to leave Fancy's Land and re-enter, sadly or thankfully but in either case inevitably, the realm of factual truth.

This fantastic opposition is intimately associated with a material one — namely, that in the system of late eighteenth-century British capitalism, the Highlands are on the *periphery* and the non-Highlands are the *core*. These terms are part of the proposition, elaborated most notably by Immanuel Wallerstein, that capitalism is constitutively a geographical phenomenon, which consistently and from the beginning has entailed a 'hierarchization of space'.[2] The fundamental unit of the capitalist system is not the individual transaction but the 'commodity chain', the extended series of linked production processes through which capital passes in its drive to increase itself. These chains, which are the operative form of the social division of labour, are not random in their geographical distribution, but tend to converge, from very diverse points of origin, on certain limited zones, which are thus the centres of power and accumulation in the system: the core. The transfer to the core of surplus from the other places, through unequal exchange along the commodity chains, is what the capitalist world-system essentially is. And to the extent that a given part of the world is assimilated into the system, and its social and economic life subordinated to the requirements of the whole, it enters into a client relationship with the core — that is, it is peripheralised.

In the main, according to Wallerstein, this geographical hierarchisation has derived its ratification and its infrastructure from the accompanying global political system of nation states. Core and periphery tend to be different 'sovereign' countries, the inertia of whose bureaucracies serves to institutionalise the differential. For many reasons, this was never a possible formula for the differentiation of the Gaeltacht: the Highlands are thus, as I've argued in an earlier chapter,[3] a case, anomalous but by no means unusual, of *instrastate* peripheralisation — a domestic 'underdeveloped country'.

This did not come about as a direct result of anyone's intentions. If we read the various commentators who have been quoted in these pages with the aim of discovering their *opinions*, it's clear that very few of them are happy with what they perceive to be happening in the Highlands. Broadly speaking, the exponents of Improvement would prefer to see the full integration of the region in the economy and society of the United Kingdom, and the romanticisers would like its historical peculiarities to be protected from systemic effects such as commercialisation and clearance by some kind of paternalistic intervention. Thus, when we say that the myth — the form of the core's *knowledge* of the periphery — is a function of domination, we don't mean simply that it is a bland tale in which the whole relationship is presented as ideally harmonious. Of course, the claim is made that the core culture is better, or that its effect on the periphery is benign. But this is not the main ideological embodiment of the assymmetrical power relations. Rather, what counts is the proposition, unchallengeably diffused and repeated throughout the discourse of Improvement, that the core's representation of the world is not a representation at all, but *reality*. The Highlands are subordinated to the sign-system of the metropolis, not on the basis that the latter is superior, but on the basis that it is inescapable. You don't have to prefer it, because it is in any case coercive.

Contemporary British politics offer an illuminating parallel. As was widely observed, Labour's defeat in the 1987 election represented a newly stark geographical polarisation of voting patterns. In the parliament that was returned, less than one twentieth of the Conservative MPs had been elected outside England, and about two thirds of them were from south of a line between the Severn and the Wash. For Labour, on the other hand, one third of the parliamentary party came from Scotland and Wales, and only about one ninth from the south and south-east of England. The immediate reasons for this peripheralisation of the Left offer no particular similarities to the situation of the Highlands at the beginning of the nineteenth century. What is recognisable, however, from the thematics of Improvement and romance, is the *valorisation*, in the media and in the Labour movement, of the dichotomy which was dramatised by the figures.

The Tory heartland is London and its increasingly broad commuter belt. Imaginatively, this enormously expanded city is the object of a very old ambivalence: like the London of adventurer folk-heroes, it is privileged, magnetic and wicked. The peripheries are then the obverse of that metropolitan image: somewhat ironically, the industrial conurbations of the north move into the rhetorical space traditionally occupied by the countryside. The opposing stereotypes which are thus put in play may be tabulated:

the core is:	*the periphery is:*
rich and successful	poor and defeated
glitz	decency
materialistic	idealistic
individualistic	communitarian
competing	caring
consumers	real people
rootless	traditional
head	heart

The first impression made by this list is of course favourable to the periphery. A simple inversion rewrites material inferiority as moral superiority: the margins are now the 'heart'. But this compensation, whatever its psychological benefits, is effectively a political *ratification* of disadvantage. The periphery, and the organisations which identify with it, absorb peripherality into their positive identity; their pride rests on their freedom from the vulgarities of the world's winners; their virtues are nourished by hard times; they are never more magnificently themselves than when their cause is hopeless.[4] Not to have won power ceases to seem like a simple failure, and comes to look like a point of honour. Conversely, electoral victory becomes problematic because of the way that defeat is inscribed on the party's image, inextricably tied up with the very values which constitute its electoral appeal and its claim on the loyalty of its activists.

This mythic bind is strikingly a replica of the one which produced the romantic Highlands, with their fine-grained loyalties and elegiac quixotism. It's not only that every line of my list of complementary stereotypes could be transferred to the Lowland–Highland opposition, and the transference substantiated from the foregoing chapters. Still more, it's that the structure which gives the list its coherence and generates fresh polarities is a duality of objective and subjective:[5] things and feelings, material gains and imaginative satisfactions, success and sensibility. Within this opposition, the 'Highlands' (that is, the periphery in mythical form) develop into the privileged home of subjectivity as such. Conceding to the metropolis the whole management of the external world and the discourses of power and money, the periphery speaks instead the language of the *purely human*. Deprived of – or free of – the mediations of material practice, the 'Highlands' form a refuge where humanity can be genuine, immediate and unconditional.

Complementing that abstracted and depoliticised theatre of humane values, the centre of power appears as the scene of the *merely* effectual. That – alas! – is just how things are. Thus the more elevated the Highland image becomes, and the more poignantly gratifying its evocations of human nobility, the more ruinously it pays for its moral splendour by its separation from practical life. Pushed to the political and cultural margins, the region is also marginalised epistemologically: London has dull and authoritative reports; Lochaber has delightful and idiomatic tales. Hence the proliferation of fictive themes in the representation – folly, imagination, superstition, vision, poetry, holiday. The Gaeltacht becomes, in every sense, an ideal country, until even those who seek to uphold its interests against the core find that they are doing so in the glowing and reverent language which ratifies its oppression.

2 NATURE

Already before the end of the eighteenth century, this language had attained the security of cliché. Here is a sample. The writer is Lady Amelia, one of the correspondents in a very minor epistolary novel of 1797.

> they are the happiest set of folks I ever saw, in a state most people would think themselves very miserable; fond of their

native rocks. The chieftain of their name sprung from the same root: The fond attachment seems to increase with every danger; but, alas! they feel no such paternal kindness as their fathers and grandfathers used to find in their chiefs. Of old, they were like children of the same family; the same easy familiarity reigned throughout, and was a great source of happiness; now the lairds has raised their rents, without pointing out to the uninstructed peasantry the art of husbandry, improvement, or cultivation ... Much blame to those who, forgetful of their country, cramp the natural freedom of these brave Highlanders, by airs of superiority and extortion, treatment their forefathers were unacquainted with; nor can the present generation relish it: their warm, grateful hearts are always ready to own a favour, but are equally alive to affronts, and ready to revenge the injury.[6]

Writing like this has representative value just because of its mindlessness. Lady Amelia seems not to understand all the things she's saying: her Highlanders are first idyllically happy and later smarting under injurious treatment; the second sentence ought to be explaining that the chief and the people share a common name and ancestry, but doesn't quite manage it; the judgement that unkind landlords are unpatriotic needs to be backed up by the 'nursery of soldiers' idea if it is to make sense. The abrupt way the children of the clan turn into 'uninstructed peasantry' when the immediate context shifts from romance to Improvement confirms the feeling that this is writing without an independent object: it is not so much a description of the Highlands, even an ill-informed one, as a series of oblivious transitions from one *ideé reçue* to the next. Contented poverty − native rocks − paternalism − danger − mercenary heritors − Improvement − natural freedom − fidelity and vindictiveness: *what everyone knows* about Highlanders in 1797 is rehearsed with the unerring confidence of a sleepwalker.

As we would expect, then, this mythic automatism executes the familiar peripheralising blend of admiration and patronage. Brave, free, warm-hearted and contented, Lady Amelia's Highlanders are also wholly incompetent, the helpless recipients of good or bad treatment, needing to be taught every art, even that of cultivating the land they have occupied for generations. The inconsistencies are unconscious because the idealisation and the dismissal are effected in the same gesture.

This passage generalises a whole structure of feeling by being derivative. What if it were to be generalised deliberately and philosophically, rather than by default? We could imagine a reflective beholder of the Highland scene, trying to raise to consciousness the contradictory pleasures which its landscapes, people and traditions afford within the culture of the metropolis. What is it, he could ask, which attracts us to these unrewarding objects?

> What could give them a claim on our love, even? It is not these objects, it is an *idea* represented by them which we love in them. In them we love ... the quiet functioning from within themselves, the existence according to their own laws, the inner necessity, the eternal unity with themselves.
> They *are* what we *were*; they are what we *should become* again. We were natural like them and our culture should lead us back to nature along the path of reason and freedom. They are, therefore, at the same time a representation of our lost childhood, which remains eternally most precious to us and thus they fill us with a certain sadness, [and] representations of our highest perfection in the ideal, so that they transport us to a state of elevated emotion.
> But their perfection is no merit of their own, since it is not the product of their own choice. They accord us, therefore, the quite singular pleasure of being our models without putting us to shame ... The essence of their character is precisely that which is lacking to the perfection of our own; what distinguishes us from them is exactly what is lacking to the divinity of theirs. We are free and they are necessary; we change, they remain one ... In *them*, therefore, we eternally see what eludes us, but for which we are called upon to struggle and which we may hope to approach in a never-ending progression, although we never reach it. *In ourselves* we see a merit which they can either never possess, like the unreasoning, or only if they travel on the same path *as us*, like children. They therefore provide us with the sweetest enjoyment of our humanity as an idea, even if they must necessarily humble themselves with regard to that *particular* condition of our humanity.

This is Friedrich Schiller, writing two years or so before Lady Amelia; and he is referring not, of course, to the Highlands, but to the objects of Nature. The extraordinary accuracy with which, nonetheless, he theorises the play of ideality and inadequacy in the romanticised Highlands is a function of the historically particular sense which he here attaches to the word Nature.

What is most striking about its use in this extract from *On the Naive and Sentimental in Literature* is the absolute and dynamic polarity of Nature on the one hand and, on the other hand, 'us'. With one exception, every sentence I have quoted contains an opposition between 'us' and 'them', often with at least one formal antithesis. The otherness of Nature is enforced over and over again. As the argument itself explains, the distinction has this controlling importance because it is constitutive: Nature is *defined* as what we are not.

It is decisively different from the Nature of the Renaissance. Take for example the famous exchange between Polixenes and Perdita in *The Winter's Tale*. Perdita is maintaining that the purposes of 'great creating nature' should not be sophisticated by grafting, Polixenes that 'nature is made better by no mean / But nature makes that mean'.[8] They are adopting opposite views, but they are agreed that the nature they are discussing is a creative and active force, and that it is possible and proper for human beings to live in accordance with its principles. These are very broadly based assumptions. Even much nearer Schiller's own age, Pope in the *Essay on Man*, for example, is effectively endorsing them. Neither Polixenes nor Perdita would understand Schiller's idea that natural objects are devoid of change, or share his sense of nature as ungraspable, an irrecoverable origin or an unattainable goal. In short, they were speakers *in* Nature, whereas Schiller speaks as one who is *outside* it. A kind of alienation seems to have occurred in the mean time.

It's tempting to conclude that man has been banished from nature, which has therefore been reduced to the non-human – the animals, vegetables and minerals of 'natural science'. But this doesn't quite match what Schiller is saying. It's clear from his examples that 'nature' can include the people and customs of the countryside as well as its flora and fauna, and that he is thinking of the emotions evoked, not only by rocks and streams, but also by ancient monuments. He is not making rigorous distinctions between the natural and the man-made. Besides, it's hard to imagine how a definingly non-human image could represent 'what we were ... what we should become again'. The separation, decisive as it is, is of another kind.

For who, in that case, are 'we' – the constituency which is so relentlessly contrasted with nature? Not simply all mankind, but particular people, or rather, people in a particular situation. If we take that question back to the extract, it's emphatically clear that the situation is that of being *in motion*: we 'were', we 'should become', we are on a 'path', we 'change'. The implied constituency is defined as being historically and irreversibly *en route*, characterised by choice, freedom, reason, homelessness; it is not too gross a simplification to say that 'we' are the subjects of *progress*.

An image from later in the essay luminously suggests the role of nature in this construction. At worst, Schiller concedes, the consciousness of freedom oppresses us: our dynamism affects us only as a lack of moral harmony, our reason only as a source of anxiety and caprice: 'We then see in irrational nature only a happier sister who remained behind in the parental home from which we rushed forth to foreign climes, in the arrogant high spirits of our freedom.'[9] In the character of the happier sister, nature provides a notional point of departure for the *übermütig* venture of 'reason and freedom', a mythic moment at which we could have been content to stay at home. It's evident that an image of this kind is necessary to the whole metaphor of 'progress', since it's not possible to conceive of movement without also imagining something that stays still. The 'great stillness'[10] of Schiller's nature thus forms itself as the obverse of great changes; its 'eternal unity' with itself as the projection of the felt self-division of modernity; its remaining behind in the parental home as a formula for the permanent nostalgia of a culture of exile. 'They are what we *were*': it is because humanity has become historical that nature has become timeless.

For Schiller's essay, the most pressing instance of great change is clearly the French Revolution. He began writing it a few months after Thermidor, and its closing sentences, reflecting on the abysmal danger that attends wrong choices on the path of freedom, are all but explicitly an epitaph for Jacobinism.[11] Less immediately, we can refer the essay's ambivalent consciousness of perfectibility to the moment of European industrial 'take-off': as capitalism approaches, for the first time, the condition of a world-system, its now apparently unlimited capacity to transform nature and custom creates a newly open future which in turn alters the meaning of the past.[12] But what is more structurally pervasive in the essay than all such referents is just the dyadic organisation of the thought which sets artificiality against nature, German against

Greek, Ariosto against Homer, the sentimental against the naive – that is, always, though on widely different time-scales, what *supervenes* against what *was there before*. These pairs are thoroughly dialectical: there seems to be no possibility of thinking a particular state of language and culture without also explicitly thinking what it is not. The naive is characterised by what has *not yet* happened to it; the sentimental is defined by its relation to a prior naivety. It's this general penetration of positive statement by the terms of 'then and now' which gives the writing its sense of fatal secondariness, its unhappy consciousness of history.

The myth of the Highlands is a myth of nature in this particular sense – nature as left behind, as lost wholeness. This is the reason why, for example, the region can appear as wild and empty and also as the scene of an elaborately articulated customary culture extending back through the centuries: the structure doesn't distinguish between inhuman nature and human antiquity, but gives the name of 'nature' to both of them, because both are able to represent in exactly the same way 'what was there before'. It is also the reason why the Highlander's attachment to his home continued as one of the most powerful beliefs about him through decades of massive emigration: whatever the evidence, nature must be native, the happier sister must not confuse our sense of home by deciding on her own account to go somewhere else.

Improvement, after all, is itself a specification of the idea of progress. It is not reducible to the application of this or that technique of production; it proposes the systemic and sustainable alteration of the social relations and attitudes of entire communities, consciously based on principles of reason and economic efficiency. This historical self-awareness has two significant consequences. Firstly, in so far as a programme of Improvement is successful, the society which emerges from it is 'artificial': its forms, manners, artefacts and so on do not emerge in theoretically innocent fashion from the texture of its life, but represent the general principles and systematic knowledge of the Improvers. Planned villages – those showpieces of enlightened estate management in the eighteenth-century Highlands[13] – are the type of this departure from the natural: their inhabitants live in someone's *idea* of how they should live. Secondly, Improvement doesn't in principle establish any limits for itself; it's a comparative concept, not an absolute one; it could always be taken further. Its implication is therefore not only that some methods and attitudes need to be changed: it is also proposing change as a way of life. As well as opposing certain customs, it is opposed to custom as such.[14]

In both these respects — the artificiality and the capacity for indefinite transformation — Improvement necessarily designates an Other which is *not* self-conscious but, as Schiller puts it, functions from within itself and exists according to its own laws; and whose time does not open out into an interminably divergent future but is circumscribed by tradition and prejudice — which is, in a word, organic. It's one of the identifiable deformations of the romance that the Highlands are forced into this imaginary role. Within the myth, as we have seen, the Highlands are devoid of indigenous conflict or innovation: the land has no history but exhibits the aspect it wore at the creation; the people, wise but not intelligent, don't reflect on their situation but merely remain true to the traditions of their ancestors. Highlanders are either children who *must*, or non-rational creatures who *cannot*, follow the developmental path of the rest of the nation. In so far as the region is now being either known or transformed, it's because imperial knowledge and power have intervened in the primal unity which obtained from the age of Ossian up until that of General Wade. An interpretive reflex of 'before and after' dominates the reading of every Highland phenomenon from the style of singing to the virtues and failings of domestic servants,[15] to such an extent that it is still difficult to grasp the simplest facts of eighteenth- and nineteenth-century Highland history without automatically having recourse to it.[16]

As far as the Highlands themselves are concerned, this duality is oppressive. By idealising the people of the region as Edenically pre-conscious, it excludes them from participation in their own postlapsarian destiny; all possible arrangements in the real world are equally unworthy of their poetical essence, so their preferences can be ignored. And by equating the indigenous with the archaic, it ensures a metropolitan monopoly on the determination of the future. It would be perverse to deny that the myth has had this crudely ideological function, or that it has served to legitimate the depressing course of Highland history within the UK over the last two centuries — the cultural patronage, the frivolity and neglect, the impoverishment of communities and the misuse of the land. This story is by no means over, and any discourse about the Highlands which continues, today, to naturalise a 'traditional Highland way of life', to make a transhistorical idyll out of pre-clearance Strathnaver or to hymn the moral savour of the golden wine of the Gaidhealtachd,[17] risks complicity with the same techniques of power. At the same time, a mythology which was *merely* an alibi for the local operations of the British state could never have generated the world-wide reverberations and bright colours of the Highland romance. To reread the whole fantastic cultural text in the light of Schiller's universalising dialectic is to discover the general Utopianism which accompanies the specific repressions. To that wider content we must finally turn.

3 COMMUNITY

Towards the end of his book *Imagined Communities*, Benedict Anderson points out, with provocative simplicity, that Marxist accounts of the formation of nations have often been able to explain everything about nationalism except one thing: its effectiveness. People love their native lands much more usually and eloquently than they hate foreigners; a moment's thought convinces us that far more people have died for their country than have killed for it.[18] Even an interpretation which defined all these individuals as dupes would still have to come to terms with the depth of their feelings.

An investigation such as mine incurs a comparable moment of blindness. As Barthes remarks of his own undertaking in *Mythologies*:

> Any myth with some degree of generality is in fact ambiguous, because it represents the very humanity of those who, having nothing, have borrowed it. To decipher the Tour de France or the 'good French Wine' is to cut oneself off from those who are entertained or warmed up by them. The mythologist is condemned to live in a theoretical sociality; for him, to be in society is, at best, to be truthful: his utmost sociality dwells in his utmost morality. His connection with the world is of the order of sarcasm.[19]

The 'generality' of the Highland myth is clearly not so complete as that of nationalism proper. People have not literally died for the Highlands. Nevertheless, if we think of its extremely various devotees — the Englishmen who have been entertained by its rock faces or warmed by the pursuit of its deer; the Lowland Scots university students who feel impelled to learn Gaelic; the piping societies of Nova Scotia; the contemporary Highlanders who know where their ancestors stood in the battle order at Culloden — it's likely that most of them could adopt Schiller's phrase: they find in the Highlands an idea which they love. The authors of nineteenth-century Highland sentimentality, such as Stewart of Garth, Osgood Mackenzie and even Queen Victoria,[20] express a powerful if precious delight in the place which certainly affected landlords' behaviour and must have mitigated on an individual level the disastrous passage of Highland economic history to which they contributed as a class. Behind such semi-indigenous figures stand the countless people who as readers, filmgoers and tourists continue in a more casual way to celebrate the Highland 'idea'. To extrapolate the profile and motivation of the idea is a complex but not very difficult task. But what about the love?

Anderson points out, later in the same chapter, that nationality commands a certain kind of loyalty which is denied to political affiliations because it is not chosen. However constructed or historically belated the nation, the individual's connection to it is given, is anterior to consciousness. Consequently, one's nationality has an inextinguishable aura of naturalness, which is reflected in the way patriotism across the world draws its imagery from kinship (motherland, *patria*, blood) and home (*Heimat*, earth, roots). Membership of this imagined community awakens a sentiment for what Anderson memorably calls 'the beauty of *gemeinschaft*'. Here, as can never be the case in political or occupational collectives held together by shared *reversible* choices, the pains of ontological fragmentation in a capitalist society, with its commodified culture and interminable mediations, are healed in imagination. It's true, of course, that this humanist balm is equally a lubricant of the very machinery which inflicts the pain: not only does it forestall the search for more concrete remedies, but also it serves to stabilise the system's unequal power relations by naturalising individual situations within them. Even so, the sentiment is not exhausted by this ideological function. The anti-systemic potential of national feeling hardly needs to be spelt out.[21]

However, the gift of communal identity, when it is offered by a nation, is always tainted. For the nation is never only the totality of the 'natural' filiations of its nationals. It is also a nation *state*, an entity which doesn't in the least resemble an organism, but is constituted by its role in the global interstate system, by the equilibrium of contending social forces within the territory of its jurisdiction, by the institutional power and cohesion of its bureaucracy, and so on. Its leaders may very likely portray themselves as the immediate representatives of the nation, and this claim is at once formally incontestable (diplomacy rests on it) and palpably a half-truth (at best, their representativeness is validated by a political mechanism). Consequently, there is always a margin by which the actually existing nation fails to realise the 'beauty of *gemeinschaft*' – the word itself, after all, is famously one half of another constitutive pairing.[22] The nation you live in never quite matches up to the one you die for.

It's as the form of this disappointment, so to speak, that the Highlands are lovable. The circumstances of their absorption into British society left them with all the differentiae of nationality and none of those of statehood: they could thus form a theatre in which the imagined community was free to flourish without incurring the tribulations of power. The unrealised possibility of a nation, they held out the image of a community whose cohesion would be purely affective; diffusing, amid the European reality of oppressive and competing states, the fragrance of a truly disinterested patriotism. That the purity is in fact guaranteed by the impossibility of realisation is tacitly acknowledged by the language of the myth, with its insistent elegiac note, its 'fondly lingering'[23] over what must pass. The pathos of its own illusoriness is the condition of the myth's universality: its appeal extends beyond its local object because it encodes a paradoxical nostalgia for a homeland which no one ever had, but which everyone has been promised.

This grain of Utopianism, wrapped up in bales of tartan, is the secret of the myth's enchantment. For example

> From the lone shieling of the misty island
>   Mountains divide us, and the waste of seas –
> Yet still the blood is strong, the heart is Highland,
>   And we in dreams behold the Hebrides.

These much-quoted lines, affecting like cheap music, owe their resonance (acoustic virtuosity apart) to a particular conjunction: they take a historically actual grief – some Highland communities, though by no means all, really did go reluctant and weeping to the emigrant ships[24] – and make it generally available by the systematic use of the definite article. Consider, for example, how much less suggestive the third line would be with the more obvious 'our'. So that the last line invites the reader into its plural subject: even if I have visited the Hebrides and found them charmless, I am not encouraged to bring that experience to bear on the reading, but rather to accept the word as simply a beautiful name for what we see in dreams. As a possible but denied wholeness of life, the Highlands accept in a lavish geographical embrace all the lost homes, everything that isn't, in the end, what it once had a right to turn out as.

The insubstantiality of Highland 'nationhood', its exceptionally pure subjectivity, is the condition of this general availability. The very emptiness of the projected home creates a space for identification. It's thus appropriate, if not inevitable, that the poem is a cross-cultural fake. Presented in 1829 as a translation of a Canadian Gaelic rowing song, it was almost certainly written in the offices of *Blackwoods Magazine* by D.M. Moir and J.G. Lockhart.[25] Exactly as in the more spectacular case of Macpherson, the Highland imagery's openness to appropriation is the outcome of a *rapprochement* between naive ethnicity and sentimental universality which is ultimately fraudulent.

Cultural criticism finds itself on familiar ground at this point. The potency of the Highland myth comes down to this: that in it the vague transcendental values of bourgeois humanism acquire the charm and definition of a particular place and time, a historically actual community. A better known instance of this magic, this marriage of the linguistically specific and the universally human to create a richly significant and politically uncontradictory vision of life, is Literature. In the institutions and academies of Literature, as if in the peripheral fastnesses of a cultural Highlands, this moralised sensuousness is preserved on terms which ensure at once its isolation from and its subordination to the discourses of power. It's a component of the Highland romance as well as an analogy. Poetry permeated the myth at every level: it was a central activity of the imagined society; it was the most important medium of the elaboration and diffusion of the myth itself; and, in a curious conflation of the other two, it was a general characteristic of the image of Highland life, conceived of as a landscape and people inherently 'poetical'. The process as a whole could be called the *literarisation* of the Highlands: the region was admitted to the privileges, and condemned to the marginality, of fiction. It thus offers to catch the student of its forms in a bind rather like the one which confronts us in the case of the literary. Seeing the myth's implicit colonialism, its co-option by militarism and rapacity, and the vulgarity and duplicity of its products from the confections of Macpherson to the shop windows of the contemporary Royal Mile, we reach reflexively for the hatchet of the demystifier. We pause on reflecting that the possibility which the myth cherishes and deforms — that beyond the complementary abstractions of Improvement and romance we could discover an authentic way of living together — is not yet conclusively either discredited or achieved.

Notes and References

Some of the primary works referred to were published anonymously. To simplify reference, I have automatically and silently adopted attributions from the catalogues of the British Library and the National Library of Scotland. Throughout the notes, the place of publication is London unless otherwise stated.

1 INTRODUCTION

1. Edward Burt, *Letters from a Gentleman in the North of Scotland*, 2 vols. (1754), vol. II, p. 10.
2. Roland Barthes, *Mythologies*, selected and translated by Annette Lavers, paperback edn (St Albans, 1973), p. 119.
3. The phrase is from Scott's 1830 introduction to the poem in *The Poetical Works of Walter Scott*, ed. J. L. Robertson (1894), p. 274. It echoes a phrase in Francis Jeffrey's review of the poem, *Edinburgh Review*, vol. 16 (1810), p. 280.
4. A. J. Youngson, *After the Forty-Five: The Economic Impact on the Scottish Highlands* (Edinburgh, 1973), especially pp. 47–100.
5. As I write this introduction, I notice the same point made by Raphael Samuel with reference to the blossoming of the 'heritage industry' in the dehistoricising wasteland of Thatcherism. See his 'Review of Robert Hewison's *The Heritage Industry*', *Guardian*, 9 October 1987. For 'Improvement' read privatisation; for the Highlands substitute, say, those working-class continuities which state power represses and then preserves (as leisure consumption goods) in industrial museums and theme parks. The past is not effaced but appropriated, dematerialised and rendered as décor in a romanticising process which is sometimes called Laura-Ashleyfication.

2 CONVERTING THE UNCOUTH SAVAGE

1. *Monthly Review*, vol. 11 (1754), p. 343.
2. William Cobbett, *The Parliamentary History of England*, 36 vols. (1806–20), vol. XIV (1813), p. 50.
3. In practice, the dominant force in Highland and Island education was the SSPCK, whose directors were consistently opposed to Gaelic from the Society's incorporation in 1709 until a change of policy in 1766. See V. E. Durkacz, *The Decline of the Celtic Languages* (Edinburgh, 1983), pp. 47–69.

4. 25 Geo. II C. 41, clause 14.
5. This paragraph is abstracted from Duncan Forbes, 'Some Thoughts Concerning the State of the Highlands of Scotland', (1746), *Culloden Papers* (1815), pp. 297–301; Andrew Fletcher, 'Proposals for Civilising the Highlands', (1747), C. S. Terry (ed.), *Albermarle Papers*, 2 vols. (Aberdeen, 1902), vol. II, pp. 480–91; 'Extracts from a MS in the possession of the Gartmore Family', (1747), in Edward Burt, *Letters from a Gentleman in the North of Scotland*, 5th edn, ed. R. Jamieson, 2 vols. (1818), vol. II, pp. 338–70; *A Second Letter to a Noble Lord, Containing a Plan for effectually uniting and sincerely attaching the Highlanders to the British Constitution* (1748); Andrew Lang (ed.), *The Highlands of Scotland in 1750* (1898); speeches in support of the Annexing Act, *Parliamentary History*, vol. XIV, pp. 1249ff.
6. See H. T. Dickinson, *Liberty and Property: Political Ideology in Eighteenth-Century Britain* (1977).
7. Lang, *The Highlands of Scotland in 1750*, p. 82.
8. *Culloden Papers*, p. 301.
9. Burt, *Letters*, vol. II, p. 340.
10. Joseph Mitchell, *The Highland Fair; or, the Union of the Clans* (1731), p. 4.
11. Mitchell, *The Highland Fair*, p. 39.
12. Lang, *The Highlands of Scotland in 1750*, p. 145.
13. Daniel Defoe, letter to Lord Harley, quoted in R. N. Salaman, *The History and Social Influence of the Potato* (Cambridge, 1949), p. 353.
14. Edward Burt, *Letters from a Gentleman in the North of Scotland*, 2 vols. (1754), vol. II, pp. 281–2.
15. Mrs Hughes of Uffington, *Letters and Recollections of Sir Walter Scott*, ed. H. G. Hutchinson, (n.d.), p. 331.
16. Tobias Smollett, *Miscellaneous Works*, ed. R. Anderson, 3rd edn, 6 vols. (Edinburgh, 1806), vol. III, p. 460.
17. See W. Donaldson, 'Bonny Highland Laddie: the Making of a Myth', *Scottish Literary Journal*, vol. 3 (2), (1976), pp. 30–50.
18. C. C. Grant, 'Highland–English as Found in Books', *Transactions of the Gaelic Society of Inverness*, vol. 15 (1888–9), pp. 172–88.
19. G. MacGregor (ed.), *Collected Writings of Dougal Graham*, 2 vols. (Glasgow, 1883), vol. I, pp. 257–73.
20. James Boswell, *Life of Johnson*, ed. R. W. Chapman, corrected by J. D. Fleeman (1970), p. 443.
21. Burt, *Letters* (1818), p. 344.
22. E. B., *The Highland Rogue* (1723); for Wade, see Burt, *Letters* (1818), vol. II, pp. 272–3.
23. Lang, *The Highlands of Scotland in 1750*, p. 82.
24. William Gilpin, *Observations, Relative Chiefly to Picturesque Beauty, Made in the Year 1776 on Several Parts of Great Britain; Particularly the High-lands of Scotland*, 2nd edn, 2 vols. (1792), vol. I, pp. 211–13.
25. T. C. Smout, *A History of the Scottish People, 1560–1830*, paperback edn (1972), pp. 321–3.
26. J. Kinsley (ed.), *The Poems and Songs of Robert Burns*, 3 vols. (Oxford, 1968), no. 580. Future references to Burns's poems will identify them simply by their 'Kinsley numbers'.

Notes 183

27. W. Donaldson, 'Bonny Highland Laddie'.
28. 'My Love was born in Aberdeen' and 'Liza Baillie', in Thomas Crawford (ed.), *Love, Labour and Liberty: the Eighteenth Century Scottish Lyric* (1976), p. 129.
29. See Walter Scott, *Rob Roy*, Border edn, 2 vols. (1893), vol. I, pp. cxi–cxii.
30. Kinsley no. 84.
31. Lang, *The Highlands of Scotland in 1750*, p. 6.
32. *The Gentleman's Magazine*, vol. 16 (1746), p. 261.
33. Thomas Newte, *Prospects and Observations on a Tour in England and Scotland* (1791), p. 227.
34. William Cleland, *A Collection of Several Poems and Verses* (1697), p. 35.
35. *The Highlander Delineated; or, The Character, Customs and Manners of the Highlanders* (1745), p. 14, where the verses are said to be 'entitled, The HIGHLANDER', and to have been 'writ near fifty years ago'.
36. James Ray, *A Compleat History of the Rebellion*, 2nd edn (1760), p. 347.
37. Daniel Defoe, *The True-Born Englishman* (1701), p. 17.
38. The greatest literary embodiment of the type is Sir Pertinax MacSycophant in Charles Macklin, *The Man of the World*, first published in 1764, London première in 1781, reprinted in *Four Comedies by Charles Macklin*, ed. J. O. Bartley (1968). MacSycophant is a wholly Lowland figure.
39. John Cleveland, *Poems* (Oxford, 1967), p. 29.
40. In *The Reprisal*, Smollett, *Miscellaneous Works*, vol. III, pp. 455–86.
41. Cobbett, *Parliamentary History*, vol. XIV, p. 9. The letter to *Old England* is reprinted in *The Thistle: a Dispassionate Examine of the Prejudices of Englishmen in general to the Scotch Nation* (1747); see pp. 43, 46.
42. Quoted in K. G. Feiling, *The Second Tory Party 1714–1832* (1938), p. 50.
43. Background in G. Nobbe, *The North Briton: A Study in Political Propaganda* (New York, 1939); see also John Brewer, 'The Earl of Bute', in H. Van Thal (ed.), *The Prime Ministers*, 2 vols. (1974), vol. I, pp. 103–13; and Bruce Lenman, *Integration, Enlightenment and Industrialisation: Scotland, 1746–1832* (1981), pp. 39–42.
44. *The North Briton*, reprinted in 3 vols. (1763), vol. I, p. 14.
45. *North Briton*, vol. I, p. 16; vol. II, p. 7.
46. *North Briton*, vol. I, pp. 47–8.
47. *The British Antidote to Caledonian Poison: Containing fifty-three Anti-ministerial . . . Prints, for those remarkable Years 1762, and 1763*, 7th edn, 2 vols. (n.d.), and *The Scots Scourge: being a Compleat Supplement to the British Antidote to Caledonian Poison*, 6th edn, 2 vols. (n.d.).
48. *Monthly Review*, vol. 28 (1763), p. 316.
49. Richard Cumberland, *The Fashionable Lover* (1772), p. 2.
50. Cumberland, *Fashionable Lover*, pp. 43, 63.
51. 'Scotch Myths', exhibition, St Andrews and Edinburgh, 1981, and film for Channel 4, 1983, both written and directed by Murray Grigor.
52. William Camden, *Britannia*, translated, revised and expanded by Edmund Gibson, 1695, facsimile edn (Newton Abbot, 1971), p. 926.

53. Andrew Henderson, *The History of the Rebellion* (Edinburgh, 1748), p. 147.
54. Ray, *Compleat History*, p. 354.
55. John Pinkerton, *An Enquiry into the History of Scotland*, 2 vols. (1790), vol. I, p. 340.
56. William Robertson, *A Sermon preached before the Society in Scotland for Promoting Christian Knowledge, Monday January 6, 1755*, 3rd edn (Edinburgh, 1759), p. 39.
57. See R. L. Meek, *Social Science and the Ignoble Savage* (Cambridge, 1976), pp. 107ff.
58. Paper reproduced from *The Craftsman*, in *Scots Magazine*, vol. 8 (1746), pp. 532–3.
59. James Steuart, *An Inquiry into the Principles of Political Oeconomy*, ed. A. S. Skinner (1966), p. 106.
60. Adam Smith, *Lectures on Jurisprudence*, ed. R. L. Meek, D. D. Raphael and P. G. Stein (Oxford, 1978), p. 224.
61. Hugh Blair, 'A Critical Dissertation on the Poems of Ossian, the Son of Fingal', in James Macpherson, *The Works of Ossian*, 3rd edn, 2 vols. (1765), vol. II, pp. 313–443 (p. 350).
62. Burt, *Letters* (1754), vol. II, pp. 92, 95, 103.
63. Samuel Johnson, *Journey*, in *Johnson's Journey to the Western Islands of Scotland and Boswell's Journal of a Tour to the Hebrides with Samuel Johnson, LL.D.*, ed. R. W. Chapman, Oxford Standard Authors (1930), p. 77. This is my edition, throughout, for both the texts it includes. Johnson's *Journey* was originally published in 1775, and Boswell's *Journal* in 1786.
64. Adam Smith, *An Inquiry into the Nature and Causes of the Wealth of Nations*, ed. R. H. Campbell, A. Skinner and W. B. Todd, 2 vols. (Oxford, 1976), vol. I, pp. 416–17.
65. Thomas Douglas, Earl of Selkirk, *Observations on the Present State of the Highlands of Scotland* (1805), pp. 12–19.

3 WARRIORS

1. James Ray, *A Compleat History of the Rebellion*, 2nd edn (1760), p. vii.
2. Alexander Cunningham, *History of Great Britain from the Revolution in 1688 to the accession of George the First*, translated from the Latin (1787), quoted in Thomas Newte, *Prospects and Observations on a Tour in England and Scotland* (1791), pp. 266–70.
3. Sir John Dalrymple, *Memoirs of Great Britain and Ireland*, 2nd edn, 3 vols. (1790), vol. II, part II, pp. 77–81.
4. Thomas Pennant, *A Tour in Scotland MDCCLXIX*, 2nd edn (1772), p. 176. The relevant chapter in Gibbon is the 26th, which appeared in 1781. Pennant made two journeys in Scotland, in 1769 and 1772, and his accounts of them were first published in Chester in 1771 and 1774 respectively. However, they were and are much more widely available in their grander London editions, and these are what I have used: that is, *A Tour in Scotland MDCCLXIX*, 2nd edn (1772),

referred to from now on as 'Pennant, 1769', and *A Tour in Scotland and Voyage to the Hebrides: MDCCLXXII*, 2nd edn, 2 vols. (1776), referred to as 'Pennant, 1772'.
5. *Gentleman's Magazine*, vol. 16 (1746), p. 153.
6. The phrase is from a poem celebrating the opening of Wade's bridge over the Tay at Aberfeldy. Alexander Robertson, *The History and Martial Achievements of the Robertsons of Strowan* (Edinburgh, 1785), part 2, p. 17.
7. David Stewart of Garth, *Sketches of the Character, Manners, and Present State of the Highlanders of Scotland*, 2 vols. (Edinburgh, 1822), vol. I, p. 278.
8. Tobias Smollett, *Miscellaneous Works*, ed. R. Anderson, 3rd edn, 6 vols. (Edinburgh, 1806), vol. III, pp. 455–86.
9. Samuel Johnson, *Journey*, in *Johnson's Journey to the Western Islands of Scotland and Boswell's Journey of a Tour to the Hebrides with Samuel Johnson, LL.D.*, ed. R. W. Chapman, Oxford Standard Authors (1930), p. 89. For an anthology of the stories, see Stewart, *Sketches of the Highlanders*, vol. I, pp. 294–360 and vol. II, pp. 18–35.
10. Charles Macklin, *Love à la Mode*, in *Four Comedies by Charles Macklin*, ed. J. O. Bartley (1968), p. 57.
11. *Scots Magazine*, vol. 24 (1762), p. 701.
12. John Knox, *A View of the British Empire*, 3rd edn, 2 vols. (1785), vol. I, p. 134.
13. *Scots Magazine*, vol. 24 (1762), p. 604.
14. John Langhorne, *Poetical Works*, 2 vols. (1804), vol. I, pp. 51–64.
15. Pitt's own phrase. See Basil Williams, *The Life of William Pitt, Earl of Chatham*, 2 vols. (1913), vol. I, p. 294.
16. See John Prebble, *Mutiny: Highland Regiments in Revolt 1743–1804*, paperback edn (Harmondsworth, 1977), pp. 95–100.
17. Quoted in Williams, *Life of Pitt*, vol. II, p. 189.
18. The phrase is the title of an immense collection of materials relating to the Forty-five, compiled in the years following by Robert Forbes. His lion is of course that of the Scottish royal standard.
19. Details, somewhat inaccurate, in Stewart, *Sketches of the Highlanders*, vol. I, p. 360.
20. The words were first published in 1765, and much reprinted. This is the text of David Herd, *Ancient and Modern Scottish Songs, Heroic Ballads, Etc*, 2 vols. (Edinburgh, 1776), vol. I, p. 116.
21. J. H. Plumb, *England in the Eighteenth Century* (Harmondsworth, 1950), p. 115.
22. Pennant, *1769*, p. 174.
23. Knox, *View of the British Empire*, vol. I, p. 133.
24. Archibald Maclaren, *The Highland Drover; or, Domhnul Dubh M'Na-Beinn at Carlisle* (Greenock, 1790), p. 18.
25. Johnson, *Journey*, pp. 39–40.
26. *The History of the Feuds and Conflicts among the Clans*, originally published Glasgow, 1764; reprinted 1780 and 1818 (Stirling, 1907).
27. William Gilpin, *Observations, Relative Chiefly to Picturesque Beauty*,

Made in the Year 1776 on Several Parts of Great Britain; Particularly the High-lands of Scotland, 2nd edn (1792), vol. I, pp. 189–206.
28. Charles Burlington, *The Modern Universal British Traveller* (1779), p. 773.
29. Dalrymple, *Memoirs of Great Britain*, vol. II, p. 88.
30. See Stewart, *Sketches*, vol. I, pp. 391–5.
31. Luke Booker, *The Highlanders, A Poem* (Stourbridge, 1787), p. 25.
32. David Carey, *Craig Phadric, Visions of Sensibility, with Legendary Tales, and Occasional Pieces* (Inverness, 1811), p. 34.
33. Alexander Campbell, *The Grampians Desolate: a Poem* (Edinburgh, 1804), p. 19.
34. Burlington, *British Traveller*, p. 772.
35. Gilpin, *Observations*, vol. I, pp. 190, 135–7, 125, 139.
36. Johnson, *Journey*, p. 249.
37. Anne Grant, *Letters from the Mountains; being the real Correspondence of a lady, between the years 1773 and 1807*, 4th edn, 3 vols. (1809), vol. I, p. 10. Anne Grant (1755–1838) is the period's most articulate example of a Highlander of sentiment. Brought up in Glasgow and North America, she moved in 1773 to the Highlands with her parents, who both had family connections there, and in 1779 she married John Grant, the Minister of Laggan on Speyside. In 1801 he died and Mrs Grant, in serious financial straits, began to publish her writings, including her poems in 1803, the first edition of her letters in 1806, and in 1811 a book of essays on Highland life. On the success of these she became something of a literary celebrity in Edinburgh as an exponent of the Highland romance.
38. This is not the Rob Roy of Wordsworth and Scott, but his son, Robin Oig.
39. Campbell, *The Grampians Desolate*, pp. 158–60.
40. R. Colvill, *The Caledonians: A Poem* (Edinburgh, 1779), p. 10.
41. Johnson, *Journey*, p. 41.
42. Adam Ferguson, *An Essay on the History of Civil Society*, ed. Duncan Forbes (Edinburgh, 1966), p. 101.
43. In the introduction to Ferguson, *Essay*, pp. xxxviii–xl.
44. Sir William Temple, *Five Miscellaneous Essays*, ed. S. H. Monk (Ann Arbor, Michigan, 1963), pp. 98–172.
45. A. Macdonald, *Alexis; or, the Young Adventurer. A Novel* (1746).
46. John Campbell, *A Full and Particular Description of the Highlands of Scotland* (1752), p. 17.
47. Printed in Pennant, *1772*, vol. II, p. 428.
48. G. Wallace, *Prospects from Hills in Fife* (Edinburgh, 1796), p. 45.
49. J. G. Lockhart, *Peter's Letters to His Kinsfolk*, '3rd edn' (in fact the second), 3 vols. (1819), vol. I, pp. 236–9.
50. See for example Robert Burns, 'Comin' o'er the Hills o' Coupar' and 'Had I the Wyte' in *The Poems and Songs of Robert Burns*, ed. J. Kinsley, 3 vols. (Oxford, 1968), nos. 177, 559. Future references to Burns's poems will identify them simply by their 'Kinsley numbers'.
51. Adam Smith, *An Inquiry into the Nature and Causes of the Wealth of*

Nations, ed. R. H. Campbell, A. Skinner and W. B. Todd, 2 vols. (Oxford, 1976), vol. II, p. 787.
52. Ferguson, *Essay*, p. 231.
53. A. Allardyce (ed.), *Scotland and Scotsmen in the Eighteenth Century, edited from the MSS of John Ramsay, Esq. of Ochtertyre*, 2 vols. (Edinburgh, 1888), vol. II, p. 408.
54. Johnson, *Journey*, p. 82.
55. Ferguson, *Essay*, p. 219.
56. Ferguson, *Essay*, p. 227.
57. Ferguson, *Essay*, p. 228.
58. It does not say so, but the point was immediately taken by sympathetic readers, who wrote of its weaning people from selfishness, or diffusing a Spartan spirit. See Ferguson, *Essay*, p. xxvii.
59. Grant, *Letters from the Mountains*, vol. I, p. 22.
60. Donald McNicol, *Remarks on Dr Samuel Johnson's Journey to the Hebrides* (1779), p. 293.
61. Anne Grant, *Essays on the Superstitions of the Highlands of Scotland*, 2 vols. (1811), vol. II, p. 143.
62. Sir John Sinclair, *An Account of the Highland Society of London* (1813), p. 5.
63. See J. Barron, *The Northern Highlands in the Nineteenth Century*, 3 vols. (Inverness, 1903–13), vol. I, p. 88.
64. Grant, *Essays*, vol. II, p. 145.
65. Quoted in Joseph Mitchell, *Reminiscences of My Life in the Highlands*, 2 vols. (1883–4), vol. I, p. 22.
66. Thomas Douglas, Earl of Selkirk, *Observations on the Present State of the Highlands of Scotland* (1805), pp. 60–74.
67. 'Amicus', *Eight Letters on the Subject of the Earl of Selkirk's Pamphlet on Highland Emigration* (Edinburgh, 1806), p. 27.
68. E.g. James Hogg's 'Donald McDonald', printed in his *Selected Poems*, ed. D. S. Mack (Oxford, 1970), p. 111.
69. D. B. Horn, 'George IV and Highland Dress', *Scottish Historical Review*, vol. 47 (1968), pp. 209–10.
70. Sir John Sinclair, *Observations on the Propriety of Preserving the ... Customs of the Ancient Inhabitants of Scotland* (1804), p. 15.
71. Mrs A. McDonald, *Evening Amusements, or, What Happens in Life, A Novel*, 2 vols. (Edinburgh, 1797), vol. I, p. 149.
72. *Fatal Follies; or, the History of the Countess of Stanmore*, 4 vols. (1788), vol. II, p. 22.
73. Johnson, *Journey*, p. 329.
74. I. G. Lindsay and M. Cosh, *Inveraray and the Dukes of Argyll* (Edinburgh, 1973), p. 200.
75. See J. Telfer Dunbar, *History of Highland Dress* (1962), p. 13.
76. Grant, *Letters from the Mountains*, vol. II, p. 227.
77. *Remarks on the People and Government of Scotland* (Edinburgh, 1747), p. 21.
78. Letter printed in C. R. Fay, *Adam Smith and the Scotland of his Day* (Cambridge, 1956), pp. 11–14.

Notes

79. Quoted in J. M. Bumsted, *The People's Clearance: Highland Emigration to British North America 1770–1815* (Edinburgh and Winnipeg, 1982), p. 83.
80. Pennant, *1772*, vol. II, p. 39; vol. I, p. 252.
81. Pennant, *1772*, vol. I, pp. 421–8.
82. John O'Keeffe, *A New Comic Opera, called the Highland Reel* (1790), p. 42.
83. Campbell, *The Grampians Desolate*, p. 27.
84. In *The Life and Songs of the Baroness Nairne*, ed. Revd C. Rogers (1849), the editor's introduction relates how the poet's father was congratulated on his unbending Jacobite principles by 'the Elector of Hanover'. Another such tale provided the germ of Sir Walter Scott's novel *Redgauntlet* (1824), which also represents the predicament of *real* Jacobitism in the new context.
85. Johnson, *Journey*, p. 294.
86. From 'Bauldy Fraser', James Hogg, *The Forest Minstrel* (Edinburgh, 1810), p. 166.
87. From 'Donald McDonald', Hogg, *Selected Poems*, p. 111.
88. Sir Alexander Boswell, 'On the Fidelity of the Highlanders in the Rebellion 1745–6', in his *Songs, Chiefly in the Scottish Dialect* (Edinburgh, 1803), p. 23.
89. 'A Birth-day Ode. December 31st 1787' (Kinsley no. 189).
90. 'O'er the Water' (Kinsley no. 211).
91. 'Orananaoig, or, The Song of death' (Kinsley no. 330).
92. C. I. Johnstone, *Clan-Albin: A National Tale*, 4 vols. (Edinburgh, 1815).
93. Walter Scott, *The Letters of Sir Walter Scott*, ed. H. J. C. Grierson, 12 vols. (1932–7), vol. II, p. 76 (20 June 1808).
94. Scott, *Letters*, vol. II, p. 159 (31 January 1809).
95. Scott, *Letters*, vol. II, p. 95 (14 October 1808).
96. Scott, *Letters*, vol. II, p. 75 (20 June 1808).
97. Scott, *Letters*, vol. II, pp. 120–3 (2 November 1808).
98. The 'Albinnich' is an ancient name for the Gaelic inhabitants of Scotland, given, for example, in William Camden's *Britannia* (translated, revised and expanded by Edmund Gibson, 1695, facsimile edn (Newton Abbot, 1971)). Both Clan-Alpine and Clan-Albin thus offer to represent the Gaeltacht in general. As for the influence of Scott's poem, one striking piece of evidence is a masquerade in C. I. Johnstone's previous novel, *The Saxon and the Gael* (4 vols. (Edinburgh, 1814), vol. II, pp. 52–9), which assumes the reader's familiarity with the *Lady*, and is otherwise incomprehensible.
99. Walter Scott, *The Lady of the Lake*, text and notes in *The Poetical Works of Walter Scott*, ed. J. L. Robertson (1894), pp. 207–312, Canto V, stanzas ix–x.
100. Tom Dibdin, *The Lady of the Lake, A Romantic Drama, in Three Acts* (n.d., but premièred 1810); T. Morton, *The Knight of Snowdoun; A Musical Drama* (1811); E. J. Eyre, *The Lady of the Lake: A Melo-Dramatic Romance, in Three Acts* (1811).
101. For example in Edward Burt, *Letters from a Gentleman in the North of*

Notes

Scotland, 2 vols. (1754), vol. II, p. 96; and A. Allardyce (ed.), *Scotland and Scotsmen in the Eighteenth Century, edited from the MSS of John Ramsay, Esq. of Ochtertyre*, 2 vols. (Edinburgh, 1888), vol. II, pp. 392–5.
102. William Robertson, *History of Scotland*, in *Works*, 8 vols. (1840), vol. I, p. 23.
103. J. G. Lockhart, *Memoirs of the Life of Sir Walter Scott*, edn in 10 vols. (Edinburgh, 1882), vol. III, p. 327.
104. Scott, *The Lady of the Lake*, Canto V, stanza xxxii.
105. J. S. Watson, *The Reign of George III 1760–1815* (Oxford, 1960), pp. 476–87.

4 THE LAND

1. L. Timperley, 'The Pattern of Landholding in Eighteenth-Century Scotland', in M.L. Parry and T.R. Slater (eds), *The Making of the Scottish Countryside*, (1980), pp. 137–54 (pp. 137–9).
2. See Christopher Hussey, *The Picturesque: Studies in a Point of View* (1927).
3. Henry Home, Lord Kames, *Elements of Criticism*, 2nd edn, 3 vols. (Edinburgh, 1763), vol. I, p. 311.
4. Kames, *Elements of Criticism*, vol. I , p. 381n.
5. Thomas Pennant, *A Tour in Scotland MDCCLXIX*, 2nd edn (1772), p. 89. And see John Knox, *A Tour through the Highlands of Scotland and the Hebride Isles in 1786* (1787), p. 9.
6. Gilpin, for instance, says that 'this lake has ever been esteemed one of the most celebrated scenes in Scotland' (William Gilpin, *Observations, Relative Chiefly to Picturesque Beauty, Made in the Year 1776 on Several Parts of Great Britain; Particularly the High-Lands of Scotland*, 2nd edn, 2 vols. (1792), vol. II, p. 15).
7. Sir William Burrell, 'Cursory Observations', 1758, National Library of Scotland, MS 2911, fo. 20.
8. Tobias Smollett, *The Expedition of Humphry Clinker*, ed. L.M. Knapp (1966), p. 248.
9. Pennant, *1769*, pp. 205–6.
10. 'Verses Wrote at an Inn', *Weekly Magazine*, vol. 37 (1777), p. 137.
11. Charles Ross, *The Traveller's Guide to Lochlomond, and its Environs* (Paisley, 1792).
12. Thomas Newte, *Prospects and Observations On a Tour in England and Scotland* (1791), p. 75
13. Rather loosely based on Longinus, and authoritatively described in S.H. Monk, *The Sublime: A Study of Critical Theories in XVIII-Century England* (1935).
14. The views Pennant admires usually have this closed character – most articulately perhaps at Inverness, where mountains form a background to the plain 'as if created as guards to the rest of the island from the fury of the boisterous north' (Pennant, *1769*, p. 148).
15. M.H. Nicolson, *Mountain Gloom and Mountain Glory: the Development of the Aesthetics of the Infinite* (New York, 1958), pp. 184–270.

16. William Derham, *Physico-Theology; or, A Demonstration of the Being and Attributes of God, from His Works of Creation* (1713), Book III, Chapter 4; cited in Gilpin, *Observations*, vol. II, p. 121n.
17. James Thomson, *The Seasons*, ed. J. Sambrook (Oxford, 1981). 'Autumn', lines 834–5.
18. John Cririe, *Scottish Scenery; or, Sketches in Verse* (1803), p. 73.
19. The traveller is instructed to do this by Mrs. S. Murray, *A Companion and Useful Guide to the Beauties of Scotland*, 2 vols. (1799, 1803), vol. I, p. 89.
20. Gilpin, *Observations*, vol. II, pp. 19–22.
21. Gilpin, *Observations*, vol. II, pp. 129–32.
22. Thomas Pennant, *A Tour in Scotland and Voyage to the Hebrides: MDCCLXXII*, 2nd edn, 2 vols. (1776), vol. I, p. 378.
23. Gilpin, *Observations*, vol. I, p. 154.
24. Charles Cordiner, *Antiquities and Scenery of the North of Scotland* (1780), p. 23
25. Robert Burns, 'The Humble Petition of Bruar Water', in *The Poems and Songs of Robert Burns*, ed. J. Kinsley, 3 vols. (Oxford, 1968), no. 172. Future references to Burns's poems will identify them simply by their 'Kinsley numbers'.
26. R.L. Brown, *Robert Burns's Tours of the Highlands and Stirlingshire 1787* (Ipswich, 1973), p. 171.
27. John Murray, 4th Duke of Atholl (1755–1830). See *Dictionary of National Biography*.
28. See Dorothy Wordsworth, *Recollections of a Tour Made in Scotland A.D. 1803*, ed. J.C. Shairp, reprint of 3rd edn (Edinburgh, 1974), p. 201.
29. For example, Samuel Johnson, *Journey*, in *Johnson's Journey to the Western Islands of Scotland and Boswell's Journal of a Tour to the Hebrides with Samuel Johnson, LL.D.*, ed. R.W. Chapman, Oxford Standard Authors (1930), pp. 126–7.
30. Cririe, *Scottish Scenery*, p. 54.
31. Gilpin, *Observations*, vol. I, p. 179.
32. Gilpin, *Observations*, vol. II, p. 112.
33. Gilpin, *Observations*, vol. I, p. 122.
34. Daniel Defoe, *Caledonia: A Poem in Honour of Scotland* (Edinburgh, 1706), p. 8.
35. Thomson, *The Seasons*, 'Autumn', ll. 919–28.
36. Virgil, *Georgics*, Book I, l. 30.
37. Antiquarians were curious about where Thule was. John o' Groats is canvassed in Pennant, *1769*, p. 196; Barra in John L. Buchanan, *A Defence of the Scots Highlanders* (1794), p. 99; other possibilities in, for example, William Camden, *Britannia* (translated, revised and expanded by Edmund Gibson, 1695, facsimile edn (Newton Abbot, 1971)), pp. 1073–88.
38. Knox, *Tour*, pp. 27, 32.
39. Defoe, *Caledonia*, p. 15.
40. Knox, *Tour*, pp. 263–5.
41. Defoe, *Caledonia*, p. 11.

Notes

42. Aaron Hill, 'To the Editor of Albania, a Poem', in John Leyden (ed.), *Scotish Descriptive Poems* (Edinburgh, 1803), p. 147.
43. D.B. Horn, 'Natural Philosophy and Mountaineering in Scotland, 1750–1850', *Scottish Studies*, vol. 7 (1963), pp. 1–17.
44. William Parsons, 'Verses written in the Island of Staffa, August 6, 1787', *European Magazine*, vol. 21 (1792), p. 309.
45. G. Wallace, *Prospects from Hills in Fife* (Edinburgh, 1796), p. 44.
46. Mr Dyer, 'Description of Dunkeld', *Scots Magazine*, vol. 60 (1798), pp. 346–9.
47. Pennant, *1772*, vol. I p. 398.
48. See Plate 4a.
49. For example, Pennant, *1772*, vol. I p. 247; Knox, *Tour*, p. 220.
50. John Walker, *Report on the Hebrides of 1764 and 1771*, ed. M.M. McKay (Edinburgh, 1980), p. 33; William Marshall, *General View of the Agriculture of the Central Highlands of Scotland* (1794), p. 52.
51. Johnson, *Journey*, p. 34.
52. Charles Churchill, 'The Prophecy of Famine', in *The Poetical Works of Charles Churchill*, ed. D. Grant (Oxford, 1956), pp. 193–210, lines 295–310
53. John Cleveland, *Poems*, (Oxford, 1967) p. 29.
54. Churchill, 'Prophecy of Famine', lines 327–8
55. D.W. Jefferson, ' "Satirical Landscape": Churchill and Crabbe', *Yearbook of English Studies*, vol. (1976), pp. 92–100.
56. Churchill, 'Prophecy of Famine', lines 275–8.
57. Churchill, 'Prophecy of Famine', lines 12–14.
58. Anthony Champion, 'From a Traveller in Wales to a Friend Travelling in Scotland, August 1772', in his *Miscellanies in Verse and Prose* (1801), pp. 80–1.
59. The source of the cliché is James Thomson's *The Castle of Indolence*, Canto I, stanza xxxviii.
60. Untitled verses in J. Elphinston, *Forty Years' Correspondence*, 8 vols. (1791–4), vol. VI, p. 208. The spelling is distractingly reformed in the original; I have restored the usual imperfections. The author is perhaps Lady Louisa Stuart, who was born in 1757. If so, she has for her retort to Churchill the ulterior motive of being Bute's daughter.
61. Gilpin, *Observations*, vol. I, p. 171
62. James Beattie, *Essays on Poetry and Music*, 3rd edn (1779), p. 169; quoted by Gilpin, *Observations*, vol. II, p. 133.
63. Mary Anne Hanway, *A Journey to the Highlands of Scotland* ([1776]), p. 78
64. Cordiner, *Antiquities and Scenery*, p. 104; Pennant, *1769*, p. 103.
65. R. Blunt (ed.), *Mrs. Montagu, 'Queen of the Blues', her letters and friendships 1762–1800*, edited by R. Blunt, 2 vols. (1923), vol. I, p. 147.
66. Quoted in I.S. Ross, 'A Bluestocking Over the Border: Mrs Elizabeth Montagu's Aesthetic Adventures in Scotland, 1766', *Huntington Library Quarterly*, vol. 28 (1965), pp. 213–33 (p. 224).
67. Hugh Blair, 'A Critical Dissertation on the Poems Ossian, the Son of Fingal', in James Macpherson, *The Works of Ossian*, 3rd edn, 2 vols. (1765), vol. II, pp. 313–443 (p. 410).

68. Malcolm Laing (ed.), *The Poems of Ossian, &c.; containing the Poetical Works of James Macpherson, Esq. in Prose and Rhyme*, 2 vols. (Edinburgh, 1805), vol. I, p. 193. All references to Macpherson's poetical works are to this, the most readily available edition, which is referred to from now on as 'Laing'. Macpherson, *The Works of Ossian*, is used only for the dissertations by Blair and by Macpherson himself, which Laing does not reproduce.
69. Macpherson, *Works of Ossian*, vol. II, p. 349.
70. Laing, vol. I, p. 240.
71. Laing, vol. II, p. 396.
72. Edmund Burke, *A Philosophical Enquiry into the Origin of our Ideas of the Sublime and Beautiful*, ed. J.T. Boulton (1958), pp. 8 and 51.
73. Burke, *Enquiry*, pp. 65–6.
74. Quoted by Hanway, *Journey*, pp. 43–6, and by several other travellers.
75. *Correspondence of Thomas Gray*, ed. P. Toynbee and L. Whibley, 3 vols. (Oxford, 1935), vol. II, p. 899.
76. Macpherson, requiring a less fastidious terminological solution, taught his readers to speak of 'the joy of grief'. See L.L. Stewart, 'Burke, Macpherson and "the joy of grief"', *ELN*, vol. 15 (1977), pp. 29–32.
77. Monk, *The Sublime*, pp. 48–9.
78. Johnson, *Journey*, pp. 35–6.
79. The Fall of Foyers, by Loch Ness, is celebrated, almost as unanimously as Loch Lomond, in terms of awe and horror which unambiguously suggest the sublime. See Johnson, *Journey*, p. 29; J. Lettice, *Letters on a Tour through various parts of Scotland in the year 1792* (1794), pp. 352–6; Mrs S. Murray, *A Companion and Useful Guide to the Beauties of Scotland*, 2 vols. (1799, 1803, vol. I, pp. 241–5; and countless others.
80. Smollett, *Humphry Clinker*, pp. 250–2.
81. Martin Martin, *A Description of the Western Islands of Scotland circa 1695*, ed. Donald J. Macleod (Stirling, 1934), pp. 156, 146, 124, 152, 192, 197, 224, 201.
82. Alexander Campbell, *The Grampians Desolate: a Poem* (Edinburgh, 1804), p. 95.
83. John Campbell, *A Full and Particular Description of the Highlands of Scotland* (1752), p. 16.
84. Anne Grant, *Letters from the Mountains; being the real Correspondence of a lady, between the years 1773 and 1807*, 4th edn, 3 vols. (1809), vol. I, p. 114.
85. See R.N. Salaman, *The History and Social Influence of the Potato* (Cambridge, 1949), pp. 364–8; Frank Fraser Darling, *West Highland Survey* (Oxford, 1955), pp. 3–13; Robin Callander, 'The Place of Trees in the Highlands', in John Hulbert (ed.), *Land Ownership and Use* (Fletcher Paper No. 2) (Dundee, 1986), pp. 29–38 (pp. 32–3).
86. From 'The Choice', in Aaron Hill, *Poems*, British Poets, 60 (Chiswick, 1822), p. 90. The context states the relationship between Improvement and sublimity with naive directness: 'On some lone

wild should my strong house be placed, / Surrounded by a vast and healthy waste: / Sterile and coarse the untried soil should be; / But forced to flourish and subdued by me.' 'Healthy' is probably a misprint for 'heathy'; the connotative interchangeability of the two epithets is nicely symptomatic.

87. 'The commercialisation of the agricultural structure in response to the chieftains' financial necessitousness ... is the great fact of eighteenth century Highland history. From it all else follows.' James Hunter, *The Making of the Crofting Community* (Edinburgh, 1976), p. 9.

88. Revd Mr Singer, 'On the Introduction of Sheep Farming into the Highlands', *Prize Essays and Transactions of the Highland Society of Scotland*, vol. 3 (1807), pp. 536–606 (p. 605).

5 GHOSTS

1. Thomas Blackwell, *An Enquiry into the Life and Writings of Homer* (1735), p. 26.
2. William Collins, 'Ode to Fear' in his *Works*, ed. R. Wendorf and C. Ryskamp (Oxford, 1979), p. 27, ll. 1–6.
3. Geoffrey Hartman, 'False Themes and Gentle Minds', in his *Beyond Formalism: Literary Essays 1958–70* (1970), pp. 283–97 (p. 291).
4. William Collins, 'Ode to a Friend on his Return &c.' in his *Works*, p. 56, ll. 13–17. This is the title on the unfinished MS. The poem is also known as 'An Ode on the Popular Superstitions of the Highlands of Scotland, Considered as the Subject of Poetry'. It was written in 1749–50, and published, after a chequered MS career, in 1788. For an account of the text, see the commentary on the poem in the edition cited.
5. See J.R. Tanner (ed.) *Private Correspondence and Miscellaneous Papers of Samuel Pepys, 1697–1703*, 2 vols. (1926), vol. I, pp. 213–25; and John Aubrey, 'An Accurate Account of Second-Sighted Men in Scotland', reprinted in *Treatises on the Second Sight* (Glasgow, 1819), pp. 207–25
6. Martin Martin, *A Description of the Western Islands of Scotland c. 1695*, ed. Donald J. Macleod (Stirling, 1934), especially pp. 321–48.
7. Martin, *Description*, p. 347.
8. Martin, *Description*, p. 89.
9. See ll. 22–5, and the note on them in R.H. Lonsdale (ed.), *The Poems of Gray, Collins and Goldsmith* (London and New York, 1969), p. 503.
10. Lines 57–69. The gap in l. 62 is one of the MS lacunae. Alexander Carlyle reasonably suggested 'piercing' when he published the poem.
11. Robert Kirk, *Secret Commonwealth*, printed from MS of 1691 (Edinburgh, 1815), p. 15.
12. Daniel Defoe, *The Second-Sighted Highlander. Being Four Visions of the Eclypse, And something of what may follow* (1715), p. 44.

13. William Duff, *An Essay on Original Genius* (1767), p. 177.
14. In James Mylne, *Poems* (Edinburgh, 1790): see p. 280.
15. Anne Grant, *Essays on the Superstitions of the Highlands of Scotland*, 2 vols. (1811), vol. II, p. 35.
16. Quoted in *The Works of John Home*, edited by Henry Mackenzie, 3 vols. (Edinburgh, 1822), vol. I, p. 100.
17. Alice Gipson, *John Home* (Caldwell, Idaho, 1916), pp. 59–61. Compare Henry Mackenzie's comments in Mackenzie (ed.), *The Works of John Home*, vol. I, p. 92.
18. *Works of John Home*, vol. I, p. 349.
19. *Report of the Committee of the Highland Society of Scotland, appointed to inquire into the nature and authenticity of the poems of Ossian*, drawn up by Henry Mackenzie (Edinburgh, 1805), pp. 66–8. Referred to in future as *Highland Society Report*.
20. The clearest and most accurate of many accounts is in R.M. Schmitz, *Hugh Blair* (New York, 1948), pp. 42–60 and 88–90.
21. Hugh Blair, *A Critical Dissertation on the Poems of Ossian, the Son of Fingal*. First published on its own in 1763, then reprinted in James Macpherson, *The Works of Ossian*, 3rd edn, 2 vols. (1765), vol. II, pp. 313–443. It was included in most standard editions of Ossian thereafter.
22. The most authoritative review of the evidence is D.S. Thomson, *The Gaelic Sources of Macpherson's Ossian* (1952).
23. The cult and the controversy are both reviewed with entertaining hostility in J.S. Smart, *James Macpherson: an Episode in Literature* (1905). The immense literature of Ossianic dissemination and reception is catalogued in G.F. Black, 'Macpherson's Ossian and the Ossianic Controversy: A Bibliography', *Bulletin of the New York Public Library*, 30 (1926), I, pp. 424–39 and II, pp. 508–24; supplemented in the same publication, 75 (1971), 465–73, by J.J. Dunn. There are also articles on Ossian in Germany, Russia and America, in *Scottish Literary News*, 3, 3 (November 1973).
24. *The Poems of Ossian, &c.; Containing the Poetical Works of James Macpherson, Esq. in Prose and Rhyme*, ed. Malcolm Laing, 2 vols. (Edinburgh, 1805) vol. II, p. 393
25. Fragment II, Laing, vol. II, p. 387.
26. Fragment III, Laing, vol. II, p. 388.
27. Geoffrey Hartman, 'Evening Star and Evening Land', in his *The Fate of Reading and Other Essays* (1975), pp. 147–78 (p. 165).
28. Blair in Macpherson, *Works of Ossian*, vol. II, p. 375.
29. In a 'Dissertation' of his own, Macpherson, *Works of Ossian*, vol. II, pp. i–xlii (p. xxviii).
30. Macpherson, 'Dissertation' in Macpherson, *Works of Ossian*, vol. II, p. xx.
31. D.T. Mackintosh, 'James Macpherson and the Book of the Dean of Lismore', *Scottish Gaelic Studies*, vol. 6 (1949), pp. 11–20.
32. Norman Ross, *Heroic Poetry from the Book of the Dean of Lismore* (Edinburgh, 1939), nos. XXI, XXVI, VII.
33. *Highland Society Report*, p. 44.

Notes 195

34. Blair, 'Critical Dissertation' in Macpherson, *Works of Ossian*, vol. II, p. 338.
35. Laing, vol. I, pp. 132–7.
36. David Hume, 'Of the Authenticity of Ossian's Poems', in *Philosophical Works*, ed. T.H. Green and T.H. Grose, 4. vols. (1874–5), vol. II, pp. 415–24 (p. 417).
37. See D.S. Thomson, 'Bogus Gaelic Literature c. 1750–1820', *Transactions of the Gaelic Society of Glasgow*, vol. 5 (1958), pp. 172–88.
38. Anne Grant, *Poems* (1803), p. 374.
39. Not only in *Douglas*, but also in Home's explicitly Ossianic tragedy, *The Fatal Discovery*, staged in 1769. See *Works of John Home*, vol. II, p. 128.
40. Laing, vol. I, p. 95.
41. Laing, I, 200.
42. In William Hazlitt, 'Lectures on the English Poets', *Complete Works of William Hazlitt*, ed. P.P. Howe, 21 vols. (1930–34), vol. V (1930), p. 18.
43. Charles Cordiner, *Antiquities and Scenery of the North of Scotland* (1780) p. 77. The quotation is from *Fingal*, Laing, vol. I, p. 89.
44. William Ross, *A Description of the Paintings in the Hall of Ossian, at Pennycuik* (Edinburgh, 1773), pp. 30, 34. Compare Laing, vol. I, pp. 320–3. The hall was in a house which is now itself a ruin.
45. P. Toynbee and L. Whibley (eds.), *Correspondence of Thomas Gray*, 3 vols. (Oxford, 1935), vol. II, p. 680 (June 1760).
46. See Samuel Johnson, *Journey*, in *Johnson's Journey to the Western Islands of Scotland and Boswell's Journal of a Tour to the Hebrides with Samuel Johnson, LL.D.*, ed. R.W. Chapman, Oxford Standard Authors (1930), pp. 106–8
47. M.P. McDiarmid, 'Ossian as Scottish Epic', *Scottish Literary News*, vol. 3, no. 3 (November 1973), pp. 4–9.
48. Bailey Saunders, *The Life and Letters of James Macpherson* (1894), pp. 32–48.
49. Laing, vol. II, p. 588.
50. Laing, vol. I, p. 321n.
51. Henry Home, Lord Kames, *Sketches of the History of Man*, 2 vols. (Edinburgh, 1774), vol. I, p. 282.
52. The hero of J.W. von Goethe, *Die Leiden des jungen Werthers*, first published 1774, edited and translated by Harry Steinhauer (New York, 1962), moves between opposed modes of being represented by Homer, who is aligned with summer, objectivity and sanity, and Ossian, whose influence over him is associated with storms, subjectivity and eventual suicide.
53. *Highland Society Report*, p. 152.
54. Walter Scott, Review of *Highland Society Report* and also of Laing, *Edinburgh Review*, vol. 6 (1805), pp. 429–62.
55. Adam Ferguson, *An Essay on the History of Civil Society*, p. 173; Edward Gibbon, *The History of the Decline and Fall of the Roman Empire*, ed. J.B. Bury, 7 vols. (1896–1900), vol. I, p. 129; John Millar, *The Origin of the Distinction of Ranks* (1779), p. 76.

56. Saunders, *Life and Letters of James Macpherson*, p. 90.
57. Blair 'Critical Dissertation', in Macpherson, *Works of Ossian*, vol. II, p. 344.
58. Blair 'Critical Dissertation', in Macpherson, *Works of Ossian*, vol. II, p. 376.
59. Thomas Newte, *Prospects and Observations on a Tour in England and Scotland* (1791), p. 235; William Gilpin, *Observations, Relative Chiefly to Picturesque Beauty Made in the Year 1776 on Several Parts of Great Britain; Particularly the High-Lands of Scotland*, 2nd edn, 2 vols. (1792), vol. I, p. 126 and 169; Thomas Pennant, *A Tour in Scotland MDCCLXIX*, 2nd edn (1772), p. 193; and Pennant, *A Tour in Scotland and Voyage to the Hebrides: MDCCLXXII*, 2nd edn, 2 vols. (1776), vol. I, p. 302.
60. Laing, vol. I, 458. For other hunters, vol. I, pp. 194, 267, 556–7.
61. *Gentleman's Magazine*, vol. 40 (1770), p. 322.
62. Printed in Charles Cordiner, *Remarkable Ruins, and Romantic Prospects, of North Britain* (1795), unpaginated. In the last sentence, 'becoming' is presumably a misprint for the less interesting 'beckoning'.
63. Laing, vol. I, p. 401.
64. Pennant, *1772*, vol. II, p. 13; Gilpin, *Observations*, vol. I, p. 174.
65. Laing's note, vol. I, p. 401, referring to James Thomson, 'Winter', ll. 66–71, in *The Seasons*, ed. J. Sambrook (Oxford, 1981).
66. Virgil, *Georgics*, Book I, ll. 357–8.
67. *Works of John Home*, vol. I, p. 330.
68. Geoffrey Hartman, *Wordsworth's Poetry 1787–1814* (New Haven and London, 1964), p. 9.
69. Dorothy Wordsworth, *Recollections of a Tour Made in Scotland A.D. 1803*, ed. J.C. Shairp, reprint of 3rd edn (Edinburgh, 1974), p. 116.
70. James Beattie, *Essays on Poetry and Music*, 3rd edn (1779), p. 169.
71. Thomas Wilkinson, whose journal Wordsworth read in MS; it was published as *Tours to the British Mountains* (1824). 'Passed a female who was reaping alone: she sung in Erse as she bended over her sickle; the sweetest human voice I ever heard: her strains were tenderly melancholy, and felt delicious, long after they were heard no more.' (p. 12).
72. Martin, *Description of the Western Islands*, p. 104.
73. A group of Highland gentleman raised a subscription to finance the publication of the Gaelic text; Macpherson was sent the money in 1784, but nothing had appeared when he died in 1796 (Saunders, *Life and Letters*, pp. 278, 300).
74. William Wordsworth, *The Prose Works*, ed. W.J.B. Owen and J.W. Smyser, 3 vols. (Oxford, 1974), vol. III, p. 77.
75. See the section 'Memorials of a Tour in Scotland, 1803', in William Wordsworth, *Poetical Works*, ed. E. de Selincourt and H. Darbishire, 5 vols. (Oxford, 1940–9), vol. III (1946), pp. 73–96. Other relevant lyrics from the tour are 'To a Highland Girl', 'Address to Kilchurn Castle', and the elegy for Ossian himself, 'Glen Almain'. The later and more programmatic lines 'Written in a Blank Leaf of Macpher-

son's Ossian', vol. IV (1947), p. 38, are a clear if pedestrian statement of the rejection of 'finished Strains' in favour of the authentic bard 'Dim-gleaming through imperfect lore'.
76. For example, see the description of Killiecrankie in the Wordsworths' own guide book, John Stoddart, *Remarks on Local Scenery and Manners in Scotland during the Years 1799 and 1800*, 2 vols. (1801), vol. II, p. 185.
77. Johnson, *Journey*, p. 134.

6 SOCIAL TRIBES

1. *The Statistical Account of Scotland*, compiled by Sir John Sinclair from the returns of parish ministers, 1791–9, is an extremely detailed if patchily systematic snapshot of Scottish society at the time, and also of the attitudes of its contributors. The reports from Highland parishes repeatedly note the advance of 'civilisation and industry'.
2. James Hunter, *The Making of the Crofting Community* (Edinburgh, 1976), p. 9.
3. See I. H. Adams, 'The Agents of Agricultural Change', in M. L. Adams and T. R. Salter (eds), *The Making of the Scottish Countryside* (1980), pp. 155–75; Eric Richards, *A History of the Highland Clearances: Agrarian Transformation and the Evictions, 1746–1886* (1982), pp. 121, 192–6, 202–3; Malcolm Gray, *The Highland Economy, 1750–1850* (Edinburgh, 1957), pp. 86–100, 124–51.
4. Hunter, *The Making of the Crofting Community*, Chapter 1.
5. This concept from Michael Hechter, *Internal Colonialism: the Celtic Fringe in British National Development, 1536–1966* (1975), though I am differing from Hechter's reading of events in Scotland.
6. Gray, *Highland Economy*, p. 148.
7. Richards, *History of the Highland Clearances*, pp. 64, 152–4.
8. N. H. Macdonald, *The Clan Ranald of Knoydart and Glengarry* (Edinburgh, 1979), pp. 134–63.
9. The incompatibility was both economic and technical: see Gray, *Highland Economy*, pp. 87–95.
10. A. J. Youngson, *After the Forty-Five: The Economic Impact on the Scottish Highlands* (Edinburgh, 1973), pp. 164–5.
11. Gray, *Highland Economy*, pp. 141, 127–8.
12. Richards, *History of the Highland Clearances*, pp. 148–9, 154.
13. Gray, *Highland Economy*, pp. 129–38.
14. For a discussion of popular resistance, see Eric Richards, *A History of the Highland Clearances, Volume 2: Emigration, Protest, Reasons* (1985), pp. 301–19.
15. Gray, *Highland Economy*, p. 151; for an example, see, I. F. Grant, *The Macleods: the History of a Clan 1200–1956* (1959), pp. 490–508.
16. Richards, *History of the Highland Clearances*, p. 146.
17. Richards, *History of the Highland Clearances*, p. 174; Gray, *Highland Economy*, pp. 155–8.
18. Gray, *Highland Economy*, pp. 181–6.

19. Gray, *Highland Economy*, p. 188.
20. Roland Barthes, *Mythologies*, selected and translated by Annette Lavers, paperback edition (St Albans, 1973), pp. 129, 151.
21. For example, Samuel Johnson, *Journey*, in *Johnson's Journey to the Western Islands of Scotland and Boswell's Journal of a Tour to the Hebrides with Samuel Johnson, LL.D.*, ed. R.W. Chapman, Oxford Standard Authors (1930), p. 417; Thomas Pennant, *A Tour in Scotland and a Voyage to the Hebrides: MDCCLXXII*, 2nd edn, 2 vols. (1776), vol. I, pp. 364–5. Material from both travellers is used polemically in 'An Address to the Lairds of Scotland', *Gentleman's Magazine*, vol. 46 (1776), pp. 397–8.
22. John Knox, *A Tour Through the Highlands of Scotland and the Hebride Isles in 1786*, (1787), p. 39.
23. J. L. Buchanan, *Travels in the Western Hebrides: from 1782 to 1790* (1793), pp. 47–78.
24. Oliver Goldsmith, 'The Deserted Village', in R. H. Lonsdale (ed.), *Poems of Gray, Collins, Goldsmith* (London and New York, 1969), pp. 669–94, ll. 51–6.
25. Quoted in Eric Richards. *The Leviathan of Wealth* (1973), p. 159.
26. Johnson, *Journey*, pp. 85–7.
27. Johnson, *Journey*, p. 81.
28. Johnson, *Journey*, p. 79.
29. 'The Emigrant. An Eclogue', by 'Scots Spy', *Weekly Magazine*, vol. 31 (1776), p. 399.
30. It was much reprinted in the following decades: see the entry on Henry Erskine (1746–1817), *Dictionary of National Biography*, and William Scott, *Beauties of Eminent Writers* (Edinburgh, 1793), p. 206.
31. For a contemporary example of the same deformation, see a pamphlet of 1773 called *The Present Conduct of the Chieftains and Proprietors of Land in the Highlands of Scotland*, by 'A Highlander'.
32. Robert Burns, 'Address of Beelzebub to the Earl of Breadalbane' (in *The Poems and Songs of Robert Burns*, ed. J. Kinsley, 3 vols. (Oxford, 1968), no. 108). The poem was not published until 1818.
33. The mechanics of this repression are detailed in J. M. Bumsted, *The People's Clearance: Highland Emigration to British North America 1770–1815* (Edinburgh and Winnipeg, 1982). See especially pp. 108–54.
34. Thomas Douglas, Earl of Selkirk, *Observations on the Present State of the Highlands of Scotland* (1805), p. 23.
35. This double bind, like much of Selkirk's thinking, is thoroughly Smithian: see Adam Smith, *An Inquiry into the Nature and Causes of the Wealth of Nations*. ed. R. H. Campbell, A. Skinner and W. B. Todd, 2 vols. (Oxford, 1976), vol. I, pp. 418–19.
36. John Cririe, *Scottish Scenery; or, Sketches in Verse* (1803), pp. 352–3.
37. Richards, *History of the Highland Clearances*, pp. 176, 185–90.
38. Richards, *History of the Highland Clearances*, p. 194.
39. Richards, *History of the Highland Clearances*, pp. 285–300.
40. K. J. Logue, *Popular Disturbances in Scotland 1780–1815* (Edinburgh, 1979), pp. 54–74, shows how direct action was focussed on the

sheep and the shepherds, failing to engage with the real agents of eviction. This tended to mean that minor acts of sabotage obscured the contest about the land by raising immediate questions of law and order, thus alienating middle-class sympathisers just when they were needed.

41. Raymond Williams, *The Country and the City* (1973), p. 78.
42. Goldsmith, 'The Deserted Village', in Lonsdale, *Poems of Gray, Collins and Goldsmith*, ll. 407–8.
43. Anne Grant, *Poems* (1803), p. 34.
44. *The Statistical Account of Scotland*, reprinted in 20 vols. (East Ardsley, 1973–), vol. XVII (1981), p. 223.
45. Youngson, *After the Forty-Five*, pp. 29 and 168–9.
46. Grant, *Poems*, p. 34.
47. Grant, *Poems*, p. 34.
48. William Marshall, *General View of the Agriculture of the Central Highlands of Scotland* (1794), p. 31.
49. Gray, *Highland Economy*, p. 39.
50. Smith, *Wealth of Nations*, p. 19.
51. Dr Rennie, 'Of those Obstacles to Improvement which are Local to the Highlands', in Sir John Sinclair (ed.), *Appendix to the General Report of the Agricultural State and Political Circumstances of Scotland*, 2 vols. (Edinburgh, 1814), vol. II, p. 395.
52. Anne Grant, *Essays on the Superstitions of the Highlands of Scotland*, 2 vols. (1811), vol. II, p. 24.
53. Smith, *Wealth of Nations*, pp. 782–3.
54. Grant, *Essays*, vol. II, p. 19.
55. Grant, *Poems*, p. 37.
56. Smith, *Wealth of Nations*, p. 31.
57. Smith, *Wealth of Nations*, p. 27.
58. Grant, *Poems*, p. 33.
59. Grant, *Poems*, p. 35.
60. James Thomson, 'Winter' in *The Seasons*, ed. J. Sambrook (Oxford, 1981) ll. 356–8.
61. Grant, *Poems*, p. 23.
62. Grant, 'Sonnet', in *Poems*, p. 204.
63. Anne Grant, *Letters from the Mountains; being the real Correspondence of a lady, between the years 1773 and 1807*, 4th edn, 3 vols. (1809), vol. III, p. 52. The letter was written in 1796.
64. 'Dissertation' (by Ramsay of Ochtertyre) in P. McDonald, *A Collection of Highland Vocal Airs* (1784), p. 14.
65. Anne Grant, *Essays On the Superstitions of the Highlands of Scotland*, 2 vols. (1811), vol. II, p. 8.
66. James Dunbar, *Essays on the History of Mankind in Rude and Cultivated Ages*, 2nd edn (1781), Essay I.
67. Dunbar, *Essays*, pp. 1, 17.
68. Dunbar, *Essays*, p. 25.
69. As reported in J. Lettice, *Letters on a Tour through various parts of Scotland in the year 1792* (1794), pp. 263–4.
70. Uncommon in English. For Mac Mhaighstir Alasdair's version of the

idea, see Malcolm Chapman, *The Gaelic Vision in Scottish Culture* (1978), p. 60.
71. J. L. Buchanan, *A Defence of the Scots Highlanders* (1794), p. 46.
72. James Macpherson, 'A Dissertation concerning the Antiquity, &c. of the Poems of Ossian the son of Fingal', in *The Works of Ossian*, 2 vols. (1765), vol. I, pp. i–xxiv (xvii).
73. Grant, *Letters from the Mountains*, vol. II, p. 94.
74. Ferrier wrote *Marriage* (1818), *The Inheritance* (1824) and *Destiny, or the Chief's Daughter* (1830); Brunton *Self-Control* (1811) and *Discipline* (1814). Except for *The Inheritance*, all these novels make significant use of Highland settings. Except for *Destiny*, they are all currently available in paperback editions.
75. Elizabeth Helme, *Duncan and Peggy: a Scottish Tale*, 2 vols. (1794), vol. I, p. 51.
76. C. I. Johnstone. *Clan-Albin: A National Tale*, 4 vols. (Edinburgh, 1815), vol. I.
77. Revd John Walker's report to the General Assembly of the Kirk, *Scots Magazine*, vol. 34 (1772), p. 289.
78. Johnson was briefly involved in the change of policy: see James Boswell, *Life of Johnson* ed. R. W. Chapman, corrected by J. O. Fleeman (1970), pp. 373–5. For the linguistic history in detail, see V. E. Durkacz, *The Decline of the Celtic Languages* (Edinburgh, 1983), especially Chapter 2.
79. Women worked on the land in the pre-clearance Highlands; they were perhaps even the main direct cultivators. See, e.g., Richards, *History of the Highland Clearances*, pp. 48, 81. They were also conspicuous in many of the instances of physical resistance to eviction: for some highly speculative deductions from this fact, see Hamish Henderson, '"Infirm of purpose! Give me the daggers!" Some thoughts on Highland History', *Cencrastus*, vol. 3 (1980), pp. 14–17.
80. A complete list of romances in which lost heirs benefit from rustic upbringings in Highland retreats would be very long. Headed, appropriately, by James Macpherson's poem *The Highlander* (1758), it could include *Llewellin: A Tale*, 3 vols. (1799); *Monteith, A Novel, Founded on Scottish History* (Gainsborough, 1805); *Glencore Tower; or, The Feuds of Scotland. A Legend of the Thirteenth Century*, 2 vols. (1806); and P. M. Darling, *The Romance of the Highlands* (Edinburgh, 1810).
81. Elizabeth Helme, *Albert; or the Wilds of Strathnavern*, new edn, 4 vols. (1821), vol. IV, pp. 139ff. First published 1799.
82. Helme, *Duncan and Peggy*, vol. II, p. 30.
83. Susan Ferrier, *Marriage, A Novel*, ed. H. Foltinek (1971), pp. 195–8.
84. Mary Johnston, *The Lairds of Glenfern; or, Highlanders of the Nineteenth Century*, 2 vols. (1816).
85. Elizabeth Helme, *St. Clair of the Isles; or, the Outlaws of Barra. A Scottish Tradition*, 3rd edn, 4 vols. (1823), vol. IV, p. 111; vol. I, p. 123. First published 1803.
86. The best example is Winpenny in C. I. Johnstone's *The Saxon and the Gaël; or, The Northern Metropolis*, 4 vols. (1814).

Notes

87. For example, Mary Brunton, *Discipline: A Novel*, 3 vols. (Edinburgh, 1814), vol. III, p. 226; Johnstone, *Clan-Albin* vol. I, pp. 12–17.
88. Brunton lived and corresponded in Edinburgh literary society 1803–18, and will certainly have known Grant's writings; for Johnstone's admiration, see *The Saxon and the Gaël*, vol. IV, p. 62.
89. Brunton, *Discipline*, vol. III, p. 153.
90. Brunton, *Discipline*, vol. III, p. 281.
91. Colonel Campbell in Helme, *Duncan and Peggy*, Captain Grant in Johnston, *The Lairds of Glenfern*, Major Douglas in Ferrier, *Marriage*, etc.
92. Duncan in Helme, *Duncan and Peggy*, Lennox in Ferrier, *Marriage*, and, most compendiously, Norman in Johnstone, *Clan-Albin*.
93. In *Waverley* (1814), *Rob Roy* (1818), and *Chronicles of the Canongate*, first series (1827).
94. For a reading from different sources of the construction of the Saxon-Celt dichotomy as a gender opposition, see Chapman, *The Gaelic Vision in Scottish Culture*, pp. 105–9.
95. Walter Scott, *The Lady of the Lake*, text and notes in *The Poetical Works of Walter Scott*, ed. J. L. Robertson (1894), Canto II, stanza xix.
96. Scott, *Lady*, Canto V, stanza vii; Canto II, stanza xviii.
97. This is the light-quality realised in Landseer's *The Monarch of the Glen* (1851), deservedly the most famous visual image of the Highland romance. Officially, the golden side-light which subtly anthropomorphises the animal's face is dawn, but the effective associations go the other way; the stag's monarchy is poignant because this is a *sporting* picture; his magnificence, like Roderick's, makes it the more certain that he will be killed.
98. Scott, *Lady*, Canto II, stanza xiv. Compare Thomas Pennant, *A Tour in Scotland MDCCLXIX*, 2nd edn (1772) pp. 176–8.
99. *Scots Magazine*, vol. 72 (1810), p. 107. For Scott's involvement, see Edgar Johnson, *The Great Unknown*, 2 vols. (1970), vol. I, p. 323.
100. Walter Scott, *The Letters of Sir Walter Scott*, ed. H. J. C. Grierson, 12 vols. (1932–7), vol. II, p. 286 (21 January 1810).
101. There were seven editions in the author's lifetime, as well as conversions for the stage and the penny magazines. See A. D. Hook, 'Jane Porter, Sir Walter Scott, and the Historical Novel', *Clio*, vol. 5, no. 2 (1976), pp. 181–92; and Montagu Summers, *A Gothic Bibliography* (1946), p. 497.
102. Postscript to the 3rd edn (1816).
103. Jane Porter, *The Scottish Chiefs. A Romance*, 5 vols. (1810), vol. II, p. 7.
104. The word is J. G. Lockhart's; his account of the occasion is in his *Memoirs of the Life of Sir Walter Scott*, edn in 10 vols (Edinburgh, 1882), vol. VII, p. 67.
105. E.g., John Prebble, *Culloden*, paperback edn (Harmondsworth, 1967), p. 313; Frank McLynn, *The Jacobites* (1985), pp. 211–12; Nigel Tranter, *The Story of Scotland* (1987), p. 239.
106. Allan Ramsay, *Works*, ed. Burns Martin and John W. Oliver, Scottish Texts Society Publications, 3rd series, vol. 19 (Edinburgh, 1951), p. 27.

107. 'Bannocks of Barley-meal', in David Herd, *Ancient and Modern Scottish Songs, Heroic Ballads, Etc.*, 2 vols. (Edinburgh, 1776), vol. II, p. 130.
108. Allardyce Nicoll, *The Garrick Stage* (Manchester, 1980), pp. 170–2.
109. See William Ferguson, *Scotland, 1689 to the Present*, paperback edn (Edinburgh, 1978), pp. 259–65. The costumes are illustrated with nice absurdity by the caricaturist John Kay: see his *A Series of Original Portraits and Caricature Etchings*, ed. Hugh Paton, 2 vols. (Edinburgh, 1877), vol. II, pp. 280, 283.
110. Sir John Sinclair, *Observations on the Propriety of preserving the ... Customs of the ancient Inhabitants of Scotland* (1804), p. 3.
111. E.g., William Robertson, in his *History of Scotland*, in *Works*, 8 vols. (1840), vol. I, p. 23.
112. In James Macpherson, *An Introduction to the History of Great Britain and Ireland* (1771).
113. David Erskine Baker, *The Muse of Ossian: A Dramatic Poem* (Edinburgh, 1763), p. 10.
114. *Caledonian Mercury*, 25 August 1810.
115. Scott, *Letters*, vol. II, pp. 286–92.
116. Scott, *The Lay of the Last Minstrel* in *Poetical Works*, pp. 1–88, Canto VI, stanza ii; *Lady*, introductory lines to Canto I.
117. J. G. Lockhart, *Peter's Letters to His Kinfolk*, 'third edition' (actually the second), 3 vols. (1819), vol. II, p. 348.
118. Scott, 'The Family Legend', in *Poetical Works*, p. 711.
119. Immanuel Wallerstein, 'One Man's Meat: The Scottish Great Leap Forward', *Review*, vol. III, no. 4 (Spring 1980), pp. 631–40.
120. N. T. Phillipson, 'Nationalism and Ideology', in J. N. Wolfe (ed.), *Government and Nationalism in Scotland* (Edinburgh, 1969), pp. 167–88.

7 HOLIDAYS

1. Anthony Champion, *Miscellanies in Verse and Prose* (1801), pp. 72–8.
2. Samuel Johnson, *Idler* no. 97 (February 1760), in W. J. Bate, J. M. Bullitt and L. F. Powell (eds), *The Yale Edition of the Works of Samuel Johnson*, Vol. II (New Haven, 1963), pp. 298–300.
3. E.g. Edward Young on the 'original' writer: 'on the strong wing of his Imagination ... we have no Home, no Thought, of our own; till the Magician drops his Pen: And then falling down into ourselves, we awake to flat Realities, lamenting the change' (*Conjectures on Original Composition* (1759), p. 13).
4. Sterne's *A Sentimental Journey* appeared in 1768.
5. James Boswell, *Journal of a Tour*, in *Johnson's Journey to the Western Islands of Scotland and Boswell's Journal of a Tour to the Hebrides with Samuel Johnson, LL.D.*, ed. R. W. Chapman, Oxford Standard Authors (1930), pp. 243, 253, 281, 379, 394.
6. Dorothy Wordsworth, *Recollections of a Tour Made in Scotland A. D. 1803*, ed. J. C. Shairp, reprint of 3rd edn, (Edinburgh, 1974), pp. 103–5.

Notes

7. Dorothy Wordsworth, *Recollections of a Tour*, pp. 221–3.
8. William Wordsworth, *Poetical Works*, ed. E. de Selincourt and H. Darbishire, 5 vols. (Oxford, 1940–9), vol. III (1946), p. 76.
9. Walter Scott, *The Lady of the Lake* text, and notes in *The Poetical Works of Walter Scott*, ed. J. L. Robertson (1894), Canto I, stanza xxxi; Canto II, stanza ii; Canto III, stanza xxix. For an oddly comparable Highland Elysium, see William Gilpin's 'reverie' of a Loch Lomond inhabited by a group of 'philosophical friends', each with his own island and boat: William Gilpin, *Observations Relative Chiefly to Picturesque Beauty, Made in the Year 1776 on Several Parts of Great Britain; Particularly the High-Lands of Scotland*, 2nd edn (1792), vol. II, pp. 33–5.
10. Anne Grant's phrase: *Memoir and Correspondence of Mrs Grant of Laggan*, ed. J. P. Grant, 3 vols. (1844), vol. I, p. 269.
11. Peter Middleton Darling, *The Romance of the Highlands*, 2 vols. (Edinburgh, 1810), vol. II, p. 134.
12. T. J. H. Curties, *The Scottish Legend; or, the Isle of Saint Clothair, A Romance*, 4 vols. (1802), vol. III, p. 193; Henry Siddons, *William Wallace: or, The Highland Hero*, 2 vols. (1791), vol. II, p. 81.
13. This is not simply an interpretive conceit. Such a relationship between masquerading and literature was realised, in the service of an orientalist myth rather than a Highland one, in the genesis of William Beckford's *Vathek* (1786). See J. W. Oliver, *The Life of William Beckford* (1932), pp. 88–91.
14. This figure was a role-model of sensibility for a few years. 'In truth, I am a strange, and wayward wight, / Fond of each dreadful, and each gentle scene' – Anne Grant, in a letter written in 1778, in *Letters from the Mountains: being the real Correspondence of a lady, between the years 1773 and 1807*, 4th edn, 3 vols. (1809), vol. II, p. 32, alluding to James Beattie's poem *The Minstrel; or, the Progress of Genius*, which had appeared in two volumes in 1771/4.
15. Ann Radcliffe, *The Castles of Athlin and Dunbayne. A Highland Story* (1789), p. 8.
16. See Edgar Johnson, *The Great Unknown*, 2 vols. (1970), vol. I, p. 336, and E. Burt, *Letters from a Gentleman in the North of Scotland*, 5th edn, ed. R. Jamieson, 2 vols. (1818), vol. I, pp. 202–3n.
17. Quoted in Scott, *The Letters of Sir Walter Scott*, ed. H. J. C. Grierson, 12 vols. (1932–7), vol. II, pp. 419–20.
18. John Stoddart, *Remarks on Local Scenery and Manners in Scotland during the Years 1799 and 1800*, 2 vols. (1801), vol. II, p. 307. Hence, presumably, the Wordsworths' desire to go there.
19. *Statistical Account*, vol. XII (1977), pp. 137–90 (p. 139). A little contest for precedence between Mrs Murray and the Revd Robertson is recorded in Elizabeth I. Spence, *Sketches of the Present Manners, Customs, and Scenery of Scotland*, 2nd edn, 2 vols. (1811), vol. I, p. 200.
20. See Patrick Graham, *Sketches Descriptive of Picturesque Scenery on the Southern Confines of Perthshire* (Edinburgh, 1806), pp. 10–18.
21. Scott's first publication, in 1796, had included his translation of the Bürger poem. See *Poetical Works*, p. 651.

22. Scott, *Lady*, Canto I, stanzas xi–xiv.
23. Spence, *Sketches*, vol. I, pp. 203–16.
24. The notable exception to this is English foxhunting, the blood sport of the agricultural revolution's heartland, and definitively a local (not a holiday) pursuit. But this is a special case of a peculiar kind: it is extremely stylised, socially and sartorially; and its material base is not food-gathering but pest control. For the story of its regularisation in the period of Improvement, and its grounding in the particular socioeconomic structure of English agrarian capitalism, see Raymond Carr, *English Fox Hunting: A History* (1976), pp. 45–64.
25. Thomas Thornton, *A Sporting Tour through the Northern Parts of England, and great part of the Highlands of Scotland* (1804), 'Advertisement'.
26. Thornton, *Sporting Tour*, p. 93.
27. John Taylor, quoted in Thomas Pennant, *A Tour in Scotland MDCCLXIX*, 2nd edn (1772), p. 108.
28. *Edinburgh Review*, vol. 5 (1804–5), p. 402.
29. Described in Duff Hart-Davis, *Monarchs of the Glen: a History of Deer-Stalking in the Scottish Highlands* (1978).
30. The *OED*'s first reference is from Scott in 1816.
31. James Holloway and Lindsay Errington, *The Discovery of Scotland*, National Gallery of Scotland exhibition catalogue (Edinburgh, 1978), pp. 103–18 (pp. 107–9).
32. Alexander Irvine, *An Inquiry into the Causes and Effects of Emigration from the Highlands* (Edinburgh, 1802), p. 56.
33. *Forest Sketches: Deer-stalking and other Sports in the Highlands Fifty Years Ago* (Edinburgh, 1865), p. xxi.
34. See J. H. Plumb, *The Commercialisation of Leisure in Eighteenth Century England* (Reading, 1973). Plumb's most significant examples, from my point of view here, are the emergence of the spa and the seaside resort as holiday (as opposed to purely medicinal) locations, and the immense growth of light reading which, besides contributing directly to the Highland cult as we have seen, also represented a major domestication of leisure.
35. Hugh Cunningham, *Leisure in the Industrial Revolution c.1780–1880* (1980), pp. 76–84; John Clarke and Chas Critcher, *The Devil Makes Work: Leisure in Capitalist Britain* (1985), p. 53.
36. James Anderson, *Observations on the Means of Exciting a Spirit of National Industry* (1777).
37. Highland Society of Scotland, 1784; British Fisheries Society, 1786. 'General View' of the agriculture of the Central Highlands, 1794; of the Northern Counties, 1795; of Perthshire, 1799; of Inverness, 1808. *Statistical Account*, 1791–99.
38. Thomas Telford's *Survey and Report*, quoted in A. J. Youngson, *After the Forty-Five: The Economic Impact on the Scottish Highlands* (Edinburgh, 1973), p. 145.
39. Sir John Dalrymple, *Memoirs of Great Britain and Ireland*, 2nd edn, 3 vols. (1790), vol. II, Part II, p. 77.

40. Eric Richards, *A History of the Highland Clearances: Agrarian Transformation and the Evictions, 1746–1886* (1982), pp. 484–5; R. N. Millman, *The Making of the Scottish Landscape* (1975), pp. 168–9.

8 THE STRUCTURE OF THE MYTH

1. The phrases are those of the unnamed lady in Charles Cordiner, *Remarkable Ruins, and Romantic Prospects, of North Britain* (1795): see above, Chapter 5, note 62.
2. Immanuel Wallerstein, *Historical Capitalism* (1983), p. 30.
3. See above, Chapter 6, section 5.
4. A TV example from the end of the 1984–5 coal strike: the news programmes, having been consistently hostile to the strikers while the struggle was actually in progress, suddenly warmed to the pride and dignity with which the South Wales coalfield *went back*.
5. See, for example, what David Edgar makes of the proposition that 'on many key issues the British *think* further to the left than they vote'. Socialist sentiments; capitalist power. David Edgar, 'Never Too Old: Learning from the Sixties', *New Socialist*, no. 38 (May 1986), pp. 16–20.
6. A. McDonald, *Evening Amusements, or, What Happens In Life, A Novel*, 2 vols. (Edinburgh, 1797), vol. I, p. 243.
7. Friedrich Schiller, *On the Naive and Sentimental in Literature*, translated by Helen Watanabe-O'Kelly (Manchester, 1981), p. 22.
8. Shakespeare, *The Winter's Tale*, IV, iv, 89–90; in *The Complete Works* (1951).
9. Schiller, *On the Naive*, p. 31. The original is perhaps more 'sentimental' here: the home is not merely parental but *'mütterlich'*, and we leave it to rush *'in die Fremde'*, which suggests alienation as well as emigration.
10. Schiller, *On the Naive*, p. 32.
11. Schiller, *On the Naive*, p. 90. For biographical corroboration of this reading, see Friedrich Schiller, *On the Aesthetic Education of Man*, ed. E. M. Wilkinson and L. A. Willoughby (Oxford, 1967), p. xvii.
12. The classic analysis of the transformation of the European sense of history at the close of the eighteenth century is the first section of Georg Lukács, *The Historical Novel*, translated by Hannah and Stanley Mitchell, paperback edn (Harmondsworth, 1969), pp. 15–29.
13. See T. C. Smout, 'The Landowner and the Planned Village in Scotland 1730–1830', in N. T. Phillipson and R. Mitchison (eds), *Scotland in the Age of Improvement* (Edinburgh, 1970), pp. 73–106.
14. 'All fixed, fast-frozen relations, with their train of ancient and venerable prejudices and opinions are swept away, all new-formed ones become antiquated before they can ossify.' From the *Communist Manifesto*: see *Karl Marx: The Essential Writings*, ed. F. L. Bender (New York, 1972), p. 244.
15. For the singing, P. McDonald, *A Collection of Highland Vocal Airs*

(1784), p. 3. The Improvement of domestic servants is the main theme and aim of Elizabeth Hamilton, *The Cottagers of Glenburnie; a Tale for the Farmer's Ingle-Nook* (Edinburgh, 1808), and a less exclusive preoccupation of Brunton and Ferrier.

16. This point is trenchantly made by Ian Carter, 'Economic Models and the Recent History of the Highlands', *Scottish Studies*, vol. 15 (1971), pp. 99–120.
17. E.g., Ian Grimble, 'Emigration in the Time of Rob Donn, 1714–1778', *Scottish Studies* vol. 7 (1963), pp. 129–53; and Hugh MacDiarmid's poem 'A Golden Wine in the Gaidhealtachd', in *The Complete Poems*, ed. Michael Grieve and W. R. Aitken, paperback edn, 2 vols. (Harmondsworth, 1985), vol. I, p. 721.
18. Benedict Anderson, *Imagined Communities: Reflections on the Origin and Spread of Nationalism* (1983), pp. 129–31.
19. Roland Barthes, *Mythologies*, translated by Annette Lavers, paperback edn (1973), p. 157.
20. David Stewart of Garth, *Sketches of the Character, Manners, and Present State of the Highlanders of Scotland*, 2 vols. (Edinburgh, 1822); Osgood Mackenzie, *A Hundred Years in the Highlands* (1921); Queen Victoria, *Leaves from the Journal of our Life in the Highlands* (1868).
21. Explored, for example, in Tom Nairn's essay 'The Modern Janus', in *The Break-Up of Britain* (1977), pp. 329–63.
22. *Gemeinschaft* and *Gesellschaft*: society-as-community and society-as-state. Title of a book by the German sociologist F. Tönnies (1887). See Raymond Williams, *Keywords* (1976), p. 66.
23. The phrase is from Wordsworth's 'Address to Kilchurn Castle, Upon Loch Awe', William Wordsworth, *Poetical Works*, ed. E. de Selincourt and H. Darbishire, 5 vols. (Oxford, 1940–9), vol. III (1946), p. 78.
24. Eric Richards, *A History of the Highland Clearances, Volume 2: Emigration, Protests, Reasons* (1985), pp. 203, 229–30.
25. E. MacCurdy, *A Literary Enigma – The Canadian Boat-Song: its Authorship and Associations* (Stirling, 1935), reviews the evidence, as well as giving the text of the poem.

Index

Alexis; or the Young Adventurer 40–1
Anderson, Benedict 176–7
Argyll, Dukes of 12, 144
  see also Inveraray
Arnold, Matthew 99
Atholl 63, 66–8, 161
Aubrey, John 89

Baillie, Joanna 139, 141–2, 145–7
ballads 13–14
Banks, Sir Joseph 71, 109
Barthes, Roland 1–2, 176
Beattie, James 76, 112, 155, 203n14
Beckford, William 203n13
Blackwell, Thomas 87
Blair, Hugh 22–3, 78–9, 96, 97–8, 108–9, 131
Boswell, Sir Alexander 53–4
Boswell, James 19, 37–8, 51–2, 151–2
Boyle, Sir Robert 89
British Antidote to Caledonian Poison 19, Plate 1a
British Fisheries Society 69, 164
Brunton, Mary 133, 135, 137, 138, 210n88
Buchanan, J. L. 119
Bürger, Gottfried 157
Burke, Edmund 80–2, 158
Burlington, Charles 36–7
Burnet, Thomas 64, 78
Burns, Robert 13, 14, 42, 54, 66–8, 122, 124
Burrell, Sir William 63, 66
Burt, Edward 1, 8, 23–4
Bute, John Stuart, 3rd Earl of 17–19, 31, 191n60

Camden, William 21
Campbell, Alexander 51, 83–4
Campbell, John 41, 84
Canadian Boat-Song 178–9

capitalism
  ideology of 3, 25, 70
  impact on Highlands 85–6, 115–18, 166–9
  and leisure 160, 162–3
  and war 29, 33, 59–60
cattle 12, 117–18, 126
Champion, Anthony 75, 149–50, 153
chiefs
  as landlords 85–6, 115–24
  as patriarchs 49–51, 55
  as sovereigns 5, 7–9, 12, 23–5, 141, 151–2
  see also clanship
childhood 133–6
Churchill, Charles 73–6, 78, 81
clanship
  as family 18, 34, 136–8
  as military unit 27–8, 39–40, 57–8
  as slavery 4, 12
  see also chiefs
Claude 75
Cleland, William 9, 15, 19
Cleveland, John 16, 74
Collins, William 83, 87–95, 97, 100–1, 114
comedy 7–8, 34, 51
community 43, 120, 128–30, 176–80
  see also clanship
Congreve, William 87
Constitution, British 6, 11, 39, 49
Cordiner, Charles 66, 77, 103–4
Corrieyairick 110–11
Cririe, John 65, 67, 123
Culloden *see* Forty-five
Cumberland, Richard 19–20
Cunningham, Alexander 27

Dalrymple, Sir John 27, 36, 164–5
Darling, P. M. 154
Defoe, Daniel 8–9, 16, 70, 92–3

Dennis, John 82
Derham, William 64
division of labour 42–3, 126–8
Duff, William 93
Dunbar, James 131–2
Dundas, Henry 49
Dunkeld 62, 109

eco-system 85–6
Edgar, David 205n5
emigration 174, 178–9
  controversy over 45–6, 119–23
  to Glasgow 10–11, 33
English
  Highland dialect of 8–9
  as metalanguage 134–5
  see also Gaelic
Errington, Lindsay 162

Ferguson, Adam 40, 42–4, 54, 108, 131
Fergusson, Sir Adam 58
Ferrier, Susan 133, 135–6
fishing 69–70
folly 81, 124, 130
Forbes, Duncan 40
Forbes, Duncan, of Culloden 6
Forfeited Estates 4–5, 115
Forty-five 2, 4, 15–17, 18–19, 27–9, 105
  official response to 4–6
  and Peninsular campaign 56
  sentimentalisation of 51–4
  see also Stuart, Prince Charles Edward
French Revolution 49, 173

Gaelic, 4, 111–13, 132–5
Garrick, David 30
George III 48, 52, 118n84
George IV 46, 52, 144
Gibbon, Edward 27–8, 108
Gilpin, William 36–7, 64–5, 67–8, 76, 110–11, 189n6, 203n9
Glencoe 78, 109
Glen Croe 63, 77–8
Glengarry, Macdonnell of 45, 117, Plate 2a
Goethe, J. W. von 106

Goldsmith, Oliver 119–22, 125, 128
Graham, Dougal 9–11
Graham, Patrick 156
Grant, Anne 186n37
  Essays 44–6, 94, 127, 131, 137
  Letters 38, 49, 84, 130, 133–5
  Poems 100–1, 125–31, 149, 160, 164
Gray, Malcolm 116
Gray, Thomas 81, 103
Grigor, Murray 20
Gunn, Neil 85

hardiness 27, 31–2, 41–2, 49
Hartman, Geoffrey 88, 98, 111
Hazlitt, William 102
health 83–4, 160
heather 1–2, 39
Hebrides 68–9, 89–90, 151–2, 178–9
Helme, Elizabeth 133, 135, 136
Henderson, Andrew 21
Highland dress 31, 46–8, 144–5
  illegality of 4, 5–6, 9, 13, 115
Highland Drover, The 33–4
Highland Regiments 7, 29–34, 40, 49–50, 117, 139
  as replicas of the clan 31, 39, 45, 57–8
Highland Rogue, The 12, 28
Highland Society
  of London 45, 46, 122
  of Scotland 86, 107, 164, Plate 2b
Highland Delineated, The 15
Hill, Aaron 192n86
History of the Feuds and Conflicts among the Clans 35–6
Hogg, James 52–3
Holloway, James 162
Home, John 88–9, 94–7, 111, 141
Horn, D. B. 71
Howell, James 73–4
Hume, David 94, 100
Hunter, James 115
hunting 6, 109–10, 158–63, 165

Index

imperialism 29, 30–3, 85, 109, 147–8
Improvement 2–3, 5, 174–5
  agrarian 61, 73–4, 125–7
  and landscape 61–2, 67–8, 72, 81–2
  and poetry 87–8, 107, 125
  refusal of 13, 54, 78, 81, 130, 160, 165
In the Garb of Old Gaul 32
industrialism 77–8, 80–1, 173
Inveraray 47, 63, 67, 142, Plate 6
Iona 114
Irvine, Alexander 162
islands 151–4

Jacobites *see* Forty-five
Johnson, Samuel
  on chiefs 23–4, 118–20, 141, 151–2
  on Highland warriors 11, 30, 35, 39, 43
  on scenery 73, 75, 82
  as tourist 19, 47, 114, 150–2
Johnston, Mary 136
Johnstone, C. I. 55, 57, 133, 136–7, 188n98

Kames, Henry Home, Lord 62, 64, 106
Killiecrankie 27, 37, 114, 197n76
Killin 76, 109
Kirk, the 4, 21–2, 134
Kirk, Robert 92
Knox, John 30, 32, 33, 70, 74, 119
Knoydart 84

labour discipline 6, 14, 33, 70, 164
Labour Party 167–8
Laing, Malcolm 105, 110, 192n68
Landseer, Edwin 201n97
Langhorne, John 31
law 11–14, 39–40
Lismore, Book of the Dean of 98
Lochaber 68, 73, 82
Lochiel, Cameron of 24, 51
Loch Katrine 63, 152–4, 156–8

Loch Lomond 38, 63–5, 83, 92, 111–12, 156, Plate 4b
Lockhart, J. G. 42, 58, 144, 146, 179
Logue, K. J. 198n40
London 13, 15, 26, 72, 135, 168
L. S., Lady 75–6

McCulloch, J. R. 119
McDiarmid, M. P. 104–5
Mackenzie, Osgood 177
Maclaren, Archibald 33–4
Macleod, Sjt. Donald 48–9
McNichol, Donald 44
Macpherson, James 30–1, 78, 96, 132, 145, 179–80, 192n76, 196n73, 200n80
  see also Ossian
Macklin, Charles 30, 183n38
magic 90–1, 157
Maitland, William 21
Marshall, William 73, 126
Martin, Martin 83, 85, 89–92, 113
Millar, John 108
Mitchell, Joseph 7–8, 51
Moir, D. M. 179
Monboddo, Lord 132
Monk, S. H. 82
Montague, Elizabeth 77–9
mountains 64–5, 71, 130
  Ben Doran 110
  Ben Lomond 63, 81
Murray, Mrs S. 156
Mylne, James 94
Mylne, Robert 47
mythology 1–2, 118, 176

Nairne, Baroness 52
Napoleonic Wars 46, 55–9, 117–18
nationalism
  British 30–1, 56, 69–70, 72
    see also imperialism
  Scottish 104–5, 107, 142–8
  sentiment of 43–4, 176–8
nature, concepts of
  anthropocentric 63–5, 68
  dialectical 171–4
  ecological 85

Index

moralistic 76, 135, 137–8
negative 70–1, 73–5
neoclassical 98–9
transcendental 79–81
neo-classicism 94–7
Nicholson, M. H. 64

O'Keeffe, John 51
Ossian 19, 23, 38, 78–82, 96–114, 161, Plate 5

pastoral 43, 74, 126–7, 129, 149–50
Pelloutier, Simon 21–2
Pennant, Thomas 19, 184n4,
  on Highland charter 27, 141
  on scenery 65–6, 72, 74, 189n14, Plate 4a
  on society 33, 50–1, 118–19
Pepys, Samuel 89
Phillipson, N. T. 147
philosophical history 22–5, 40–2, 108, 131
Pinkerton, John 21
Pitt, William (the Elder) 29–33, 36–7, 45, 49
Plumb, J. H. 32–3, 204n34
poetry
  as displacement 125, 179–80
  Highlanders peculiarity adapted to 2, 45, 128–31, 149–50
  as religion 99–100
  and Second Sight 93–4
  self-referring 95, 100–1
politeness 107–8, 129, 137–8
Pope, Alexander 61, 74, 87, 172
Porter, Jane 139, 143–5, 147
property 6, 11, 162–3

Radcliffe, Anne 155, 156
Ramsay, Allan 104, 144
Rawlinson, Thomas 48
Ray, James 21
Richards, Eric 117, 124, 200n79
rivers 64–5, 66–7
road-building 9–10, 70–1, 87
Rob Roy 12, 14, 38
Robertson, James 156
Robertson, William 21–2

Roman Empire 27–8, 32, 69–70, 145
Rosa, Salvator 75
Runciman, Alexander 103; Plate 5b

Samuel, Raphael 181n5
Schiller, Friedrich 171–6
Scotland
  as imaginary country 88, 146–8
  conflated with Highlands 16–17, 20, 144–7
  prejudice against 16–20, 73–4, Plate 1
  see also nationalism
Scott, Walter 8, 83, 107, 139–40, 144–7
  The Lady of the Lake 2, 55–9, 140–6, 153–4, 155–8, 161–2, 165
Scrope, William 161
Second Sight 76, 89, 91–4, 101
Selkirk, Thomas Douglas, Earl of 25, 46, 54, 122–3
sensibility 20, 77–9, 99, 129–31, 155, 169
Seven Years' War 18, 29–33, 36, 40, 48–9
Shakespeare, William 29, 151, 154, 172
sheep 86, 117–18, 124, 125–6, 150
Sinclair, Sir John 45, 46, 48, 115, 145, 156, 158
Statistical Account of Scotland 125, 131, 164–5, 197n1
Smith, Adam 22, 24, 42, 61, 126–8
Smollett, Tobias 9, 16, 19, 21, 63, 83–5
Spence, Elizabeth 158
Steuart, Sir James 22
Stewart, David, of Garth 177
Stoddart, John 156
Stuart, Prince Charles Edward 1, 19, 20, 29, 52–4, 151

Tacitus 21, 27–8
Telford, Thomas 164–5
Temple, Sir William 40

Index

Thomson, James 65, 69–70, 73, 110–11, 129
Thornton, Thomas 159–62, 163, 165
tourism 20, 149–58, 163, 165
  and Ossian 109–11, 114
  picturesque 37, 62–4, 76–7
Trossachs 58–9, 141, 155–7
True Highlander 44–6

violence 36–41
Virgil 69–70, 75, 110–11
Victoria, Queen 177
Voltaire 94

Wade, General 12, 70–1
Walker, John 72–3

Wallerstein, Immanuel 147, 166–7
War of American Independence 31, 39, 48–9
waterfalls 37, 82
weather 110–11
Wilkes, John 17–18
Wilkinson, Thomas 196n71
Williams, Raymond 125
Wolfe, General 30, 48
women 133–4, 139–40
Wordsworth, Dorothy 111–12, 152, 155, 164
Wordsworth, William 111–14, 152–3, 155, 157, 164, 196n75

Young, Edward 202n3
Youngson, A. J. 3